Praise

"Jake Hinkson is the Roger Ebert of film noir. His stylish prose bristles with memorable insights and the kind of fun only a true movie lover can bring to the table."

—Ed Gorman, co-founder of *Mystery Scene* and winner of the Anthony Award for Best Critical Work for *The Fine Art of Murder*

"Newcomers to noir and connoisseurs alike can both revel in Jake Hinkson's riffs on the subject. He brings to the films a wealth of insight, valuable context, and—most vitally—real passion and a sense of fun. It was a privilege to publish many of these pieces the first time around, and it's a pleasure to read them again in this smart and savvy collection."

—Eddie Muller, author of *Dark City* and president of the Film Noir Foundation

"If you want to learn more about film noir, read *The Blind Alley*. Jake Hinkson is like a literary Reed Hadley. His lively, informative essays comprise an essential voice over tour of the characters and foibles of film noir."

—Alan K. Rode, author of *Charles McGraw: Film Noir Tough Guy* and *Sit On The Camera, Pant Like a Tiger: The Life and Films of Michael Curtiz*

"In *The Blind Alley*, Jake Hinkson ventures down some of the darkest and most unfamiliar back streets of film noir. A knowledgeable and passionate tour guide, Hinkson illuminates neglected corners with insightful essays on noir's treatment of subjects from religion to childhood, lesbianism to the "crisis pregnancy." Incisive profiles of overlooked figures—Norman Foster, Richard Quine, Tom Neal, Mickey Rooney—rescue their contributions from the shadows while revealing lives often more noir than their films. *The Blind Alley* is especially to be treasured for its loving tributes to women who never quite had the careers they deserved, but who left their indelible mark on noir, among them Peggie Castle, Martha Vickers, and Thelma Ritter. For the noir fan, delving into this collection is like opening a box of extra-dark chocolates."

—Imogen Sara Smith, author of *In Lonely Places: Film Noir Beyond The City*

"Even though it is hard to believe that there are any dark corners left in the study of classic film noir, Jake Hinkson in *The Blind Alley* manages to shine light into a few of its more obscure niches with perceptive and entertaining studies of character actors like the redoubtable Art Smith, unrecognized femme fatales like Peggie Castle and Joan Dixon, as well as taking on neglected social issues in noir such as lesbianism and unwanted pregnancy."

—James Ursini, author of *The Noir Style* and editor of the *Film Noir Reader* series

"Jake Hinkson's concise, highly readable essays cover the wide waterfront of film noir, offering insightful new perspectives both on monumental films like *Double Indemnity* and *Touch of Evil* and overlooked figures such as Peggie Castle and Norman Foster. A must-have collection for every student of this eternally fascinating genre."

—Dave Kehr, author of *When Movies Mattered: Reviews From a Transformative Decade*

A Broken River Books collection

Broken River Books
10765 SW Murdock Lane
Apt. G6
Tigard, OR 97224

Copyright © 2015 by Jake Hinkson

Cover art and design copyright © 2015 by Matthew Revert
www.matthewrevert.com

Interior design by J David Osborne

All rights reserved. No part of this book may be reproduced or transmitted in any form or by any means, electronic or mechanical, including photocopying, recording, or by any information storage and retrieval system, without the written consent of the publisher, except where permitted by law.

ISBN: 978-1-940885-16-2

Printed in the USA.

THE BLIND ALLEY

JAKE HINKSON

BROKEN RIVER BOOKS
PORTLAND, OR

For
Susan Paschal Hinkson

Beautiful Mother Dear

CONTENTS

Introduction   1

I
THE BEGINNING AND THE END

1	1944 and the Birth of Film Noir	7
2	The God-Haunted Street of No Return	33

II
BLIND ALLEYS

3	Hell Itself Couldn't Be a Stranger Place	43
4	All Kinds of Women	63
5	At the Center of The Storm	75
6	The Passion of the Chump	83
7	The Little Story of Right-Hand/Left-Hand	91
8	Women in Trouble	101
9	Hearing Voices	119
10	Through the Camera's I	127
11	God's Murderous Men	137
12	Children of the Night	147

III

FACES FROM THE SHADOW GALLERY

13	The Girl They Loved to Kill	163
14	The Broken Man	187
15	What Shows And What Doesn't	207
16	The Crooked Road of Richard Quine	227
17	The Long Wait of Norman Foster	235
18	Journeyman	245
19	No One Escapes	253
20	Fate Slaps Down Andy Hardy	259

IV

MUG SHOTS

21	Hard Luck Ladies	271
22	Notes From the Goon Squad	285
23	The Nothing Man	297
24	The Altars of Forgotten Women	301

"Mothers of America
let your kids go to
the movies!
get them out of the house so they won't
    know what you're up to
it's true that fresh air is good for the
    body

    but what about the soul
that grows in darkness, embossed by
    silvery images"

—from Frank O'Hara's
"Ave Maria"

INTRODUCTION

In his essay collection *Pulphead*, the author John Jeremiah Sullivan writes of the blues archivist James McKune, "He was interested…in culturally precious things that had been accidently snagged and preserved by stray cogs of the anarchic capitalist threshing machine." When I read that line it jumped out at me as being a pretty good description of most noir geeks. After all, the great majority of movies that we define as classic noir were created to be instantly disposable entertainments. They were considered by many of the people who bankrolled them, made them, and first watched them to be as culturally important as a tub of popcorn. As a result, not long after they were first released, many of these films were essentially discarded, left to disintegrate in various storage units while time and tastes marched on to the next new thing.

Then a weird thing happened. The rise of television, and the need to fill late night airtime with cheap material, meant these films were dusted off and given a brief second life. That's when the geeks took over.

Where most people saw campy dreck, the geeks saw priceless artifacts of a forgotten culture. America is a country that prides itself on heritage and tradition even as it regularly sweeps its culture into history's garbage pile. The geeks rooted through the dumpsters and pulled out works of genius.

I use the word "geek" not just with respect and admiration but with fraternity. The book you're holding in your hands was written by a man obsessed with the flickering shadows of history that we call movies. Over the past ten years or so, I've had the opportunity to write and research extensively for the Film Noir Foundation and to lend my efforts to the cause of rescuing and restoring these old crime films. I've had the pleasure of working with some of the most important people in the current field of noir studies and restoration. It's been the most gratifying period of my working life, but perhaps the best thing about it has been the opportunity to explore the lives of so many different people—not just well known figures like Orson Welles or Robert Mitchum, but all-but-forgotten figures such as Norman Foster and Peggie Castle.

Noir is big right now, of course, and the market is full of terrific books covering a variety of topics. What I want to do with *The Blind Alley* is to recover some of those culturally precious things that have nearly slipped away, even in the current boom of noir studies.

Part One of the book, The Beginning and the End, is a brief introduction to some key films and filmmakers. Because noir is a retrospective genre—which is to say that "film noir" is a unifying concept that critics adopted to classify the mystery stories and b-movie potboilers of an earlier era—it is necessary for any writing on the subject to establish some perimeters for the genre. In this section, I try to identify when the classic era of noir began, who its key practitioners were, and exactly how and when it came to an end.

In Part Two, Blind Alleys, the focus narrows to areas that remain either underexplored, misunderstood, or completely ignored in recent noir studies—among them: the impact of Orson Welles, the complicated figure of the lesbian *butch fatale*, the prevalence of religious fanatics, the robust sub-genre of films about unwed mothers, the conflicted view of children, and noir's formal experimentations with voiceover and the subjective camera.

Part Three, Faces From the Shadow Gallery, is dedicated to profiles of overlooked figures. I'm particularly proud of this section since it includes two of my favorite pieces—a six thousand word profile on the tragic Peggie Castle ("The Girl They Loved to Kill"), a woman whose life continues to haunt me; and a five thousand word piece on Tom Neal ("The Broken Man"), a man whose violent life encapsulates the darkest part of the Hollywood story. These two pieces represent the first extensive work published on the lives of these two actors. This section also includes work on character actors Frank Lovejoy and Art Smith; overlooked directors Richard Quine, Norman Foster, and Felix Feist; and the unappreciated noir work of Mickey Rooney.

Part Four, Mug Shots, are short sketches of some of the unheralded actors who filled the margins—and occasionally held the center—of film noir.

Since this book collects the work of one writer, it is idiosyncratic in its focus and, perhaps, downright eccentric in some of the opinions expressed. I'm not only fine with that, I suspect that such a unity of personality is chief among this collection's strengths. I hope you enjoy reading the book as much as I enjoyed writing it.

I

THE BEGINNING AND THE END

1944 AND THE BIRTH OF FILM NOIR

In 2014, film noir turned 70. While there had been some intermittent movies leading up to the birth of the classic noir, in 1944 the dahlia bloomed with six key films: *Double Indemnity*, *Laura*, *Murder My Sweet*, *Phantom Lady*, *When Strangers Marry*, and *The Woman In The Window*. In these films you have many of the key figures in noir making some of their first forays into the genre (directors Billy Wilder, Otto Preminger, Fritz Lang, and Robert Siodmak; writers Raymond Chandler, Cornell Woolrich, Vera Caspary, Phillip Yordan; actors Robert Mitchum, Barbara Stanwyck, Joan Bennett, Dana Andrews—just to name a few). This onslaught of darkness came in the wake of the bleakest days (from the American perspective, anyway) of WWII. The basis of many of these films were older properties, but it is the way these films came out—physically darker, psychologically denser, and ultimately more pessimistic—that marks the real birth of film noir.

I. *Double Indemnity*

Double Indemnity might well be the most famous of all film noirs, and there are good reasons for its outsized reputation. It is a hugely entertaining film of great technical accomplishment—and if that sounds like mannered praise, it's because I've never really fallen in love with this movie.

It tells the story of an insurance agent named Walter Neff. As the movie begins, he stumbles into his company's office building in the middle of the night and heads to the office of his claims manager, Barton Keyes. He takes out Keyes's Dictaphone and begins to confess to a murder. This leads to a flashback structure in which we see hotshot salesman Neff pay a visit to the Dietrichson house. Mr. Dietrichson isn't home, but Mrs. Dietrichson is there wearing only a towel and an anklet. Before long, Neff and Mrs. Dietrichson are trading barbs and sharing drinks, and the young housewife starts talking to the insurance man about maybe getting her much older husband some life insurance. It doesn't take long for Neff to see where this is going, but he's already hooked on Mrs. Dietrichson. A few clandestine meetings later, Neff has engineered the perfect murder. He and Mrs. Dietrichson kill her husband, make it look like an accident, and sit back while the cops fall for it. Now all they have to worry about is the scrappy little claims manager Mr. Keyes.

The making of *Double Indemnity*—particularly the writing of the script—is the stuff of movie legend. Adapted from the novel by James M. Cain, the screenplay was written by director Billy Wilder and novelist Raymond Chandler. This was an impossibly talented duo, though not exactly the match made in heaven that it might have looked like on paper. Chandler was curmudgeonly under the best of circumstances, and he neither approved of Cain's book ("Everything Cain touches smells like a billygoat") nor enjoyed working with Wilder ("an agonizing experience"). Perhaps those fat studio paychecks gave him the strength to endure.

The script produced by the two men, however, is a classic of noir screenwriting. The banter between Neff and Mrs. Dietrichson is as crisp, and artificial, as a new three-dollar bill. Like this from their first meeting:

Mrs. Dietrichson: I wonder if I know what you mean.
Neff: I wonder if you wonder.

And this toward the end of the film:

Mrs. Dietrichson: We're both rotten.
Neff: Only you're a little more rotten.

My favorite bit is this tossed off exchange between Mr. Norton, the head of the insurance company, and Keyes, the claims manager:

Norton: The witness from the train, what was his name?
Keyes: His name was Jackson. Probably still is.

Double Indemnity was justly famous at the time for

the wit and snap of these lines, and more than any other single movie, this one laid a lot of groundwork for how people talk to each other in a film noir. It wasn't all wisecracks, though. Wilder and Chandler also worked in haunting passages that presaged the doom-obsessed denizens of the dark city who would follow in their wake.

Neff: As I was walking down the street to the drugstore, suddenly it came over me that everything could go wrong…I couldn't hear my own footsteps. It was the walk of a dead man.

As good as all this is, however, the script remains a curious combination of Cain's gritty realism and Chandler's rather Victorian sensibilities. Like Cain's *The Postman Always Rings Twice*, *Double Indemnity* broke new ground in terms of its lurid subject matter. Simply put, in the thirties and early forties most movies were not about the claustrophobic psyches of murderers. Cain had based his characters on Ruth Snyder and Judd Gray, a real life duo who murdered Snyder's husband and tried to collect on a forged insurance policy, yet the film version is hardly an attempt at realism in any sense we would understand the term today. Of course, today pornography and cable news have rendered real sex and violence in enough clinical detail that no mystery exists for film to exploit, but in 1944, most everything had to be done through coded language—language tame enough for Sunday school teachers. Even then it could get you into trouble.

Like so much noir, *Double Indemnity*, benefits

from the tension resulting from the pull of opposites. Holding it altogether was the personality of Billy Wilder, Hollywood's reining misanthrope and the quickest wit in town. Wilder kept what he wanted from Cain's novel, extracted gold from Chandler and, together with his director of photography, John Seitz, gave the film a lush visual style that nevertheless captured the tawdriness of the story. Venetian blinds had appeared in movies before this one, but in *Double Indemnity* the lazy daylight shifts through the blinds in the middle of the day and corrupts a normal house into something sinister. The Dietrichson home is like a cave with sunlight seeping through. (Wilder and Seitz would use the same look in *Sunset Blvd*—shorthand for the dark underbelly of California.) Other times, as in the scenes set in Jerry's supermarket, the lighting is harsh and flat. Neff and Mrs. Dietrichson wander the aisles of cheap, neatly stacked merchandise—the embodiment of California's wartime image as the land of plenty—and plot a murder. American society never had a more cheerfully vicious critic in Hollywood than Billy Wilder. His image of the banality of evil, of murder hatched on the baby food aisle, had its fullest expression here.

Walter Neff and Mrs. Dietrichson, played by Fred MacMurray and Barbara Stanwyck, would become the archetypal antihero and femme fatale, but a lamentable inclination toward honesty forces me to admit that they're not my favorite screen couple. MacMurray does a capable job as Neff, playing him with a Dick Powell-like smugness, but I can't help myself—I wish Powell would have played the role. (To see MacMurray at his noir best, by the way, see him in the underrated *Pushover* with Kim Novak.)

Here's the larger (and, I'm sure, more unforgivable) heresy: I'm just not a huge Stanwyck fan. As much as I like her, I've never loved her. For more than a few people, however, she is the queen of noir. Here is what is inarguable: with *Double Indemnity* Stanwyck forged the image of the femme fatale and set the standard by which all others are measured. So why my reserve? Something about her leaves me cold. To put it bluntly, Stanwyck doesn't turn me on. I've watched many a femme fatale lead many a befuddled man to his doom, and I've found that for the story to really work on me I have to identify with the antihero's lust and longing. I can understand killing for Jane Greer. Or Lizabeth Scott. Or Audrey Totter. I just don't think I'd kill for Barbara Stanwyck. It doesn't help that in this film she's wearing a wig that makes her look, in the words of one studio executive at the time, "like George Washington." But it's more than the wig and sex appeal. Stanwyck lacks warmth. I know she's supposed to be a cold-blooded killer; I just don't understand why someone would be drawn to her in the first place—where's the heat that sparks the flame? In her screwball comedies for Capra and Sturges, she had a tomboyish charm that, for my money, was far more appealing. (My favorite Stanwyck is the Stanwyck of *Ball Of Fire*.) In so many of her noirs, though, her charisma fails to work on me.

It's okay if I say that I like, rather than love, *Double Indemnity*. It doesn't need me to love it. It's a giant of film noir. Hell, for a lot of people, it is *the* giant of film noir. Timing is everything, and Wilder/MacMurray/

Stanwyck got to the party first. With this film, they created the prototypical femme fatale story.

II. *Laura*

Laura is among the best known of all noirs. I'm not exactly sure why that is, though I suspect it has something to do with this intriguing premise: a cop investigating the murder of a beautiful young socialite named Laura Hunt finds himself falling in love with the dead woman. I'll try not to say too much more than that about the plot since this is a mystery and the basic set-up seems to be enough for most people at the outset. What is intriguing about this synopsis, however, is that it actually leaves out the main character.

The main character is neither the murdered Laura (Gene Tierney) nor the cop Mark McPherson (Dana Andrews) who finds himself falling in love with the portrait of her that hangs over her fireplace. No, the main character of the film is Laura's friend and mentor, Waldo Lydecker, played with acid charm by Clifton Webb. He's a newspaper columnist who observes the murder investigation with absolute contempt for everyone involved. It's Lydecker's withering scorn and urbane sophistication which make *Laura* something of an anomaly in noir. These kinds of movies aren't usually narrated by people who could blend into the cocktail party scene in *All About Eve*. Lydecker sort of classes everything up. Credit should go to screenwriters Jay Dratler, Samuel Hoffenstein, and Betty Reinhardt, working closely from Vera Caspary's novel. Lydecker never has a boring line of dialogue, and Clifton Webb makes the most of his opportunity here. He was primarily a stage actor when he made this film, but it launched his career in Hollywood. He played smug sophisticates—either dramatically or comically—for the rest of his time in movies.

Good as he is here, Webb isn't the whole show. Director Otto Preminger has an impressive cast on hand to play the assorted social climbers and millionaires who comprise the cop's list of suspects. A young Vincent Price is excellent as the scion of a washed-up Southern aristocracy who lives off his ability to charm wealthy women like Laura. Judith Anderson plays another of Price's benefactors, a rich widow who might have been willing to get Laura out of the way in the race for Price's affections. Anderson was often cast as frigid she-monsters, but her performance here is surprisingly sympathetic. She's probably the most honest person in the movie.

Against this colorful cast of uptown characters, Dana Andrews provides a solid foundation as the cop McPherson. He's something of an enigma himself. Among this group of talkers, McPherson is quiet, watchful, and suspicious of everyone. Andrews was ideal for the role because his specialty was a certain mournful intelligence. (He would use this quality in other excellent noirs like *Where The Sidewalk Ends* and *Fallen Angel.*) His thoughts seemed to trouble him, and this is the right quality for McPherson, who never expresses what he's really thinking. I've always felt that the plot transitions into his obsession with Laura a little too quickly—it just seems to happen out of the blue one night—but this isn't the fault of Andrews. There seems to be a scene missing, one which would bridge the investigation and the obsession.

The key to this missing element is found in the source novel *Laura*, written by the brilliant novelist/playwright/screenwriter Vera Caspary. (The story had a circuitous route the screen. Caspary had originally conceived the idea as the basis of a screenplay but after being laid off by Paramount Studios, she turned it into a book. Preminger read it and immediately seized on it as great material for a movie. Needing the money, Caspary sold the rights to the book to 20th Century Fox for a pittance and then watched as the movie became a sensation.) In the novel, the point of view floats between characters, so while we get Lydecker narrating the beginning, we get McPherson's obsession from the inside. Preminger and his screenwriters kept much of Caspary's novel, but they jettisoned the multiple points of view, which creates a bit of narrative confusion as the movie progresses.

Still, perhaps it all works because Gene Tierney was the perfect actor to play the enigmatic Laura Hunt. It wasn't simply that she was beautiful, it's that she had a peculiar passivity which seemed to draw people nearer to her. No director knew this better than Preminger, and he utilized this aspect of her personality in several films (including *Whirlpool* and *Where The Sidewalk Ends*) but found its richest expression available in *Laura*. Everyone in the film projects their hopes, fears and obsessions onto her because her beauty is as ethereally empty as a movie screen. The following year Tierney would plumb those empty depths with a harrowing performance in *Leave Her To Heaven*, but here Preminger uses her emptiness as a vacuum which the other characters fill with their hopes and fears and desires. Only after the film has delivered up its secrets and revealed its mysteries do you realize that its true subject is the way Laura Hunt is a convenient catalyst for the obsessions of everyone around her. *Laura* is one of the few classic mysteries where the solution actually has resonance, where it reconfigures the meaning of what you've seen before.

III. *Murder, My Sweet*

Raymond Chandler's Philip Marlowe is the most famous private eye to ever walk the mean streets of American crime fiction. He's gotten more traction than Sam Spade (who only headlined one novel and a handful of stories by Dashiell Hammet), and he's outlasted his most famous successor, Mickey Spillane's Mike Hammer. As a literary creation, he's iconic: the raincoat and snap brim hat, the cigarettes, the smartass remarks, the office bottle, the tendency to get knocked over the head and wake up next to a dead body. He is a pivotal American heroic archetype, the lonely but honest private investigator. If the English have Sherlock Holmes, then Americans have Phillip Marlowe.

In many ways, Chandler was an impressive writer with a distinctive vision, but he was also blessed to work at just the right time. He famously disdained Hollywood, but Hollywood loved his laconic P.I. and adapted him to the screen several times. The most famous incarnation was Howard Hawks' version of *The Big Sleep* starring Humphrey Boart, but Marlowe actually got his start a little earlier when Dick Powell played him for director Edward Dmytryk in *Murder, My Sweet*.

The film is based on Chandler's second Marlowe novel, *Farwell, My Lovely*. The complicated story centers around a towering ex-boxer named Moose Malloy (Mike Mazurki) who is recently out of prison and looking for his long lost love, a dancer named Velma. He engages Marlowe to track her down, but soon the private eye has another client, a foppish gent named Lindsay Marriott (Douglas Walton). He wants Marlowe to accompany him to retrieve a stolen jade necklace. Marlowe tags along to a midnight meeting in the woods, but someone saps him on the back of the head. When he wakes up, Marriott is dead. He discovers that the stolen necklace belonged to the beautiful Helen Grayle (Clare Trevor), the much younger wife of a rich old man. Mrs. Grayle doesn't seem in a terrible hurry to get her necklace back, and her stepdaughter, Ann (Anne Shirley) confides to Marlowe that there's something funny going on between Mrs. Grayle and a sham doctor named Jules Amthor (Otto Kruger).

And so on and so forth. I've seen this movie many times, and I've read the novel twice, but I don't think I could pass a test on the story's plot. Chandler was never much of a plotter, really. He once wrote that the talent to construct a good puzzle is not necessarily to be found in the same brain that can write believable characters and dialogue. *The Big Sleep* is famously confusing, but for my money *Murder, My Sweet* is even more baffling. Part of the problem is that Dmytryk lets the exposition bog down a bit, especially toward the end. Hawks kept

The Big Sleep going so fast that it was only afterwards that you realized you didn't know what the hell had happened. Here, Dmytryk occasionally slows things down to try to iron out the details, to the detriment of both the pace and the plot.

What's important here, though, is that *Murder, My Sweet* is really a movie about tone and style—and in this respect it's almost shockingly good. It smartly rigs up a flashback device to allow Marlowe to narrate his adventure while being questioned by the cops (a far better idea than Robert Montgomery's goofy subjective camera in *Lady in The Lake*). It also employs a terrific score by the great Roy Webb that manages to be both intimately smoky and epic at the same time, in much the same way the scores of *The Maltese Falcon* and *The Big Sleep* gave their pictures the feeling of nightbound urban adventure.

Dmytryk's most important collaborator here is veteran RKO cinematographer Harry Wild. Together on this film they helped create the look of film noir. There's an early shot of Marlowe sitting in his office at night, smoking and looking out the window as neon signs for Chinese food reflect off the glass. This single shot is damn near a dictionary definition of the noir style of high contrast black and white, with light scrupulously used to frame faces and capture drifts of smoke. And the entire film is just as beautiful.

Of course, a Philip Marlowe movie is only as good as its Philip Marlowe and *Murder, My Sweet* has a fascinating lead performance from Dick Powell. At the time, Powell was most notable as a song and dance man (in fact, the legend goes that the studio changed the name of the movie from *Farewell, My Lovely* because it sounded too much like a musical), and this film marked his entrance into tough guy territory. Interestingly though, Powell isn't much of a tough guy. There's a smug quality about him—and he delivers the wisecracks with relish—but there was also a faint whiff of the maladroit about Dick Powell. He takes the requisite cracks on the noggin with aplomb, but he lacks Bogart's steel spine. Understand, though, that this isn't a criticism. You could even argue that Powell's portrayal hews closer to the Marlowe of the books. Unlike Spillane's borderline psychotic Mike Hammer, Chandler's Marlowe is essentially a sensitive man with a tough shell. His interactions with the ugliness of the underworld always take a toll on him, and Powell's vulnerable enough that you're not sure if he'll make it through in one piece. It's difficult to imagine Bogart enduring the strange sequence here in which Powell is drugged by a quack doctor and fumbles through a surrealist landscape, nor is it easy to picture big Mike Mazurki manhandling Bogart like a cheap rag doll. Powell's performance gives the movie the center of ambiguity that is lacking in *The Big Sleep*.

Of course, *The Big Sleep* is more famous and features a more highly regarded director and bigger stars, but—make no mistake—*Murder, My Sweet* is equally indispensable. More than any other Marlowe film, it positions the detective story firmly within the decidedly unheroic milieu of film noir.

IV. *Phantom Lady*

Sometimes when you're watching a movie there comes a moment so wonderful that it strikes you like a revelation. You realize in an instant that you've lucked into something terrific. The first time I saw *Phantom Lady*, that moment hit me at about the ten minute mark. In the film, Alan Curtis plays a civil engineer who has just had a fight with his wife. He heads to a bar for a drink, and while he's there he meets a sad woman wearing a peculiar hat. She doesn't seem to be in a mood to talk to anyone, but eventually Curtis convinces her to go to a show. She agrees, but on one condition: they will not exchange names. He agrees, pays for their drinks, and they take a cab to the show. Nothing much happens at the show and once it's over, Curtis and the woman say goodnight.

Then comes The Moment. Curtis returns home to find three men waiting for him. Who are they? We don't know at first, but slowly we get the idea they're cops. They direct Curtis to his bedroom. His wife has been murdered.

The quiet and suspenseful way this scene unfolds is a harbinger of the film to come. More than anything else, *Phantom Lady* is a triumph of style. The first ten minutes of the film are good, but The Style really kicks in the moment Curtis walks into his apartment to find his wife murdered. The shot begins in the dark (setting up a motif of beginning scenes in the pitch black). The cops speak in clipped sentences. When Curtis goes to his room to view his wife's strangled corpse, we begin

The Blind Alley

with a strange shot of the door (setting up another motif: there's a lot of business with doors in the course of the film), and then he enters the room. There's no music, just the silence of the moment punctuated by dialog. As Curtis tries to explain to the cops that he had nothing to do with his wife's murder, his alibi unfolds in a terrific shot. Curtis is on the left side of the frame, with a huge portrait of his wife over his shoulder in the middle of the frame, and an unimpressed cop smacking gum in the bottom right of the frame. The scene ends with the three cops surrounding Curtis as the camera creeps in on him. You could watch the shot with the sound off and know what's happening.

He's in trouble. Before he knows it, he'll be railroaded into the clink (filmed in an inventive courtroom scene that avoids every cliché of courtroom scenes). His only friend is his secretary, Carol (played with pluck by the almost unbelievably beautiful Ella Raines). She's able to convince the inspector on the case, Burgess (the always dependable Thomas Gomez) to reopen his investigation. If they can find the mysterious woman in the strange hat, then they can prove Curtis's alibi. This is a great set-up, but the story adapted from the novel by Cornell Woolrich is really just an excuse for scenes of suspense, as Carol travels into a seedy underworld to track down the woman and, maybe, the real killer. Now here's the funny thing: I can tell you the killer is played by Franchot Tone in a good performance as a psycho, but as many times as I've seen this movie I cannot remember *why* he killed Curtis's wife. That goes to show that, as is often the case with a Woolrich mystery, the questions are more interesting than the answers. What matters is how it's all handled.

Today, Cornel Woolrich is probably best remembered as the author of the short story "It Had To Be Murder" which formed the basis for Hitchcock's *Rear Window*, but he was in fact among the most prolific of all pulp writers. Author Woody Haut, in his excellent study *Heartbreak and Vine: The Fate of Hardboiled Writers in Hollywood*, puts Woolrich's credits at twenty-two novels and 350 short stories. Perhaps as impressive as his literary output were the seventeen adaptations of his work that Hollywood produced between 1938 and 1956.

It was the bizarrely off-center quality of his writing that led to a profusion of Woolrich movies. Like a dimestore Kafka, Woolrich wrote almost exclusively about a world of ever-encroaching doom, of mysterious people who show up in the middle of the night to persecute confused protagonists for crimes they have not committed. He was the master of the set up. A man spying on his neighbors thinks he's witnessed a murder (*Rear Window*). A woman in a train accident assumes the identity of a dead woman (*No Man of Her Own*). A man awakens from a violent nightmare to find actual blood on his hands (*Fear in the Night*). A sham fortune teller discovers to his horror that he can actually see into the future (*Night of a Thousand Eyes*). A little boy known for telling fibs witnesses a murder, but no one will believe him (*The Window*). One of Woolrich's favorite tropes was the amnesia story: a man wakes up to discover that he's apparently done something awful. The cause of his amnesia can be a falling rock (*Street of Chance*) or an all-night bender (*Fall Guy*), but the

The Blind Alley

result is the same. Confusion. Guilt. Terror.

And on and on. Hollywood lapped up these stories at an astounding rate, and while masters like Hammet, Chandler, and Cain scored impressive hits, none of them churned out prose like Woolrich. He seemed to wake up from a different nightmare every morning and run to his typewriter.

Woolrich was himself, alas, pretty much a miserable son of a bitch. His biographer Francis M. Nevins once described his life as "wretched." Also like Kafka (who was something of his literary soul mate), his relationships to both sex and death were complicated. A self-hating gay man who tormented a young wife for a short time before retreating to booze-soaked codependency with his beloved/despised mother, as a person Woolrich was as unpleasant as many of his darkest scenarios. In his autobiography *Blues of a Lifetime*, he wrote of a childhood epiphany that "I would surely die finally…I had that trapped feeling like some sort of poor insect that you've put inside a downturned glass." He channeled that vision not only into a life of debauchery and cruelty but also into his fiction. After his mother died, however, Woolrich's literary output stagnated and his drinking exploded. By the time he died in 1968, he'd all but been forgotten by most people, his legacy a fraction of that of Hammet and Chandler.

Yet his twisted tales of sinners and weaklings caught in fate's unforgiving maw shaped noir more than the work of any other author. *Phantom Lady* is the first mature treatment of his work, and the credit for this goes to director Robert Siodmak. He had come up in the bustling German film industry during the twenties alongside future masters of noir like Edgar G. Ulmer, Billy Wilder, and Fred Zinnemann. There must have been something in the water over there (something called Expressionism perhaps). Like many people, Siodmak fled Germany when the Nazis came to power in 1933, and he eventually found his way to America. By 1944, he was establishing a career as a master of suspense, though of course his notoriety would pale in comparison to *the* Master of Suspense, Alfred Hitchcock. Siodmak's reputation has grown over the years, and one can only hope that it continues to grow, especially now that film noir seems to be going through a resurgence in popularity. Siodmak would be on anyone's short list of the genre's great practitioners, and his list of impressive credits includes masterpieces like *The Killers, Cry of the City,* and *Criss Cross*.

And, of course, *Phantom Lady*. Working with the great cinematographer Elwood Bredell, Siodmak created the kind of film that operates as a functioning definition of the noir style, utilizing a precise application of silence and sound, slanted angles, shadows, pools of light, slicked streets—and so much more. Of the landmark noirs of 1944, this one is probably the most visually beautiful. It is not to be missed.

V. *When Strangers Marry*

While many scholars peg *Double Indemnity* as the first fully formed noir in terms of both style and theme, you can see the genre's style and ethos taking shape in earlier proto-noirs like *Stranger On The Third Floor* (1940), *I Wake Up Screaming* (1941) and *Street Of Chance* (1942).

The Blind Alley

By 1944 you can see all of this coming together in the low-budget mystery-romance *When Strangers Marry*. The film is an interesting specimen of the emerging noir style, but it is of particular importance because it launched the criminal career of noir's greatest leading man.

The film stars a young Kim Hunter, in her first starring role, as a naïve newlywed named Millie Baxter. She's newly arrived in New York City looking for her husband, a traveling salesman named Paul Baxter. This Baxter is a heck of a guy. He swept Millie off her feet, married her, and then beat it out of town. Now he's sent for her, but when she arrives at the hotel, Baxter is nowhere around. He seems to be hiding out, and the film is not very subtle in suggesting that Baxter might have something to do with a recent murder in Philadelphia. Did Millie's new husband—who is essentially a stranger to her—strangle another man with silk stockings in a hotel room and then make off with ten thousand dollars? I'll leave that for the film to reveal, though I will say that it does not explore the kinky undertones implicit in the question.

Instead, the film directs us to the relationship between Millie and an old boyfriend, another traveling salesman named Fred Graham. (Millie is apparently a traveling salesman groupie.) Fred is supportive and understanding and clearly still in love with Millie. He's also played by a young Robert Mitchum. Will he be the hero of the film? Let's put it this way, in a movie like this, he's either the hero or the villain waiting to reveal himself. There is really no other option.

When Strangers Marry was written by Phillip

Yordan—though it's more correct to say that it was rewritten by Yordan since his usual practice was to farm out projects to underlings. On this film, he and director Castle came up with the story, then Yordan had a first time screenwriter named Dennis J. Cooper take a crack at it, at which point Yordan came in a did a rewrite. The results are not a high point in the history of noir screenwriting. The plot careens around like a drunk driver, while the dialog sometimes feels clunky and expository. And Millie, naïve to a fault, makes for a particularly hapless leading lady.

Still, the noir ethos is already in place here. A mood of unease hovers over everything, and the plot and all the characters are driven by a single unifying principal: no one can really know anyone else. Moreover, the style of the film fits this theme, an early demonstration of noir moodiness. Shadows and low angle shots predominate, with human figures cut out of blackness by sheer white light. In the film's best sequence, Millie stands in a cheap hotel room late at night while the flashing lights of the nightclub across the street plunge her in and out of darkness.

The film was directed by William Castle, an often underestimated director who did his share of noir work before becoming famous later on as a producer/director of cheesy horror movies marketed with outrageous gimmicks. Perhaps in part to rectify the undervaluing of Castle's work some critics have rather overpraised *When Strangers Marry*. (Film historian Don Miller called it the finest B-movie ever made.) While Castle's accomplishment is impressive—all the more impressive when you consider that the movie was made for fifty grand over the course of a single week—it is not a masterpiece. It lacks the fierce fire in the belly of something like 1945's low budget *Detour*. So while *When Strangers Marry* is a fun movie, and a notable addition to the body of noir, it doesn't linger in the imagination in the manner of the best films.

It is, however, a must for fans of Robert Mitchum—and who the hell isn't a fan of Mitchum? Twenty-seven years old and still a relative newcomer to films (he was mostly shooting cheapie Westerns before this film), he strides through this movie like he was born inside a film noir. It's not the best performance he ever gave, but one is struck by just how much he already seems like…well, Robert Mitchum.

The critical reception of *When Strangers Marry* was excellent considering that the film had been distributed by the Poverty Row studio of Monogram. An early admirer of the movie was the writer/director/star of *Citizen Kane*, Orson Welles. Writing in his newspaper column *Orson Welles's Almanac*, Welles declared the film better directed than either Wilder's *Double Indemnity* (Paramount) or Preminger's *Laura* (20th Century Fox). While that is a debatable assertion, Welles was correct to align the three films which—along with Siodmak's *Phantom Lady* (Universal), Lang's *The Woman in The Window* (RKO) and Dmytryk's *Murder My Sweet* (RKO)—represented the full flowering of noir across the studio system in 1944. Of the six films, Castle's was the smallest in budget and scope, but this only goes to show the way the noir ethos permeated the business from the top (Paramount, Universal) to the middle (Fox, RKO) to the bottom (Monogram).

VI. *The Woman In The Window*

The Woman In The Window is the kind of film that comes right up to the edge of greatness and then swerves at the last moment. That's a shame, but the film is still an essential member of noir's class of 1944.

The movie stands at the crossroads in the career of star Edward G. Robinson. In the thirties, he had been one of the premier tommy gun-toting hoodlums at Warner Brothers, but in the forties, as the gangster picture gave way to the film noir, Robinson moved on to play a far different kind of character. In 1944, he made the pivotal *Double Indemnity*, playing the fast-talking insurance investigator. But that same year he made *The Woman In The Window*, the first of the middle-aged loser roles he would play in later films like *Scarlett Street* and *The Red House*.

The Woman In The Window concerns a mild-mannered professor named Richard Wanley. He's happily married to a frumpy wife and together they have a couple of contented-looking kids. When the family goes out of town for the week, Wanley meets some of the boys at the club for brandy and cigars. Life, he says with a sigh, is a little dull. The only hint of excitement is a new portrait of a woman in a gallery window next to the club. Wanley is staring longingly at this vision of beauty one night when the woman herself walks up to him on the street. Her name is Alice Reed (Joan Bennett), and if she seems overly impressed that the squat, mid-life crisis in front of her is smitten by her beauty, well, that only adds to the excitement.

The Blind Alley

Soon, Alice has talked Wanley into joining her back at her apartment where they drink and smoke and talk the night away (while a large, soft-looking bed looms through the open bedroom door). Wanley is almost deliriously happy with this turn of events. Hell, who wouldn't be?

Then a cab pulls up in the rain and an angry man bursts through the door and demands to know what Wanley is doing in Alice Reed's apartment. The man strikes Alice, jumps on Wanley and starts to choke him. Alice thrusts a pair of scissors into Wanley's hand and he kills the man.

Now, in classic noir fashion, what started out as a possible night of adultery has become, in just a couple of minutes, a case of murder. Wanley and Alice decide not to call the cops for fear that they won't be believed (and, it is implied, so that Mrs. Wanley will not be forced to wonder what her husband was doing in the younger woman's apartment). Their attempts to dispose of the body, to avoid detection by a fast-acting police force, and to deal with a slimy blackmailer played by the prince of sleaze, Dan Duryea, form the bulk of the rest of the film. The movie proceeds in beautifully grim style right up to the final moments...

But more on that in a second. First, what must be acknowledged is the sheer skill on display here. The film was directed by Fritz Lang and demonstrates, once again, how early the great director got to the noir party. Of course, he'd been instrumental in developing the German Expressionism that preceded the noir era, and his early work in Hollywood (in films like the 1936 *Fury*) helped pave the way, but here we have

Lang fashioning a fully developed film noir. It was perfect material for him, enlisting his skill as a pitiless observer of human weakness. Working with his gifted cinematographer Milton Krasner, Lang damn near nails down exactly what a film noir is supposed to look like with this movie. *The Woman In The Window* takes place in a 3 AM world of rain-slicked streets and cigarette smoke, a world where sexy young women and befuddled middle-aged men frantically debate how to best get rid of dead bodies.

The key performances here are from Robinson and Bennett. That same year, Robinson played a similar kind of role for laughs in *Mr. Winkle Goes To War*. It made sense, really. He had never been an imposing physical presence; as a thug, all he'd ever run on was crazy eyes and a fast mouth. Here is the Edward G. Robinson of noir, though: scared of sex, bewildered by age, wholly incapable of managing the situation he has stumbled into. His counterpoint is Joan Bennett. Beautiful, exuding fearlessness—she is not just a sexual fantasy, she's a fantasy of youthful heedlessness. Against all reason, Bennett and Robinson are a perfect screen duo, the nightmare version of the May-September romance.

And yet, despite having all this talent marshaled to such great effect, *The Woman In The Window* misses greatness in its final moments with one of the worst endings in all of noir. Of this ending, I will say nothing more except that it ends this dark tale with a wink rather than a bang.

What I will point out instead is the happy fact that one year later this same creative team took up essentially the same material—middle-aged married dullard Robinson gets caught up with sexpot Bennett and slimeball Duryea—and brought it to glorious fruition with *Scarlet Street*. That film is an incomparable masterpiece, one of the premier works of noir art. *The Woman In The Window*, then, can be seen as an early draft, incomplete but fascinating in its own right.

By the end of 1944, film noir was in full bloom. In the years to come, many of the directors, writers, actors, cinematographers, and producers who made *Double Indemnity*, *Laura*, *Murder My Sweet*, *Phantom Lady*, *When Strangers Marry*, and *The Woman In the Window* would go on to create more masterpieces (or near masterpieces) of the genre. They would be joined by virtually all of Hollywood at one time or another, from the pinnacle of the power structure (MGM, the world's most powerful studio, produced gems like 1949's *Act of Violence* and 1950's *The Asphalt Jungle*) to Poverty Row studios that shot movies for pennies (lowly PRC produced 1945's *Detour*, perhaps the purest distillation of the noir ethos ever made). 1944 was just a harbinger of the dark—and darkly wonderful—movies still to come over the next twenty years.

THE GOD-HAUNTED STREETS OF NO RETURN
SAMUEL FULLER AND THE CREATION OF NEO-NOIR

Classic film noir was in its last throes as the 1960s began. Many of the genre's most important directors and stars were either dead or relegated to television, and the B-movie production machine—at least the machine as most people had known it — was dying with the major studios. As the studio system collapsed, however, a new kind of noir began to emerge. The first filmmaker to fully capture the spirit of the new noir was the wild man of American cinema, writer/director Samuel Fuller. An unbending iconoclast, he had labored in the studios for years (issuing, among other interesting films, the 1953 noir masterpiece *Pickup on South Street*), but in the 1960s the big boys booted him out. Fuller seized this opportunity to do his most interesting work. Toiling at the economic margins of an industry in chaos, he dealt the classic noir era its death blows with the creation of two indispensable films: *Shock Corridor* (1963) and *The Naked Kiss* (1964). These low-budget epics showed film noir, in an increasingly manic style, emerging not out of the postwar trauma of the forties and fifties but out of the rising turbulence of the 1960s. While Fuller's films fearlessly reflected the American scourges of racism, Cold War politics, and sexual hypocrisy, these were not good liberal message movies. These were movies that portrayed an America that seemed to have lost its collective mind, an America beginning to come apart at the social seams, an America that looks more like America today than the America of the 1940s and 1950s. This is where classic noir died and neo-noir was born.

I. The American Madhouse

Shock Corridor follows an ambitious reporter named Johnny Barrett (Peter Breck) as he goes undercover in an insane asylum in order to investigate a murder. As he searches for the murderer among the patients and staff of the institution, his hold on reality gradually weakens. In the end, he finds the killer but sinks into madness. This plot structure is relatively simple by noir standards, and the murder investigation itself is really just a clothesline for scenes. But, God, what scenes. Fuller's depiction of American neurosis still has the power to startle and provoke. *Shock Corridor* may well be the most artistically significant American movie of 1963—and perhaps of the first half of the 1960s.

Barrett's odyssey through the mental hospital is clearly designed as a journey through various forms of social psychosis. The inmates roam one endless hallway called The Street, and as Barrett makes his way up this "god-haunted street of no return" he is like Conrad's Marlow traveling ever further toward the heart of darkness. The gallery of characters he meets are Fuller's masterstroke, embracing the director's love of misfits and societal castoffs. The most lively of the bunch is the rotund Pagliacci (played by the invaluable Larry Tucker) who sings *La Bohème* and shoves several sticks of gum into Barrett's mouth to help him sleep.

But Pagliacci is simply the affable doorman of this crazy ward. Wandering amongst the catatonics is a former Communist from the Bible belt who, rejected by his family and friends for his beliefs, has gone insane and now believes he's the Confederate General Jeb Stuart. There's the former nuclear scientist who draws stick figures in crayon and plays hide and seek. The most affecting character is the schizophrenic former Civil Rights worker, a black man who has assumed the persona of a violent white racist.

Each of these characters represents some distinct form of American madness, but each one also has resonance as an individual. In the hallway of this corrupt mental institution, none of them have access to any kind of real help, and each is left to be consumed by his own particular American fixation. James Best is terrific as the haunted ex-Commie who was raised on a poor farm and "fed bigotry for breakfast and ignorance for supper." As the ex-scientist fixated on the coming nuclear holocaust, Gene Evans slips between erudition and childishness like a man who's lost his mind and his bearings. And as Trent, the former student protester, Hari Rhodes delivers an extraordinary performance which just about stops the movie. Spewing racist bile and trying to inaugurate a chapter of the Ku Klux Klan, Rhodes creates a character driven insane by the hypocrisy at the heart of American society in the early

1960s. What all of these characters have in common is a sense of thwarted progress — politically, scientifically, morally. Following the disgrace of McCarthyism, the existential terror of the Cuban Missile Crisis, and the violent reaction to the Civil Rights movement, *Shock Corridor* takes little comfort in the idealistic aims of postwar liberals.

Writing about Edgar G. Ulmer's 1945 masterpiece *Detour*, the scholar James Naremore observed that the film was "so far down the economic and cultural scale of things that it virtually escapes commodification, and can be viewed as a kind of subversive or vanguard art." This is true of *Shock Corridor* as well because, like Ulmer, Fuller embraces his low budget and makes it essential to the aesthetic of the film. Take, for instance, his use of shadows and sets. While the play of darkness and light is an essential element of most noirs, here Fuller does something you rarely see. As his characters shuffle among the cheap sets—most of the movie takes place in a single hallway—they cast long, prominent shadows *inside*. There's no sky in this movie, not even the night sky. No sense of the outside world whatsoever pierces through. Everything is confined to this madhouse. As characters whisper and wail, they are trailed by shadows that hover like specters close at hand. That's Fuller's vision of America in 1963, a place undone by fears of the future and haunted by ghosts of a dead past.

II. A Woman On The Edge

A former crime reporter, Fuller understood the impact of a splashy headline, and as a director he converted this understanding into a style that grabbed the audience from the first frame. That's nowhere more true than in his follow up to *Shock Corridor*, 1964's *The Naked Kiss*, a film with one of the all-time great opening scenes. The movie starts without warning: a woman is slapping a man around as violent jazz music boils away underneath the action. He begs her to stop. They wrestle, and when he grabs her hair a wig whips off her bald head. Now she's really pissed. After she's beaten him senseless, she rolls him for seventy-five bucks. Then the bald woman picks up her wig, goes to a mirror and puts herself together. Only then, beneath a jarringly lush and romantic score, do the credits roll.

The woman is a prostitute named Kelly. After she rolls the guy—whom we later learn is her pimp—she skips town and winds up in a quiet little place called Grantville. Apparently the town has one cop, a plainclothes captain named Griff. By all appearances, Griff's job consists mainly of hanging out at the bus station waiting for hookers to pull into town. He and Kelly have a twenty dollar tryst (she talks him up from ten dollars), and then he tells her to get out of town.

Kelly doesn't leave, though. Deciding to stick around and make a new life for herself, she takes a job at the hospital where she works in the ward for sick kids. She also meets the richest man in town, JL Grant, a scion of old money who's lucky enough to live in a town that bears his family name. They fall in love—much to the resentment of Grant's best friend, Griff the cop.

The film packs some big surprises in its last thirty minutes or so, and you are strongly urged not to find out anymore about the plot if you can avoid it. Fuller takes *The Naked Kiss* into areas that are still surprising to viewers today. The last time I watched this film, I saw it with three friends who had never seen it before and during the scenes of revelation near the end, people audibly gasped.

The Naked Kiss was shot for about ten cents and looks like it, but as with *Shock Corridor* Fuller works within these limitations like the pulp novelists he so closely resembles. Fast and efficient, he also had the good fortune not to be a perfectionist. His independent features are frenetic, but they're not sloppy. He loves jarring visuals, and *The Naked Kiss,* with its ubiquitous shadows and slanted cameras, is noir down to its bones. Working without money or sets or stars, he created a film that is nevertheless, in its wild-ass way, the visual superior of bigger budgeted and more politely directed movies.

While he didn't have stars, he did have actors. The film is grounded by the fierce performance of Constance Towers as Kelly. This may be the toughest broad who ever stalked through a film noir. With a soft spot for kids and old people, she is otherwise a steel pillar. She thumps a lot of heads in this movie, more perhaps than any female heroine who preceded her in American movies. There's simply no precedent for the scene where she stomps into a brothel and slaps around a madam who has been trying to recruit one of her friends. Kelly pounces on the woman and makes her eat twenty-five bucks in wadded up bribe money.

Fuller was after more than just cheap thrills, though. An iconoclast with a revulsion for pretense, he casts his pitiless eye on polite society's view of itself. Every real crime in this film—that is every crime, Fuller seems to say, worth caring about—is enabled and obscured under the guise of decency and decorum. The only person with any honor worth respecting is Kelly. A precursor to later cinematic heralds of the counterculture like Bonnie and Clyde, this violent prostitute is pure outcast antihero, the spiritual superior to all the hypocrites and liars masquerading as decent citizens.

III. Fake Realism

While Fuller represented a break from the conventions of the classic studio style, he was not a realist. Far from it. He liked grittiness for its own sake, and he loved art's ability to translate emotion and struggle from the shifting currents of life to a more manageable form. "Reality," he once said, "is a bunch of damn bullshit." His theory, as least as I interpret it, was that since reality could never be less than everything and everyone all at once, the representation of reality in art was impossible. "Realism" was just another concocted film aesthetic. An artist was not in business to put real life on screen; he was in business to recreate life in a way that made it interesting or insightful for the viewer. This guiding principle led Fuller to create a gonzo noir style that is not for everyone. His emotions are enormous. Subtlety is not a concept he finds the least bit interesting. Fuller doesn't go over the top from time to time. He blasts over the top in the first scene and never looks back. *Shock Corridor* and *The Naked Kiss* are thoroughly bizarre movies precisely because they reference the classic American style while shattering it into a million pieces. His films are concerned, first and forever, with impact—with speed and shock and sensation. While many critics at the time found him crass and low-class, he told an interviewer in 1965 that his style had formed before he even became a reporter. As a newsie hawking papers on the streets of New York City, he said, "I leaned early that it is not the headline that counts but how hard you shout it."

In 1963 and 1964, he needed to shout it loud. The American cinema of the early 1960s had largely calcified in style and ambition, as Hollywood faced an existential crisis brought on by age and television and compounded by social forces which were just beginning to pull the country apart. Watching *Shock Corridor* and *The Naked Kiss*, you can see the old give way to the new. Both of these films brought much needed wit and style to bear on the subject of America—in particular the America that was running full-speed into the tumult of a decade marked by assassination, war, racial violence, and what many people feared would be a full-scale social meltdown. Sam Fuller, working in the economic hinterlands with his courageous casts, reconfigured the scope and language of film noir to mark the final collapse of the American Dream into the American Nightmare. In doing so, he changed film—and film noir—forever.

II

BLIND ALLEYS:

A COLLECTION OF ESSAYS

HELL ITSELF COULDN'T BE A STRANGER PLACE
ORSON WELLES AND FILM NOIR

By 1943, Orson Welles was virtually washed-up in Hollywood. He had arrived in town trailing clouds of glory in 1939, a 24-year old wunderkind from New York who had just leapt to superstardom with his "War of the Worlds" radio broadcast. By impersonating a series of panicked news bulletins, Welles had terrified listeners and seized international headlines—and secured an offer to make films at RKO Pictures. Embracing film like a man falling in love, he directed *Citizen Kane* and *The Magnificent Ambersons*, produced *Journey into Fear*, and attempted to make a documentary about South America called *It's All True*. Yet aside from some highbrow recognition all of these projects were loud flops and just three years after granting Welles carte blanche, RKO booted him off the studio lot. By 1943, he knew if he was going to survive in Hollywood he desperately needed to establish himself as a commercially viable filmmaker.

Not surprisingly, Welles choose to go into the thriller business. Given his association with high art and

Shakespeare, it might be easy to overlook his lifelong fondness for hardboiled crime stories, but he read pulp voraciously and even claimed to have ghostwritten some dime novels during his youthful sojourns in Europe (an unsubstantiated boast probably more revealing in spirit than in fact). His first big success on the air was as the voice of the Shadow, and he adapted Hammett's *The Glass Key* for radio in 1939. Upon arriving at RKO, in fact, one of his first projects was an unrealized adaptation of Nicholas Blake's thriller *Smiler With a Knife*—a clear sign that Welles had always wanted the suspense genre to be the bread-and-butter part of his Hollywood operation. Getting fired from RKO made this desire a necessity.

Of course, like everyone else making crime pictures in those days, he had no idea he was helping to create a new genre of American film called *noir*. As both an iconoclast and an egotist, it is unlikely he saw himself as part of a trend, and even more unlikely that he would have wanted to be a part of any such association. He was simply being himself. What is fascinating, however, is how naturally noir seemed to come to Orson Welles.

Hollywood

He took his first shot at the thriller genre while still at RKO with an adaption of Eric Ambler's *Journey into Fear* (1942), a project that hints at the kind of dual-purposed production unit Welles envisioned at the studio. If *Citizen Kane* and *The Magnificent Ambersons* were art, *Journey into Fear* was commerce. He assigned directing duties to a journeyman director named Norman Foster, co-wrote the screenplay with

The Blind Alley

Joseph Cotton, tapped Cotton to play the lead, and cast himself in a supporting role. Since Welles designed the film, intending until the last moment to direct it, some critics and historians give him de facto co-directing credit. In truth, though he did direct the final scene (in postproduction), for most of the shoot he functioned more like a producer in the Selznick mode. He oversaw all aspects of production, but since he was in South America making *It's All True* during much of the shoot, Foster (a good director who later made the excellent noirs *Kiss the Blood Off My Hands* and *Woman on the Run*) was the man standing next to the camera while the film was rolling.

Alas, the movie was shot and edited as Welles's situation at RKO imploded. *Citizen Kane* had enraged publisher William Randolph Hearst (on whom it was partly based) and exasperated most of the Hollywood establishment that feared him. Welles's follow-up film *The Magnificent Ambersons* was deemed too dark for a country heading to war, and his involvement with Brazilian socialists during the filming of *It's All True* had stirred more controversy. Welles's champion at the studio, George Shaffer, was fired and replaced by executives sick of the boy genius from New York. The new management yanked funding for postproduction on *Journey into Fear* and transferred Foster to another project.

The resulting film is a disaster. There are things to admire, such as the opening crane lift into an assassin's apartment as he prepares to go find his prey, or the beautifully shot fight scene on a rain-swept windowsill, but in a way, *Journey Into Fear* became a textbook example of how to destroy a movie through editing. The central story of a naval engineer (Joseph Cotton) being hunted by a shadowy band of Nazis across Europe is nearly impossible to follow, and the whole affair zigzags confusingly for sixty-eight minutes (truncated from 102 minutes) before arbitrarily arriving at a conclusion. Dumped on the market without fanfare, the little thriller ultimately lost $193,000. Welles's plan to establish a profitable sideline in thrillers was off to a bad start.

After being banished from RKO, he accepted an offer from Bill Goetz, head of the newly-formed International Pictures, to direct *The Stranger* (1946), the noirish story of a small town woman (Loretta Young) who discovers that she's married to a Nazi mastermind named Franz Kindler (Welles). Alas, there were strings attached. As Welles later explained to critic Peter Cowie, "[*The Stranger*] is the only picture I have made in which I did not at least expect to function as a producer." That distinction was key. Welles's goal from the beginning of the project was to demonstrate to Hollywood that he could work as a director for hire—or a "director within the producer system" as he later explained it to Peter Bogdanovich.

While the idea of presenting the small town American idyll as a cover for a sociopathic racist engaged Welles, for the most part he kept both his style and irony in check. (One notable exception comes in the film's terrific set piece: a murder in the woods at the edge of town—a long, single shot that mixes suspense with the morbidly funny image of Franz Kindler strangling a religious fanatic to death as the man prays for the restitution of Kindler's soul). Goetz and producer Sam Spiegel rejected the director's idea to cast Agnes Moorehead as the investigator hunting Kindler, casting instead Edward G. Robinson in fast talking *Double Indemnity* mode. Likewise, an opening sequence in South America—the "only chance to be visually interesting in the picture" according to Welles—was quashed as too arty. Other scenes that would have complicated Kindler's character were either cut by editor Ernest Nims or rejected outright by the producers. When Spiegel insisted on more close-ups for Loretta Young, Welles refused. This led to a protracted fight, with Welles finally getting his way. Young, for her part, loved Welles—later telling Spiegel biographer Natasha Fraser-Cavassoni that she had a "smashing crush" on the "enormously sensitive "director. Still, she and Welles created few onscreen sparks in their narrowly defined roles of victim and villain.

While *The Stranger* was his most financially successful film as a director (grossing $3,216,000 against a budget of a little over a million dollars), Welles always spoke about it as if it were a distinctly unloved child. In deferring to Goetz and Spiegel and delivering a routine thriller about a monster, he'd repressed his own sense of the dichotomy of human character. As both a writer and a director, he was obsessed by the nuances of personality, the ways in which a character can be both good and evil, strong and weak, admirable and damnable. Once that sense was gone, there was no idea left for him to dramatize onscreen, only plot points to check off on his way to a violent climax. Of his films, the director insisted, *The Stranger* was "the one…of which I am least the author."

He had more freedom, at least in the beginning, with his next picture *The Lady from Shanghai* (1947). Here Welles plays an Irish boxer named Michael O'Sullivan who stumbles into the convoluted intrigues of a nasty set of characters: the beautiful Elsa Bannister; her crippled, brilliant lawyer husband, Arthur Bannister; and Arthur's ghoulishly strange partner, George Grisby. The ace in the hole was Welles's wife, Rita Hayworth, who would play Elsa. Because she was Columbia's top star, Welles seemed to take her presence in the film as a form of leverage with studio head Harry Cohn. He'd had enough of holding back on *The Stranger*. This time around he went for a knockout.

The resulting film was, in the estimation of critic Andrè Bazin, "the most demented work of [Welles's] career." Certainly it is noir, but it is grotesque even by the standards of the genre. Hayworth looks beautiful, but Welles dyed her hair platinum and cropped it close, giving her beauty an icy glow. Nearly everyone else in the cast looks like a gargoyle. From the sweaty creepiness of Glenn Anders to the Cubist misshapenness of Everett Sloan, Welles relentlessly accentuates physical abnormality with lurching close-ups. There is a near constant swirl of action as characters cross in front of each other in overlapping lines of movement (and speak at cross purposes in overlapping dialog). Toward the end, Welles finds himself stumbling through an amusement park "crazy house," and his brief trip through its comic horrors echoes the comic horrors of the plot. Fittingly, the sequence ends with the famous shootout in a hall of mirrors, the multiplicity of the characters reflected by the multiplicity of their images.

For all its originality, however, the film flummoxed Harry Cohn, who ordered the 155-minute rough cut amputated to 88-minutes. Despite the incomprehensible plot, Welles's style seems to have been the main sticking point. For instance, he had filmed the opening sequence in three complicated long shots (akin to the opening of *Touch of Evil*), but these shots were diced up in the editing room and slapped together to approximate a conventional shot-reverse-shot style. To smooth over the resulting jumble, the dialog between Welles and Hayworth was replaced by a last minute voiceover. Likewise, Welles's ideas for the score were rejected in favor of one song ("Please Don't Kiss Me") repeated in nearly every scene.

The biggest loss was the crazy house sequence. "Hell itself couldn't be a stranger place" is how the script described it, but Columbia's top editor Viola Lawrence slashed down this surrealist *tour de force* to a few glancing shots. What we're left with is weird and wonderful, but it's only a mouthwatering glimpse of the Caligari-like insanity the director intended.

Furious at what had been done to his film, Welles sent Cohn a scathing memo, defending the "quality of freshness and strangeness" he'd labored to give the film. When Cohn swatted away these concerns, Welles took his directing credit off the picture.

Even unsigned, however, it remains distinctly a movie by Orson Welles and marks his defiant plunge into noir's darkest depths. If *The Stranger* was his attempt to replicate the studio aesthetic, *The Lady from Shanghai* was his first concerted effort to present a crime story in his increasingly turbulent style. It's easy to see why Raymond Borde and Etienne Chaumeton highlighted the film as an exemplar of noir filmmaking in their landmark 1955 study *Panorama du film noir Amèrican 1941-1953*. Like a pulp Venus de Milo, *The Lady from Shanghai* is a work of art haunted by disfigurement but marked by real inspiration.

It had become clear by this time that Welles was simply not a Hollywood filmmaker. The problem wasn't that he was too brilliant—one need only look at people like Hitchcock or Siodmak to see great artists who could flourish within the studio system—but neither was the answer as simplistic as the "overrated, reckless genius" moniker Welles was forced to wear for most of his life. While he went over budget on many of his projects (a recent article by Vincent L. Barnett in *Film History* suggests Welles lost RKO well over a million dollars), this hardly made him an anomaly in Hollywood. If the studios had had faith in the finished product as a commercial property, one suspects no frenzied reshoots and last-minute editing overhauls would have been deemed necessary. Therein lies the problem: Welles did not make commercially viable properties.

The key to understanding Welles's aesthetics is to understand that he was obsessed with fragmentation, disintegration, and chaos—not only as themes and subjects, but as *mise-en-scène* and visual metaphor. He was drawn to the falling apart of people, ideas, beliefs, even systems of morality. In this respect, he was perfectly in tune with the emerging noir style. Where he fell out of tune was in the way he framed his images and paced his scenes, to say nothing of his resistance to tweaking these oddities for commercial considerations. In framing his shots, he privileged spatial dislocation and vertiginous movement—often at the expense of narrative clarity and audience identification. Ruin and chaos were not only the most persistent themes of his work, they were the constant substance of his images. He seemed to want his audience to stagger out of the theater. In a Welles film, the center is in a constant state of frenzied collapse. Either because of stubbornness or a temperamental inability, he never married this style to convention in a way that pleased the studios. Whether you judge this as a mark of integrity or petty insolence depends largely on your reaction to the films themselves.

Europe

After *The Lady from Shanghai,* Welles swung by Republic Pictures on his way out of town to make a noirish adaption of *Macbeth* (1948), a fascinating experiment in combining the aesthetics of theater and cinema. The film was the darkest, most grisly adaptation of a Shakespeare play up to that point, but it did nothing to elevate Welles's standing in Hollywood.

He left for Europe and pieced together financing for his four-years-in-the-making adaptation of *Othello* (1952). Part of the funding came from a thriller directed by Carol Reed and starring his old pal Joseph Cotton, *The Third Man* (1949). It would turn out to be the biggest hit of Welles's career, though he forewent a profit-sharing deal in favor of a flat fee which he channeled back into *Othello*.

Because *The Third Man* looks in some respects like a Welles film, speculation has existed for decades about the extent of his participation in its creation, but Welles himself remained insistent that he was merely a happy actor-for-hire on the project. What is beyond question is that while he only appears in the film for about fifteen minutes, his character, Harry Lime, dominates the whole of it. Reed gives him perhaps the best entrance in movie history, and Welles's one verified contribution to the script—Lime's speech about the cuckoo clock—is the most famous scene in the movie. In just a few minutes onscreen, Welles is able to nail the amoral charm of Harry Lime, but what often goes unacknowledged is that aside from the scene by the Ferris wheel, Welles gives an almost entirely silent performance. The last ten minutes of the film—as he runs through the sewers trying to elude capture—are largely dialog free, yet his acting here is vital. As his boyish face gives way to panic, his fear doesn't illicit pleasure from the viewer but rather a strange kind of sympathy. Behind his bluster and mystery, Harry Lime is revealed to be a mere mortal. When Welles wordlessly beseeches Cotton to put him out of his misery, the moment is tragic rather than triumphant.

While Welles was by all accounts a bad businessman, he *was* able to spin off the massive success of *The Third Man* into a new revenue stream. He recorded (and helped write) fifty-two episodes of a weekly radio program called *The Lives of Harry Lime* wherein the drug-dealing murderer became a kind of rakish

The Blind Alley

international adventurer. For one of the episodes he concocted a mysterious European businessman named Arkadin. He liked the character so much that Arkadin became the basis for his next film.

No one is quite sure how many different versions of Welles's 1955 crime drama *Mr. Arkadin* are floating around out there. The film was taken away from Welles by producer Louis Dolivet before he had the chance to edit it, and over the years many different versions (at least seven) have surfaced in different formats. In 2006, the Criterion Collection released a box set featuring three versions of the film, one of which was a new "comprehensive version" integrating material from different sources. While Criterion's box set is a spectacular piece of scholarship and restoration, there is one problem: *Mr. Arkadin* isn't a particularly good movie.

The plot is structured as a mystery told in flashbacks. A shady character named Guy Van Stratten (Robert Arden) is hired by an even shadier character named Gregory Arkadin (Welles), a billionaire with underworld connections who claims he suffers from amnesia. He wants Van Stratten to investigate his past and discover his true identity, but the deeper Van Stratten looks into the past, the more dead people start showing up. Turns out Arkadin is using the investigation to find and knock off anyone who could reveal the truth of his identity. Van Stratten begins to suspect he might be next on Arkadin's hit list.

This suspense plot lacks forward momentum because we never much care about the thinly drawn characters. While Akim Tamiroff, Michael Redgrave, and Mischa

Auer have fun in comically grotesque supporting roles, the center of the film is dragged down by the uninspired performances of the central cast, particularly Robert Arden and Welles himself.

Of course, the primary pleasure of a Welles film is the visual texture of the thing, and *Mr. Arkadin*, for all its faults, is always interesting to look at. The opening shots of Arden trekking through a ruined city in the falling snow have an ominous beauty, and Akim Tamiroff's weird attic hideout is a juicy bit of demented set design. Visually, the highlight of the movie is a masquerade ball at Arkadin's mansion, a tour de force displaying Welles's ability to blend artifice and anarchy.

But what does this all add up to? Not much. Since Welles was never able to edit his film, *Mr. Arkadin* never assumed its final shape, but even an editor of his skill would have had trouble breathing life into the central story. Even in its restored form, *Mr. Arkadin* remains Welles's weakest film.

Luckily, however, his pulp triumph was right around the corner.

One More Night in Hollywood

Despite his struggles directing in Hollywood, Welles had stayed in business there as a movie star. Once he started really packing on the pounds in the fifties, however, he became a self-described "ham actor," a celebrity supporting-player enlisted to class up productions with his marquee name. He was originally slated to perform this function in a cops and robbers picture called *Badge of Evil* starring Charlton Heston, but when Heston suggested to Universal that Welles direct the picture, the studio reluctantly agreed. Seizing his opportunity, Welles changed the title and rewrote the script, transforming the standard little thriller into something truly bizarre.

The result, *Touch of Evil*, is one of the great pieces of cinematic trash. It's a frantic film, wildly over the top, in love with its own squalor, infatuated with the feel and smell of decay. Among the director's attempts at pulp, it is his masterpiece.

At its center is Welles himself, grotesque in the role of a bloated, degenerate cop named Hank Quinlan. In his small Texas border town, Quinlan is a legend, a redneck Sherlock Holmes who always gets his man. When a car bomb suddenly explodes on his side of the border, killing a rich developer and his girlfriend, Quinlan sets out to find the killer. Also investigating the bombing is a Mexican narcotics officer named Mike Vargas (Charlton Heston), a newlywed in town with his wife Susie (Janet Leigh). Vargas thinks the bombing might have something to do with a high profile case he's working on involving a Mexican drug cartel headed by a goofball named Uncle Joe Grandi (Akim Tamiroff). Quinlan doesn't want Vargas messing around in his investigation, probably because he's already decided the killer is the young Mexican who has been dating the dead man's daughter.

The film is a boxing match between the two lawmen, one corrupt and disintegrating, the other upright and honest to a fault. Surrounding them, in a torrent of activity, is a sprawling cast of oddities headed by Quinlan's fidgety, overly faithful sidekick Menzies (Joseph Calleia). The film has the feel—both visually and thematically—of a spiral. Action drifts back and forth across the border, characters and plotlines swerve in and out of focus, but at the center of it, circling each other like fighters, are Quinlan and Vargas, each convinced that he is right, each increasingly convinced that the other is a bigger problem than the killer. By the end, they've both compromised themselves, and one of them lies dead, sinking into a drainage ditch between their two countries.

Touch of Evil is, in many ways, a culmination of everything Welles thought about pulp art. He had struggled before to get his vision of noir to the screen, and he directed this movie as if it might be his last chance (which it was). Pushed along by Henry Mancini's blistering score, the film is relentless. Camera setups—including, of course, the famous three minute opening shot—swing in and demand attention. Trash blows down streets, people scurry in and out of frames (Akim Tamiroff unspools pages of dialog while running). Crane shots swoop up and down, shadows splash across walls. The film is a whirlpool from start to finish.

Not only is it packed with visual details, it also indulges Welles's affection for vignettes. Take the scene late in the film in which Quinlan crosses the border and stumbles across a house-of-ill-repute he used to frequent. Still manning the house, with steaming bowls of chili in the kitchen and a tinkling pianola in the parlor, is Tanya (Marlene Dietrich, laconic as ever). She takes one look at Quinlan and tells him the truth, "You're a mess, honey."

And he is. Hank Quinlan is one of Welles's great creations. The director had always been obsessed with old men—they were a constant in his work—but he had a brutal ambivalence about their disintegration. Hank Quinlan is a monster—albeit a human one—and Welles is unflinching in his embrace of the big man's fall.

A film this manic can't be perfect. Dennis Weaver's Night Man—the twitchy manager of an isolated motel where Susie Vargas is terrorized by thugs—is the most grating character Welles ever put on screen (which, given the director's fondness for absurdist clowns, is saying quite a lot). But pointing out the excesses of a film that luxuriates in excess is like criticizing a musical for having too much singing and dancing. *Touch of Evil* is exactly what it wants to be, a wild night in a sleazy town.

Alas, Universal was not impressed. The studio had been sending Welles encouraging messages throughout filming, but when it all came together…the film was just too much. By that point, Welles had gone down to Mexico to work on *Don Quixote*, and the film was reedited in his absence. His triumphant return to Hollywood seemed to have come to nothing.

Over time, however, *Touch of Evil* was recognized as a masterpiece and restored to something close to Welles's original cut. Paul Schrader in his influential 1971 essay "Notes on Film Noir" called it "film noir's epitaph," and many critics have followed his lead in regarding the film as the close of the noir cycle. While that's up for debate, the film did mark the last time Welles was able to bring a thriller to the screen. It was not, however, his last voyage into the larger noir universe.

Film Noir as European Art Film

An unexpected opportunity to direct again came in 1961 when Welles was approached by independent producer Alexander Salkind and asked to choose from a list of properties to direct. Welles opted to make an adaptation of Kafka's *The Trial*. The result is a European art film suffused with his noir vision.

The setup is pure Kafka: a man named Joseph K wakes up one morning to find that he is being persecuted for some unknown offense. He stumbles from one bizarre confrontation with the law to another, but he is never told what he's charged with. Welles, unencumbered by a need to reflect reality, takes this surreal premise and runs with it.

And what a vision he creates: the architecture is constantly closing in on Joseph K (the wonderfully maladroit Anthony Perkins), the camera forever angled so as to make the ceilings press down. Angles are sharpened like knives, and the film is full of sight lines of maddening symmetrical perfection. When K goes to work, it is at an office straight out of Vidor's *The Crowd*, with desks and florescent lights perfectly aligned and stretching off into infinity. Even in scenes shot outside, Welles emphasizes plain building facades with long lines of bare windows. K is like a man caught inside a machine about to crush him to pieces. Shot largely in and around Paris's abandoned Gare d'Orsay, the film is full of huge spaces overhung with iron rafters. Welles makes an epic out of these caverns. His ambition is to give us a dreamlike world, a nightmare we can't see through. That it was filmed without many sets at all and still achieves this otherworldly quality is a testament to Welles's ability to shoot on location, as well as a testament to the innate midnight weirdness of certain sections of Paris, Rome, and Zagreb.

Enjoying more freedom than he'd had on any film since *Citizen Kane*, Welles perfected the uniquely disjointed *mise-en-scène* that had gotten him into such trouble in Hollywood. As his cinematographer Edmond Richard later explained it in *Orson Welles At Work*, "[Welles] had key positions where his actors would stop...In moving from one point to another, every eccentricity was permitted; in the key positions he wanted to see their eyes. This created an extraordinarily dynamic and syncopated rhythm: movement, pause; movement, pause. Even in complicated movements... of fifty meters, in an S shape, going up, going down, there would be infernal positions that had to be linked in a single movement."

While visually and thematically the film has much in common with film noir, it also has a distinctly expressionist, allegorical quality. If *The Trial* isn't quite a noir, it emanates from the same dark region of the mind that produced something like *Stranger on the Third Floor* (1940). Whatever label you attach to it, it is one of Welles's great achievements.

Rosebud

After *The Trial*, Welles spent a few years making highbrow fare for the Europeans. In 1965, he made the film many Wellesians consider his masterpiece, *Falstaff (Chimes at Midnight)*, an original script culled together from several Shakespeare plays about Falstaff, the disgraced old knight and "misleader of youth" Welles was born to play. In 1968, he directed, wrote, and costarred in a color adaptation of Isak Dinesen's *The Immortal Story* with Jeanne Moreau for French television. And in 1973, he directed *F for Fake,* an essay film that is part documentary, part creative nonfiction. It is a meditation on art and forgery—and one of his best films.

By then, however, the money had dried up in Europe. Welles may have been a great artist, but he was never box office gold. He was barely box office bronze. He returned to America and took roles in films that were beneath him. He channeled the money back into his projects like *The Other Side of the Wind*, a drama featuring John Huston, Peter Bogdanovich, and his buddy from his RKO days, *Journey into Fear* director Norman Foster.

He still dabbled in pulp, too. He shot an adaptation of Charles Williams's *Dead Calm* called *The Deep* with Laurence Harvey, working on it until Harvey died. He planned an adaptation of Jim Thompson's *A Hell of a Woman* with director Gary Graver, but like almost all of his projects in the seventies and eighties, it had to be shelved for lack of funds. Hollywood, which had never liked Welles, had now forgotten him. He was

The Blind Alley

old and broke in a town where only youth and money mattered. In 1985, at the age of 70, he died at home working on a script.

There is a heartbreaking bargain you have to make with Orson Welles. Much of his work—more than that of any other major director aside from Jean Vigo—comes to us in damaged shape. When you consider that he was making difficult films to begin with, the full picture begins to emerge.

Orson Welles was either too much of an artist or too much of an egomaniac—perhaps both—to ever fully commit to genre, even for the duration of a single film. He liked genre but viewed it as a beginning, a jumping off place. This was no less true for a thriller than for a Shakespeare adaptation. His instinct was to be, as he once angrily wrote Harry Cohn, "original, or at the least somewhat oblique." Win or lose—and he lost often—his films were stamped with the conviction that cinema was an instrument of experimentation and poetry, not formula.

In some ways, this brings us back to his first film, *Citizen Kane*. A flop upon first release, it influenced, directly or indirectly, almost everyone and everything that came after it. After being studied with Talmudic intensity by film geeks for nearly seventy years, it's been enshrined as something approaching the Ur-text of modern film. Yet its reputation as the so-called "Greatest Movie Ever Made" threatens to render it a museum piece, like something Charles Foster Kane would have boxed up in his warehouse—an odd fate for a film that crackles with a giddy delight in the possibilities of cinema.

It is neither a crime film nor a thriller—indeed part of its appeal is that it defies easy categorization—but it contains many distinctly noir elements: chiaroscuro lighting, slanted angles, narrative disorientation, a sense of futility, a downbeat ending. Its fundamental story of a poor boy gaining the world but losing his soul is the American Dream turned gothic nightmare. Welles didn't invent film noir, but his contribution to its creation is difficult to overestimate.

Indeed, his immediate impact on noir was profound. Consider the talent he helped bring to Hollywood: actors Ray Collins, Joseph Cotton, Ted de Corsia, Norman Lloyd, Agnes Moorehead, Erskine Sanford, Everett Sloane, Paul Stewart; producer John Houseman; composer Bernard Herrmann; director John Berry. Consider his direct influence on noir directors like Berry, William Castle, Norman Foster, and Robert Wise. Or consider the stylistic influence of *Citizen Kane*, *The Lady from Shanghai*, *Touch of Evil* and *The Trial*.

Most of all, consider the worldview permeating almost all his work. Welles was an artist with something to say. From his first film until his last, his movies presented a distinct vision, a distinctly *noir* vision, of life as a strange place, one we're all struggling to survive.

ALL KINDS OF WOMEN
THE LESBIAN PRESENCE IN FILM NOIR

There are no lesbians in classic film noir, and the reason for this is quite simple. Lesbians didn't exist back then.

Well, they didn't *officially* exist. Sure, there were places in L.A. that catered to the all-girl set, upscale nightclubs like Tess's Café Internationale and middle-class bars like the If Club and the Paradise Club. Actors such as Margaret Lindsay (*Scarlett Street*), Ona Munson (*The Red House*), and Patsy Kelly (*The Naked Kiss*) either lived openly with their partners or carried on affairs with other women while hidden behind "lavender marriages" to gay men. And rumors swirled about big name stars like Marlene Dietrich, Barbara Stanwyck, and Lizabeth Scott. On the nation's screens, however, lesbians didn't even rate the kind of offensive portrayals accorded to other minorities. According to the Hays Code, absolutely no manner of "sex perversion" was permitted onscreen—a rule so ironclad that not even the implication of homosexuality was permissible. In the culture at large, moreover, homosexuality was rarely if ever spoken about in the open. It wasn't that people were in the closet—it's that the closet wasn't even supposed to exist.

So there are no lesbians in noir. Implications, however, are funny things. After all, what implies homosexuality and what doesn't—or more importantly, what implied homosexuality in 1947? Because film is primarily a visual medium, images carry information before it is transferred through dialog or stated in exposition. As Josef von Sternberg (no stranger to weaving lesbian inferences into his films) said, "Each picture transliterates a thousand words." To put it somewhat differently, we read the pictures that flicker on the screen. Through the images and actions presented to us we read characters as good or bad, trustworthy or diabolical. And we read some images as straight and some as queer. When Bogart sniffs Peter Lorre's perfumed business card and raises his eyebrows in *The Maltese Falcon*, we're invited to infer a meaning about the effete little man that the censors would never have allowed to be stated outright. As it happens, though, nearly everyone who's ever seen the film has assumed that Joel Cairo is gay. The figure of the slightly comic gay villain pops up occasionally in noir, as he did in the hardboiled fiction that preceded it in the twenties and thirties.

Lesbianism, however, comes to us through slightly different signifiers. Unlike male homosexuality in noir, which was denoted by a broad femininity in men, lesbianism was signified not just by female-masculinity but by a complex contempt for femininity itself. While implied lesbians were almost exclusively represented as villains, they were seldom objects of comic derision.

Lesbians were always presented as far more threatening, their masculinity an implicit threat to the male hegemony of the social order.

The Butch Fatale

Consider noir's chief lesbian villain, Hope Emerson. At 6'2" and 230 pounds, Emerson not only dwarfed all her female costars she also loomed over most of her leading men as well. With a large forehead, thick jowls, and a long beaked nose, Emerson looked like a heavy, and Hollywood, being Hollywood, quickly cast her in a series of violent, sexually ambiguous roles.

Born in Iowa in 1897, Emerson was an unlikely candidate for the role of Hollywood bad guy. A comic by nature and training, she started out in vaudeville playing piano and swapping jokes in a comedy team with her mother, Josie. She toured stages all around the country, working with funnyman Billy House and serving for a while as the sidekick to a sham mystic, a la *Nightmare Alley*. By the thirties, she'd made it to the stages and radios of New York City, stealing the show in productions like *Lysistrata* (playing an Amazon) and the hillbilly musical *Swing Your Lady*. To help pay the bills in between gigs, she worked the New York nightclub circuit, singing risqué tunes for largely gay crowds at clubs like Fifth Avenue One in Greenwich Village.

Then in the late forties, Emerson went out to Hollywood and became a villain. Her first role in a major production was as the hulking masseuse Rose Given in Siodmak's *Cry of the City*. Her first appearance in the film is unforgettable: walking through a house in the middle of the night, turning on lights in each successive room, she grows ever larger as she approaches the camera. She towers over her 5'8" costar, Richard Conte. He's Martin Rome, an escaped convict and smooth-talking ladies man who has easily manipulated every other woman in the film. He's come to Rose Given for help retrieving some stolen jewels, and he begins flirting with her almost immediately. When she offers him a back rub, his flirtations seem to have worked.

Rose is different from the other women in the film, though. As her hands move up his back, he rolls his eyes in pleasure. Yet her banter grows odd. She talks about fat old women trying to stave off age with money and jewelry, and then she clamps down on his throat and his entire neck disappears between her huge mitts. The woman's threat to the man here has nothing to do with sex or seduction, it's purely violent. Like some kind of female Mike Mazurki, she looks as if she could pop off his head like a champagne cork. The scene is the rare example in film noir—indeed in all classic film—of a woman terrorizing a man with her bare hands.

It's the blurring of lines between the traditional representations of masculinity and femininity—and their corresponding relationship to dominance and passivity—that marks the scene as a queer moment. Rose Given isn't a femme fatale. She's a butch fatale. In noir's milieu of male anxiety, the butch holds a special place. Her threat to the male isn't based on a feminine manipulation of male sexual desire but rather through the usurpation of his role as the dominant masculine presence.

In Nicholas Ray's *In a Lonely Place* (1950) we have the curious figure of Martha (Ruth Gillette) the husky-voiced butch masseuse who hovers over naked Laurel Gray (Gloria Graham), rubbing her too hard while poking into her private life. After Laurel fires her for badmouthing boyfriend Dix Steele (Humphrey Bogart), Martha snaps, "I'll get out, Angel, but you'll beg me to come back when you're in trouble. You will, Angel, because you don't have anybody else." These could easily be the words of a spurned lover, and Martha's jealous assertion that Laurel will crawl back to her when things go wrong, it should be noted, turns out to be right. Once she becomes afraid of Dix, Laurel does indeed call Martha first—a strong suggestion that Martha fills the masculine void whenever Laurel is between men. Dix seems to intuit this when he jealously intercepts a phone call from Martha meant for Laurel.

The butch fatale wasn't merely a danger to the male ego, however. Most of the time she was seen as a sexualized threat to the female. This was never more apparent than the women-in-prison film, the butch equivalent of the classic studio "woman's picture."

Women Without Men

In a deftly argued essay in the pages of the *Noir City Sentinel*, Alan K. Rode sought to rescue the classic 1950 women-in-prison picture, *Caged* from the misapplied label of camp and restore it to its rightful place among the very best noirs of the period. One factor that necessitated Rode's essay is the film's lesbian overtones—and the assumption in some quarters that homosexuality automatically equals camp (which might account for why the film was released as a "camp classic" in the first place).

No, *Caged* is not camp. But it is queer. Again we find the colossal figure of Hope Emerson, here starring as Evelyn Harper, a sadistic prison matron who taunts and tortures the "tramps" unlucky enough to be incarcerated under her watch. Locked into an ideological battle with the spinsterish warden played by Agnes Moorehead (herself a decidedly queer figure), Miss Harper is a sadistic monster. But her conflicts with the inmates have a kinky quality. In one of the film's most memorable moments, Miss Harper, dressed up for an evening on the town with a man she says is waiting for her outside, preens in front of the inmates. We never see this man, nor is he ever referred to again. Did Miss Harper walk outside the prison and catch the bus home alone? Given what we know of her character, that would make more sense than the romantic scenario Harper outlines for the girls. In her book *Female Masculinity*, cultural critic Judith Halberstam notes that Harper "indulges herself in 'feminine comforts'…not, one feels, for the pleasure she gains from femininity but because femininity is what is denied to the inmates."

Indeed, the central drama of *Caged* is a prolonged attack on the femininity of the main character, Marie Allen (played by Eleanor Parker). She's warned by Moorehead at the beginning of the film, "You'll find all kinds of women in here." She's appraised by another inmate, a glamorous butch vice queen played by Lee Patrick, who looks her up and down and calls her "a cute trick." Near the end of film, Marie finally snaps and attacks Miss Harper, a fight in which the matron's uniform is ripped and her undergarments are exposed. Once Marie has been subdued, Harper, with her scratches and bra strap still visible, drags the inmate downstairs and shaves her head—a chilling scene that has long been read by critics as a symbolic rape.

Emerson's butch villain in *Caged* is offset, however, by the sympathetic treatment of another of the film's butch characters, an inmate named Kitty Stark. Played with wonderful understatement by Betty Garde, Kitty first appears as a menacing force. Block-shouldered and short-haired, she arrives in the film trailed by two slightly more femme sidekicks (Jan Sterling and Joan Miller). She's given a dead husband and snatches of dialog to provide the requisite heterosexual cover, but Kitty Stark is as butch as they come. Near the middle of the film, as she and Marie lie together on a cot—Marie on her back, Kitty propped up on an elbow gazing down at her—Kitty coos, "If you stay in here too long, you don't think about guys at all. You just…get out of the habit." Things will turn out hard for Kitty—after an altercation with Harper she'll become a tragic figure. Yet in some ways she emerges as a hero at the end. In a fitting piece of irony, she's also the one who finally takes care of the dreaded Harper, butch to butch.

The sexually repressed butch prison guard found her most psychopathic expression a few years later in 1955's *Women's Prison*. The film stars a steely Ida Lupino as warden Amelia van Zandt, an authoritarian so frigid and heartless that repressed lesbianism seems to have transmogrified completely into psychosexual-sadism. The film is overly simplistic, even by the conventions of the women in prison film, but with this performance, Lupino pretty much wrote the book on how you pull off the she's-so-repressed-she's-sexy pulp lesbian archetype. A coldly beautiful short-haired woman with no family who beats one of her inmates for getting pregnant… that's a barely concealed subtext.

Within a few years, the lesbian subtext would begin forcing its way into the text of films.

(un)Bound…More or Less

By the late fifties, Hollywood was lagging behind the publishing world, where lesbian potboilers had become a powerful fixture of paperback imprints like Gold Medal Books. Tereska Torres sold 2 million copies of her autobiographical *Women's Barracks* in 1950, while Marijane Meaker published the first lesbian pulp novel *Spring Fire* under the name Vin Packer in 1952. When that book sold an astounding 1.5 million copies, lesbian pulp poured out by writers like Meaker's lover Patricia Highsmith (*The Price of Salt*), Ann Bannon (*Odd Girl Out*) and Valerie Taylor (*The Girls in 3-B*). None of this success translated into representation in Hollywood films, but during the fifties and sixties, lesbian characters became more obvious, if not necessarily more sympathetic.

Orson Welles contributed a gruesome addition to the pantheon of noir lesbians with his inclusion of Mercedes McCambridge in *Touch of Evil* (1958). McCambridge had already issued her performance as Emma Small in Nicholas Ray's 1954 Sapphic shoot 'em up, *Johnny Guitar*. As with everything else in *Touch of Evil*, however, Welles took the butch archetype one step further. When Janet Leigh is cornered in a seedy hotel room by a group of junkies, the threat of gang rape is made all the more real when a door opens and a short-haired, leather-wearing McCambridge creeps in. When the leader of the gang tells her to leave, McCambridge grunts, "Lemme stay. I want to watch." This is followed by a close-up of the leader licking his lips and ordering his thugs to grab Janet Leigh and, "Hold her legs." The presence of the butch hoodlum in a scene designed to infer a sexual assault is as explicit as Welles could be in 1958. The scene is hardly a shining moment in the history of lesbian representation in mainstream American film, but it is the most overt moment since a tuxedo-wearing Marlene Dietrich kissed a girl in *Morocco*.

Lesbianism would finally make it into the text of films in the sixties with William Wyler's *The Children's Hour* (1961) and Robert Aldrich's *The Killing of Sister George* (1968). It's purest noir incarnation, however, might well have been Edward Dmytryk's *Walk on the Wild Side* (1962). Here, Barbara Stanwyck plays Jo Courtney, a New Orleans madam who is obsessed with one of her working girls, Hallie Gerard (the French actor Capucine). The movie is supposed to be the story of Hallie's star-crossed love affair with a romantic drifter named Dove Linkhorn (played by a bored-looking Laurence Harvey), but this bland relationship is overshadowed by Jo's fixation on Hallie.

Of course the L-word is never used, but the script gives Jo an uncommonly frank obsession with Hallie, keeping her in a room above the brothel so the younger woman can lounge and drink and make ghoulish sculptures of the madam. Hallie is unhappy living like this, but Jo won't let her leave. When Dove tries to take Hallie away, Jo has him beaten up and framed for statutory rape. *Walk on the Wild Side*, while presenting Jo as the film's antagonist, does at least humanize her to the extent that it allows her a genuine emotional stake in the drama. She's the bad guy here, but there is no doubt that she loves Hallie. Moreover, since Harvey and Capucine lack any chemistry, Jo and Hallie become the de facto center of the film.

The script gives Jo a husband, of course, a self-hating amputee played by Karl Swenson. She treats him like a nonentity, and when he's excited to find that Hallie might be leaving, Jo snaps, "You'd like that, wouldn't you?" Stanwyck gives a performance that moves between cool calculation and uncontrollable rage. It's one of the actor's most interesting parts, and Stanwyck plays it like she means it, as when she tells Swenson, "Don't talk to me about love! What do you know? What does any man know?"

Walk on the Wild Side is a flawed film in many ways, but it did nudge the closet door open. In the decades that followed, neo-noir would become more comfortable with lesbian text and subtext, and films like *Basic Instinct*, *Mulholland Drive*, and *The Black Dahlia* dealt with lesbian or bisexual female characters with varying degrees of success and intelligence.

The main lesbian duo in neo-noir, however, are the protagonists of *Bound* (1996). Here the butch-femme dynamic is allowed to occupy the center of the film, a privileged space in which the heroes, butch Corky (Gina Gershon) and femme Violet (Jennifer Tilly) attempt to steal millions of dollars from a gangster played by Joe Pantoliano. The lesbianism of the characters is in no way downplayed or obscured, but neither is it much remarked upon outside of the set-up of the film. The plot could be easily be about a man and a woman—indeed, noir is rife with variations on this very premise. Once the story starts to twist and turn, the sexuality of the characters becomes a simple fact. Since this is a crime thriller and not a drama about sexual identity, that's as it should be. *Bound*'s lasting contribution to noir is that it finally gives us a lesbian couple that is formed and tested along the conventional genre-lines usually reserved for straight couples.

Throughout much of the classic period of noir, the lesbian represented a danger to the social order, to male privilege in particular and to heterosexual stability in general. The misogyny and heterosexism implicit in these representations speak volumes about the anxieties surrounding shifting gender norms in post-war America, but they tell us little or nothing about the gay subculture that was alive and well at the time. The first lesbian rights organization, Daughters of Bilitis, was founded in 1955, and lesbians had been working in Hollywood from the beginning, from director Dorothy Arzner to legendary costume designer Edith Head, though most kept their love lives—and by extension their subculture—secret. The veil of history is simply the beginning when trying to piece together the record of gay culture. Someone like Hope Emerson, who never married and left most of her estate to the woman she lived with the last years of her life, is often claimed by authors of gay history as a lesbian, but gay history is almost by definition a mystery without a solution, the search for artifacts of a culture that wasn't supposed to exist. While Hollywood films are inexact time capsules—history refracted by artistic interpretation and commercial imperative—they do give us some idea of how this culture began to stir in the mainstream consciousness during the middle of the twentieth century. It wasn't always pretty, but then again history never is.

AT THE CENTER OF THE STORM

HE RAN ALL THE WAY AND THE HOLLYWOOD BLACKLIST

He was born Jacob Julius Garfinkle, a poor Jewish kid from the Lower East Side of New York City. He spent some time in street gangs and ended up in a Bronx school for troubled youth. After winning a state debating contest, he attended drama school and hit the stage as a member of the Group Theater. It wasn't long before Hollywood came courting and cast him in Michael Curtiz's smash hit *Four Daughters* in 1938. Overnight he became a movie star. The legend of John Garfield was born.

Thirteen years later, it ended with a thud. Accused of being a Communist and hounded by the House Un-American Activities Committee, Garfield died of a heart attack, a frightened, broken man. It was a terrible way to go, but he'd already amassed an impressive body of work that would outlive him. He had made a special mark in the dark underworld of film noir, lusting after Lana Turner in *The Postman Always Rings Twice*, boxing his way to redemption in *Body and Soul*, and losing everything in *Force of Evil*. Cinematically, he came to his bitter end facedown in a gutter in *He Ran All the Way*.

In the film, Garfield plays Nick Robey, a simpleminded stickup man who pulls a payroll job that goes horribly wrong. Nick's accomplice ends up captured but not before Nick guns down a cop. Frantic, he hides in a public pool and picks up Peggy Dobbs (Shelly Winters) a sweet neighborhood girl. He teaches her how to swim and she takes him home to meet her parents and her little brother. Boiling with paranoia, sure the cops are hot on his trail, Nick pulls a gun and takes the Dobbs family hostage.

He Ran All the Way has an impressive pedigree. It was directed by John Berry and photographed by James Wong Howe. In addition to Garfield and Winters, it stars Wallace Ford, Selena Royle, Norman Lloyd, and Gladys George. The screenplay credited to Guy Endore and Hugo Butler was mostly written by the great Dalton Trumbo. It's an impressive group of people collaborating on a taunt, dark crime picture. What makes *He Ran All the Way* particularly fascinating, however, is that it seems to have been at the center of the Communist witch hunts in the fifties. It wasn't just Garfield's problem. The lives and careers of a shocking number of people involved in this film were crushed by the House Un-American Activities Committee's investigation into suspected Communist subversion in Hollywood.

All of the writers on the project found themselves in trouble with redbaiters. The script (based off Sam Ross's novel) was originally written by Dalton Trumbo, one of the original Hollywood Ten who had refused to testify before HUAC in 1947 and wound up serving a year in prison for contempt of Congress. Because Trumbo was banned from working in Hollywood at the time, he used a front on the project, novelist and screenwriter Guy Endore (*Tomorrow Is Another Day*). This proved ironic since Endore, a member of the Communist Party, was soon to be blacklisted himself. He sold some occasional scripts under an alias, but Endore's career in American film was essentially ruined. Likewise, the third writer on the project, Hugo Butler (who did a minor rewrite of the script and received screenplay credit with Endore) dodged a HUAC subpoena and was forced to leave his career behind. Both he and Trumbo relocated to Mexico with their wives. Trumbo continued turning out high quality work like Losey's *The Prowler* and Haskin's *The Boss*. Most notably, he wrote *Roman Holiday* which won his front, Ian McLellan Hunter, an Oscar for best screenplay (Trumbo was given posthumous credit in 1993). Butler, however, was a changed man. He did some work in Mexico and Italy, wrote some scripts for fellow blacklistee Joseph Losey, even directed a film under another name, but he became increasingly embittered and ill. In 1968, he died at age fifty-three.

Director John Berry had started out in the leftist theater world in New York. An early disciple of Orson Welles (he once called Welles "my spiritual father"), he thought theater a progressive medium and far superior to the crass commercialism of film. Soon though, he was tempted out to Hollywood where he was assigned to study Billy Wilder on the set of *Double Indemnity*. In 1949, he turned in a gem with *Tension*, starring femme fatale Audrey Totter at her sexiest and meanest. It was a suspenseful piece of work, one which should have led to bigger projects, but his next film had a far greater impact on his career—and his life. *The Hollywood Ten* (1950) was a fifteen minute documentary defending Trumbo and the rest of the Hollywood writers and directors who had stood up to the original congressional investigation into Hollywood's politics in 1947. Even while he was making *He Ran All The Way*, Berry knew that things were going to get tough. Then on April 25, 1951 one of the Hollywood Ten, director Edward Dmytryk, flipped and turned informer. One of first names he gave the Committee: John Berry. When the FBI showed up at his door to serve him with a subpoena, Berry climbed out his back window and fled the country. He relocated to France and started making films, including the impressive *Ca va barder* and *Je suis un sentimental*. He even did an adaption of *He Ran All The Way* for French television. By his own admission, though, he never recovered his career's momentum.

The list of blacklisted *He Ran All The Way* collaborators goes on. Associate producer Paul Trivers saw his career evaporate overnight. Actor Norman Lloyd, who plays Garfield's accomplice in the payroll heist, was a out of work for years after being blacklisted until Alfred Hitchcock threw him a lifeline in the late fifties and hired him to help produce *Alfred Hitchcock Presents*. Selena Royle, who plays Winters's mother, had worked steadily for years as an admired supporting player, but when her name appeared in a list of "Red Fascists" in the rightwing publication *Red Channels*, she was ordered to testify before HUAC. When she refused, her career was finished. She moved to Mexico, like many blacklist refugees, where she would live out the rest of her life writing travel guides and assembling cookbooks with titles like *Pheasants For Peasants* and *A Gringa's Guide To Mexican Cooking*. While cinematographer James Wong Howe wasn't blacklisted, HUAC made no secret that it considered him suspicious, and that whiff of controversy alone complicated the early fifties for the legendary DP. Shelly Winters also avoided a direct confrontation with the Committee, but during the hearings she quit Hollywood in disgust. As she told the San Francisco Film Festival years later, "It was all because of the Communist Scare…I couldn't stand what was happening."

These people were all small fish, though. What the Committee really wanted was someone big. That meant a bona fide movie star, and almost from the beginning they had their eye on John Garfield. He was dragged before the Committee where he denied knowing anything about Communism. He denied having ever met a single Communist. These were blatant lies (his wife had been a party member), but Garfield himself had never been a party member, and he had no desire to put the finger on any of his friends just to save his career. The Committee asked him about John Berry and Hugo Butler, both of whom had fled the country. Garfield said nothing. They asked him who wrote *He Ran All The Way*, and he didn't mention Trumbo. Still, the Committee hounded him, kept after him about an issue of *The Daily Worker* that he admitted to once having read, pressed him on the difference between being a liberal and being a pink-o. Mostly, though, they wanted names. It was all the Committee ever seemed to want: just give us the names of some of your friends, and we'll let you go. When Garfield refused to turn rat, HUAC gave his testimony to the FBI and asked them to build a perjury case. The studios stopped hiring him. One of the biggest movie stars of the 1940s—a man with two Oscar nominations and millions of fans—was done in Hollywood. The FBI started tailing him, eventually compiling a thousand page file on the comings and goings of an out-of-work actor. Panicked, Garfield wrote an article for *Look* magazine called "I Was A Sucker For A Left Hook" in which he denounced Communism and said he'd been duped into supporting various leftist causes. It read like a pathetic plea for absolution, and the magazine refused to publish it. "I'll act anywhere," he told a columnist in late 1951. But his career was over. In May of 1952, he died suddenly of a heart attack.

Asked about Garfield's death, John Berry mused later, "The tension was enormous. The temptation to play ball must have crossed his mind. This may sound romantic, but I think what happened was, faced with this option, Julius Garfinkle of the Bronx said to John Garfield of Hollywood, 'You can't do this to me.' And John Garfield packed his bags and died. The only way to clear himself was to rat, and he couldn't do that."

Yet John Garfield continues to live on, one of the great doomed men of film noir, and one of his best performances appears in *He Ran All The Way*, which was to be his final film. Berry later told interviewer Patrick McGilligan that the cast and crew were under a great deal of strain at the time the movie was made.

The Blind Alley

"[The movie is] about doom," he said. "That's not coincidental."

The film shows the director at his best. Because of Howe's exquisite deep focus photography, Berry is able to utilize the front of the image to great, jarring effect—often foregrounding an actor's face in a tight close-up while allowing another plane of action to unfold behind him. And while the script has lapses (neither Shelly Winters nor her parents seem to notice that she's brought home an anxious, stuttering mess of a man until he pulls out a gun), it still crackles with great lines: when Garfield's booze-swilling mother tells him, "If you were a man, you'd be out lookin' for a job," he snaps back, "And if you were a man, I'd kick your teeth in." The cast is uniformly good. Winters played needy, self-deluded women better than anyone, and Gladys George, sucking down Pabst Blue Ribbon for breakfast, steals every scene she's in.

Ultimately, however, the film belongs to its doomed star. Though Garfield looks pale and punchy, he's still absolutely riveting. A natural earthiness emanates from those stock shoulders, that big sweaty forehead, and that unmistakable New York voice. His eyes—dark and soulful—always appear to be shadowboxing with his thoughts. Garfield's face had always seemed to project worry, and in the way he combined everyguy authenticity with a bubbling neurosis, he presaged the Method actors like Brando and Dean who would follow him. In a way, he had outgrown this kind of role. Films like Polonsky's *Force of Evil* and Curtiz's *The Breaking Point* had showed that he could play a smart guy with moral complications as well as dumb palookas and lusty dimwits. Still, what he does here, in his last film, he did as well as anybody. The film's final image, of Garfield face down in a gutter, is a remarkable noir visual, a fitting end to a tragic career.

THE PASSION OF THE CHUMP

THE SYNOPTIC MITCHUM

During his long stint in Noir City, Robert Mitchum played everything from upright heroes to the nastiest of villains, but first and foremost he was the definitive sap. More than any other actor, Mitchum created the pivotal figure of the lovesick antihero with tragic taste in women. Here is a guy destined to die for love. We find the core aspects of this persona in three films he made at RKO between 1947 and 1953: *Out of the Past, Where Danger Lives,* and *Angel Face.* These films feature the actor in strikingly similar scenarios which develop and resolve in parallel fashion.

In each film:

Mitchum is a seemingly stable professional who, through his job, meets a beautiful woman.

Although she has money and is already involved with another man, this woman has a pathological need to control Mitchum.

Mitchum has a relationship with a virtuous but somewhat boring nice girl. At some point, he will reject this woman.

Before the femme fatale completely bonds herself to Mitchum, she will kill the other man.

Realizing that the femme fatale is crazy, Mitchum will try—and fail—to leave her.

The film will climax with the femme fatale's attempt to murder Mitchum.

The similarities between these films are fascinating, and through this repetition of scenes and situations, we see a persona take shape which is more resonant than any specific character the actor portrays. In a way, 'Mitchum' becomes our central character, and the three films become retellings of his story. Just as interesting are the differences between the films, each one a variation on the theme of Mitchum's martyrdom at the hands of a femme fatale.

I. The Gospel According to Tourneur: A Graceful Defeat

Jacques Tourneur's *Out of the Past* (1947) sets up the basic framework of the Mitchum persona we'll see developed in all three films. Here, he plays a private detective hired to track down sexy Jane Greer and the forty thousand dollars she's stolen from her gangster boyfriend Kirk Douglas. Of course, once he finds Greer, Mitchum falls helplessly in love with her. They run off together, but when she commits a murder to protect the forty grand, he realizes she's not exactly a timid damsel in distress. He quits the detective business and tries to settle down with nice girl Virginia Huston, but before long he's drawn back into Greer's web. He dies at the end, the victim of film noir's signature turn of fate: he met the wrong woman.

The Blind Alley

Tourneur's variation on the chump's gospel is notable for its lush romanticism. Beginning beside a pristine mountain river, the film starts off on a note of pastoral simplicity and contentment. As Mitchum begins his steep descent into the nocturnal world of Greer and Douglas, however, both Roy Webb's score and Nicholas Musuraca's exquisite cinematography transition seamlessly to fit the moody urban nightscapes. Packed full of witty dialog and dramatic plot twists, *Out of The Past* is the kind of classic old Hollywood melodrama that ends on a glorious note of self-sacrifice. After Mitchum dies helping bring Greer to justice, his young confidant lies to Huston, telling her that Mitchum died trying to escape with Greer. It's a symbolic rejection, designed to help the good girl get on with her life, and it ends the film on a moment of grace. With this final gesture, the film establishes Mitchum's antiheroic persona as a figure of romantic fatalism. His entanglement with Greer is more bad luck than anything else, and while he dies in the end, he still manages to keep a measure of his integrity. This is a small victory, but it is as close to heroism as an antihero can get.

II. The Gospel According to Farrow: Sin and Consequence

In John Farrow's *Where Danger Lives* (1950), Mitchum takes a turn for the worse. This time he's a doctor who exercises extremely poor judgment by falling for a beautiful young woman (Faith Domergue) who has tried to commit suicide. Mitchum blows off his sturdy nurse girlfriend (Maureen O'Sullivan) to try to rescue Domergue from her rich, controlling father

(Claude Rains), only to find out that Rains is actually Domergue's husband. After Rains whacks him over the head with a heavy fire poker, Mitchum knocks out the older man. Floating in and out of a concussion-induced mental fog, Mitchum doesn't see Domergue smoother Rains with a pillow, and once she convinces him that he killed Rains, they take off for Mexico. They wind up on the border, holed up in a cheap hotel where Domergue smothers a nearly comatose Mitchum with a pillow and then leaves him for dead like a crushed cockroach. Somehow he survives and even lives to see Domergue gunned down by the cops. In the end, he's reunited with O'Sullivan.

In *Where Danger Lives* we see Mitchum stripped of any agency, his heroic swagger all but lost in the baffling swirl of events. Knocked over the head about fifteen minutes in, for most of the movie he's essentially Domergue's woozy puppet. We have good reason to think that he would do the right thing if he were able, but concussions have a way of complicating your moral reasoning.

Still, Mitchum's crucial mistake comes early in the film. We're not necessarily reading too much into Farrow's devout Catholicism, or into the fact that Maureen O'Sullivan was his wife, if we observe that the film is essentially a cautionary tale about being tempted away from a steady (if dull) good girl by a sexy (if psychopathic) bad girl. The antihero squeaks by in the end, but he's been punished for his transgression. The film complicates and darkens the basic situation of *Out of the Past* by depriving Mitchum of much of his moral autonomy. Gone is the heroic last gesture.

In this telling of Mitchum's tale, he is a sinner/victim. He falls for the wrong woman, and so he is concussed, smothered, and shot. That should have taught him his lesson. Of course, it didn't.

III. The Gospel According to Preminger: The Tunnel at the End of the Light

In Otto Preminger's *Angel Face* (1953), the darkest of the three films, Mitchum plays an ambulance driver who blows off his nurse girlfriend played by Mona Freeman (note to nurses: don't date Mitchum) in favor of a sexy, spoiled rich girl played by Jean Simmons. Simmons is obsessed with her pathetic drunk of a father, but after she inadvertently kills him while trying to bump off her despised stepmother, she latches onto Mitchum. They're both tried for murder and in an attempt to gain the sympathy of the jury, they get married (in a wedding even more grotesque than a similarly freakish wedding in *Where Danger Lives*). After they're acquitted, Mitchum can't bring himself to stay with her. He tries to go back to the good girl, but this time she rejects him. She's moved on with her life, so he goes back to Simmons. Eventually he tries to leave her, but—to put it mildly—she's not having it.

Angel Face is ultimately the bleakest telling of Mitchum's tale. Here, he finds no redemption from a good woman, no salvation in a *deus ex machina*, and no final gesture with which he can squeeze out some consolation as he stares into the abyss. The antihero is truly anti-heroic and finds himself outwitted at every turn by the femme fatale.

Of the three films, *Angel Face* is also the starkest in its interrogation of the man's attraction to the woman. He's not a villain himself (after all, he does try to leave her), but one can't help thinking that Freeman is right to reject him at the end. Mitchum's chief adversary in the film is his own attraction to the femme fatale. He's drawn to her, for reasons beyond sex and money, by some deeper connection—some germ of personal weakness—and Preminger is brutal in his assessment of where that weakness will ultimately lead.

Mitchum's story is, in some ways, the central myth of film noir: the downfall of the antihero at the hands of the femme fatale. While *Out of the Past* views this story in grandly tragic terms, *Where Danger Lives* sees it as a twisted cautionary tale. *Angel Face*, on the other hand, unfolds as an existential study of unfathomable desire. What stays intriguingly the same throughout these films is Robert Mitchum himself. He's handsome, resourceful, and effortlessly cool, but he is finally helpless in the presence of the wrong woman. From film to film, his persona grows increasingly dark, passive, and hopeless, and by the end Mitchum achieves a potent cumulative power. At the time, of course, it was just a matter of RKO typecasting, but the final effect of seeing the actor playing variations on the same sequence of scenes is that he becomes the embodiment of a certain form of male weakness. What ties these key performances together is a consistent worldview that seemed as natural to the actor as the swagger in his walk. Mitchum was the great cinematic poet of life's essential meaninglessness. If he lacked the anxiety and neurosis that drove other noir stalwarts like Bogart or Robert Ryan, his biographer, Lee Server, summed up Mitchum's attitude when he swiped one of the actor's great lines from *Out Of The Past* for the title of a 2002 biography: *Baby, I Don't Care*. That passivity in the face of sure destruction is the essence of the Mitchum you find in his synoptic RKO films.

THE LITTLE STORY OF RIGHT-HAND/ LEFT-HAND
DAVIS GRUBB, CHARLES LAUGHTON AND
The Night Of The Hunter

Davis Grubb was still an unknown copywriter living and working in Philadelphia when producer Paul Gregory came across the prepublication galleys of Grubb's debut novel, *The Night Of The Hunter*. Gregory scooped up the book for his business partner Charles Laughton, who had been looking for a property to direct. After he read it, an excited Laughton told the producer, "You've got your finger right on my pulse. I would love to direct this."

What Laughton responded to so viscerally was Grubb's bizarre blend of Southern Gothic nightmare and children's fable. The book concerns a serial killer named Harry Powell—most often referred to simply as "Preacher"—who roams West Virginia during the Depression with LOVE and HATE tattooed on his knuckles, killing "unclean" women and pinching their money. While doing time for stealing a car, Preacher meets Ben Harper, a condemned man who has hidden $10,000 from a bank heist. After Harper goes to the gallows, Preacher tracks down his widow, lonely Willa

Harper, and her children, nine-year-old John and four-year-old Pearl. Preacher woos the grieving widow, marries her, and sets to work looking for the money, which he believes Ben Harper has entrusted with John. This leads to a battle of wills between the boy and the evil man of god.

Laughton and Gregory put together a production team with a deep bench of talent, and their adaptation of *The Night Of The Hunter* is, above all, a triumph of collaboration. Laughton relied heavily on both his cinematographer Stanley Cortiz and his art director Hilyard Brown. He enlisted the writer James Agee to pen the screenplay. For the role of Preacher, he handpicked Robert Mitchum—an actor whose gifts were matched only by his indifference—and engaged him as perhaps no other director ever had, prompting the actor to become an active participant in the formation of scenes. In a practically unheard of gesture, Laughton even had the film's composer Walter Schumann on the set during filming. Perhaps no other collaborator, however, was as important to *The Night Of The Hunter* as the author of the original novel.

It is taking nothing away from Laughton or his production team to say that much of what one loves about the movie has its genesis in Davis Grubb's book. Indeed, it shows what an intelligent and perceptive adaptor Laughton was in having Agee hew so closely to the source material. Even the rhythms of Grubb's strange novel are echoed in the imagery of film. Watch the scene of Preacher at the striptease, burning with righteous fury, his switchblade flicking phallically through his pocket, and then read Grubb's description:

The Blind Alley

He would pay his money and go into a burlesque show and sit in the front row watching it all and rub the knife in his pocket with sweating fingers; seething in a quiet convulsion of outrage and nausea at all that ocean of undulating womanhood beyond the lights; his nose growing full of it: the choking miasma of girl smell and cheap perfume and stogie smoke and man smell and the breath of ten cent mountain corn liquor souring in the steamy air; and he would stumble out at last into the enchanted night, into the glitter and razzle-dazzle of the midnight April street, his whole spirit luminous with an enraptured and blessed fury at the world these whores had made.

Laughton and his team translated not just the scene (with Agee adding the knife through the pocket bit) but also the simmering grotesquery of Grubb's West Virginian vision.

Davis Alexander Grubb was born on July 23, 1919 in Moundsville, WV, a town situated along the Ohio River and the setting for nearly all the author's work. For a time, Grubb's life seemed blessed. Since his grandfather William Davis Alexander had helped found the Mercantile Bank in Moundsville, his family was held in high regard in the community. The son of an architect father and a resolute child-welfare worker mother, Grubb was drawn at an early age to storytelling and later claimed to have been primarily influenced by the old men of the town who sat around telling tales by the river.

There were other early, less idyllic, influences that would eventually find their way into Grubb's work. Moundsville was home to the West Virginia State

Penitentiary, a hulking gray complex that Grubb passed every day on his walk to school. The daily reminder of hopeless men locked away in stone cells behind those high walls fixed an image in the young boy's mind which would later resurface during his description of Ben Harper's imprisonment.

During this same period, Grubb's family became friendly with the evangelist Will Stidger, the famous radio preacher who during the Depression had a five-day-a-week broadcast. By that point, Stidger had already served as the inspiration for Sinclair Lewis's *Elmer Gantry*. Young Davis Grubb hovered under the stairs or at the back of the kitchen as the boisterous (and grossly opportunistic) preacher regaled listeners with tales of his travels. While Grubb was transfixed by Stidger's prowess as a raconteur, he also developed a distinct suspicion of organized religion and self-proclaimed men of god. "I had a chip on my shoulder about preachers," he would later recount, "from childhood."

About this time, the family luck ran out. His father's business failed in the early thirties, not long after the birth of Grubb's younger brother. The family was evicted from their home just before Christmas in 1934, a humiliation that stayed with Grubb the rest of his life. His father suffered a heart attack soon after and died. Still a teenager, Davis Grubb had seen his life come apart in the midst of the worst economic crisis in American history. His vision as a writer would be forever shaped by his perception of life's fragility.

Around the time he graduated high school and prepared to leave to study design in Philadelphia,

The Blind Alley

Grubb had another pivotal experience. As his brother Louis would later tell the tale, Grubb stopped into a bar one day and sat down next to a man drinking a beer. "Dave looked over and saw that the man had LOVE tattooed on one hand, and HATE on the other. Dave was so horrified he got up and left." If this story is to be believed, then one can only assume Grubb's horror must have given way to elation when he realized what a great image the tattooed hands would make in a novel.

Grubb landed a job as a page at NBC in New York and worked for a time as a radio announcer and scriptwriter. While he'd been writing stories for a while—successfully placing pieces in *Good Housekeeping, Colliers, The Saturday Evening Post*, and others—he knew he needed steady employment. He soon found his way into advertising in Philadelphia, working as both an artist and copywriter, and it was there, in a six-week fit of inspiration, that he wrote *The Night Of The Hunter*.

His writing bore the marks of his literary influences—the lyrical Southern gothic of William Faulkner, the rich eye for landscape and regional detail of Rebecca West, and, perhaps most profoundly, the apocalyptic vision of poet William Blake. Yet Grubb's novel was distinctly his own creation. It combined his love of his native Ohio River region, along with his distrust of religious authority and a concern, inherited from his mother, for the well being of children. It also proved to be a good place to use those tattooed knuckles.

Grubb was stunned to learn that his unpublished manuscript had been discovered by the great Charles Laughton, of whom Grubb had long been a fan.

Laughton travelled to Philadelphia, where Grubb still worked his day job in advertising, and spent five days with the writer discussing the project. Laughton asked Grubb to draw sketches of characters and scenes, and Grubb agreed, eventually completing 119 storyboard-like illustrations. Grubb would later argue that he was "not only the author of the novel from which the screenplay was adapted but was the actual scene designer as well." This is a large claim, but looking at the sketches Grubb drew (some of which are collected on the recently released Criterion Collection edition of the film) it is difficult to deny that, at the very least, Grubb played an abnormally large role in the visual conception of many scenes in the movie. For instance, one of the film's great arresting images, the ghostly vision of Willa Harper at the bottom of the Ohio River, is based on an eerily beautiful illustration by Grubb. (Grubb's sketches were eventually bought by director Martin Scorsese who has since donated them to the Academy of Motion Pictures Arts and Sciences.)

So why didn't Grubb write the screenplay? The answer is unclear. In later years, Grubb would blame himself for turning down the job. Producer Paul Gregory, in an interview with Mitchum biographer Lee Server, remembered the writer as an unreliable eccentric, "an odd man, to say the least." As Gregory remembered it, Grubb was incredibly difficult to talk to, a closed-mouth loner who couldn't bring himself to leave Philadelphia.

Hiring James Agee (who'd written a draft of *The African Queen*) to adapt the screenplay seemed like a good idea, but when Agee turned in a script that was far too long, nearly twice as long as the eventual shooting script, Laughton went to work whittling it down to a manageable length. In a letter Agee would later write to Gregory arguing that Laughton should take sole screenwriting credit on the picture, he added "I fully concur with Charles' suggestion; that in all reference to the initial novel we give maximal credit to Davis Grubb—who after all furnished much more of a movie story than is ordinarily done by a novelist." Tellingly, Laughton's final script is a remarkably close adaptation of Grubb's novel.

As Laughton's biographer Simon Callow has noted, "It's as if the novel had been written for Charles Laughton because it concerned everything which inspired him." Laughton was simpatico not only with Grubb's distain for religious hypocrisy but also his concern for the lives of children. Both novel and film derive much of their power from being situated in the point of view of their young protagonists. Laughton said he read the novel, and envisioned the film, as a "nightmarish Mother Goose story."

To that end, Laughton grasped that the figure of Rachel Cooper, played in the film with grit and vigor by Lillian Gish, was pivotal to the story. She is the counterbalance to Preacher, the Love that overcomes Hate. Doubtless, many filmmakers would have cut her role, or switched it to a more conventional hero, or perhaps sexed it up by making Rachel a young woman. But as Paul Gregory later told Preston Neal Jones, author of the indispensable *Heaven & Hell to Play With: The Filming of The Night Of The Hunter*, Laughton felt that adapting the novel "was a marvelous opportunity to show that God's glory was really in the little old farm woman, and not in the Bible-totin' son of a bitch."

Laughton's crucial contribution to the movie, besides the sheer skill he exhibited in bringing Grubb's vision to the screen, was to extrapolate from the material a distinctly comic element. The *grotesque*, in both literature and film, is a mishmash of horror and absurdity. The audience isn't sure whether to cringe or laugh. To this end, Laughton and Mitchum turn Preacher into a comic ghoul (something of a staple in children's literature). If the image of Preacher chasing the children up the stairs looks like a still from a Wiley Coyote cartoon, it is because Laughton masterfully interpreted the scene with the absurdist flair of a child's imagination. Mitchum, the great jazzman of cinematic insolence, plays Preacher with all the smarmy charm of the Big Bad Wolf knocking at the door. The actor's palpable delight in satirizing authority and piety gives the character an almost giddy quality that isn't present in the book.

Though the filming process was largely a time of happy collaboration, everyone involved was disappointed by the reception of the film. The studio had no idea what to do with Laughton's weird children's nightmare and tried to sell it as a sexy thriller (because nothing says sexy like a psychopathic preacher). Audiences stayed away and critics largely ignored it. Laughton, crushed, never directed another film.

Grubb seemed to shake off the disappointment and turned again to his writing. Over the next twenty-five years, he published nine more novels (all very different, most very good), as well as numerous short stories.

The Blind Alley

A few of his stories were adapted for television—for shows such as *The Alfred Hitchcock Hour* and *Rod Serling's Night Gallery*—and one novel, *Fools' Parade*, concerning a trio of ex-convicts in the Depression-era West Virginia, was made into a movie with Jimmy Stewart in 1971. Though he was never to crack into the public consciousness in the same way again, Grubb made a living as a working writer the rest of his life.

By the end of his life, though, he was virtually forgotten, living in the Hotel Gore in Clarksburg, WV, dying of lung cancer and forever clacking away on a new book. He was something of the town eccentric, a shaggy-haired philosopher dressed in a white three-piece suit, waiting impatiently for the world to catch up to his greatness. He was a sick man, however, and he spent his last year in a race to finish a final novel, *Ancient Lights*. He completed it just before his death on July 24, 1980.

Since he was an endless experimenter, Davis Grubb remains hard to pin down, but as studies of Appalachian culture have grown over the years, the reputation of this odd, idiosyncratic writer has stayed alive. It doesn't hurt that the film version of *The Night Of The Hunter* has finally gained, after its initial commercial failure, the reputation and standing it deserves. Hailed now as a masterpiece, it was placed on the National Film Registry in 1992. Critics, filmmakers, and audiences have continued to discover and rediscover the strange little film—a testament to, among other things, the power of a strange little book.

WOMEN IN TROUBLE
THE CRISIS PREGNANCY IN FILM NOIR

The way people talked about it back then was vague. "She got into trouble," they would say. *She* was usually quite young, often just a teenage girl. She would get into trouble, and then she would disappear for a while. When she came back—if she came back—she might seem different. Or she might simply slip back into her old life, keeping her sorrows a secret.

The "crisis pregnancy" slowly began to make its way into the plots of films in the late forties, a troubling shadow side of the baby boom. Unplanned pregnancies, forced adoptions, and abortions were nothing new, of course, but their increase happened to overlap the noir era, making the subject of crisis pregnancy hard to ignore as prospective material. Census data shows that the rate of births by unwed girls (ages 15-19) was about 6.58 per 1,000 births in 1940. By 1945, the number had risen to 8.55. It kept rising. In 1950, it was 10.56. In 1955 it was 12.52. By 1957, the number was 13.11, meaning that the rate had effectively doubled in less than twenty years.

Unplanned pregnancy was a dangerous subject to tackle, for more than one reason. Most obviously, it implied that people were having sex—a reality the Hays Code still forbade mentioning onscreen. Worse still, it implied unmarried women were having sex, which was verboten both because it admitted, however obliquely, that women might be subject to their own sexual impulses and because it demonstrated to the great unwashed public that marriage wasn't necessarily a prerequisite for sex. Lastly, a plotline dealing with an unintended pregnancy seemed to strike at the image of a robust nation of intact nuclear families full of happy children being raised by mutually contented parents. A girl in trouble was not just seen as a disgrace, she was a threat to the community's sense of itself. As such, she needed to be kept out of view. As Alice McDermott would come to describe the era in her novel *That Night*, "Unwed mothers at that time…fell somewhere between criminals and patients, and like criminals and patients, they were prescribed an exact and fortifying treatment, they were made to disappear."

Abandoning the Woman in Trouble

At least in the movies, that disappearance was permanent. More often than not when an unwed girl gets pregnant in a film of this era, she ends up dying. In films as varied as *Abandoned, Mystery Street, Letter From An Unknown Woman, A Place In the Sun,* and *A Kiss Before Dying,* the plot hinges on the death of a girl "in trouble." The complicated question of what to do with an unmarried pregnant woman, at least from a studio or screenwriter's perspective was simple: Kill her off. This let movies have it both ways. They could deal with a racy subject, but they could also restore order, with the young mother sacrificed on the altar of the happy ending.

One of the first films to deal with the subject was ripped from the headlines. *Abandoned* (1949) was originally released in October of 1949 under the title *Abandoned Woman* and was based on articles appearing in the *Los Angeles Mirror* (the *LA Times*'s new afternoon tabloid) about the thriving black market for babies in LA.

The film begins in the middle of the night with an upset young woman named Paula Considine (Gale Storm) walking into the LA police station to report the disappearance of her sister, Mary. The bored cops in the missing persons bureau don't much care about her sister, but there's a friendly reporter there, Mark Sitko (Dennis O'Keefe), just hanging around looking for trouble. Mark takes an immediate liking to Paula and offers to help her find her sister.

Soon they track down Mary at the city morgue, an apparent suicide. We find out that the young woman, unmarried and pregnant, found herself involved in the underworld market for healthy babies. Mark and Paula set out to find Mary's baby and break up the racket run by a kindly-faced but ruthless old lady named Mrs. Leona Donner (Marjorie Rambeau) and her rich assortment of thugs, including Raymond Burr, Mike Mazurki, David Clarke, and Will Kuluva.

Though the screenplay is attributed to screenwriter Irwin Gielgud, author of such dubious cinematic classics as *Amazon Quest* and *I Was A Shoplifter*, it also has an "additional dialog" credit for William Bowers. After a career in journalism, Bowers had become a crack screenwriter with noir credits (some uncredited) that included *The Web, Pitfall, Criss Cross*, and *Cry Danger*. He's responsible for the film's abundance of snappy lines—as when O'Keefe, upon searching Burr and finding a weapon, cracks, "I guess you couldn't sleep, so you decided to take your gun out for a walk."

Despite the one-liners and the moral uprightness of Mark and Paula, *Abandoned* is still a surprisingly dark hued film for its time. Though we never meet Mary, her crisis pregnancy forms the basis of the film's drama. We learn that she kept the details of her ordeal to herself, and that she never made mention of the father of her child. All we know about her is that she was a small town girl who came to Los Angeles, got pregnant, and was then pulled down into the underworld of a black market baby ring. The evil in the film is personified by Marjorie Rambeau in a great performance as Mrs. Donner. She's a bad bit of business, a sweet-smiling old lady who hands out Bibles to troubled, unwed mothers and then sells their children to the highest bidder. Though the film spends essentially no time mourning Mary's death, it avoids assigning blame to her for putting herself into Mrs. Donner's clutches or for getting pregnant in the first place.

There is moralizing around the margins, though. A subplot involves Mary's roommate at the Salvation Army's home for unwed mothers, a young mother-to-be named Dottie (Meg Randall). She admits that Mary would get mad at her when "I used to say to her that I thought we'd be better off if we never even saw our children." A Major from the Salvation Army informs Dottie that "No girl ever emotionally releases her baby. Before, she may think she doesn't want it, but after…" Apparently that speech, and Dottie's role in finding Mary's killers, do the trick. Dottie appears at the end of the film, in a hasty scene of forced frivolity in which Mark and Paula announce that they're newly married and adopting Mary's baby. Dottie herself is now giddy about *her* new baby. Whatever problems first landed her in a Salvation Home for indigent unwed mothers go unmentioned, swept aside in favor of a happy ending.

Other films dealt differently with the death of the unwed mother. Ophüls's romantic melodrama *Letter From An Unknown Woman* (1948) plays the moment as an almost ritualistic sacrifice—the young woman dies just after childbirth, paying the ultimate price for her love of a man who has never fully loved her back. As Andrew Sarris would later note, "*Letter From An Unknown Woman* is as fully suffused with tragic inexorability and lyrical feeling as the European classics of Ophüls." The film is a tragedy, in other words, in which the pregnancy and its aftermath are almost preordained for the sake of the melodrama. While Ophüls's film is a brilliantly realized work of art, the unwed mother's death here works in the same way it worked in lesser films: it restores the pre-established order. At the base level of the censor, her tragedy works as an illustration of the pitfalls of premarital sex.

In *A Kiss Before Dying* (1956), Joanne Woodward plays Dorie Kingship, a young woman who makes the catastrophic mistake of falling for Bud Corliss, a charming heel played Robert Wagoner. Woodward here is a classic victim, a nice girl involved with a particularly sinister l'homme fatale. Tellingly, part of what works in the villain's favor is the young woman's gendered sense of guilt. Upon discovering she is pregnant with his child she tells Bud, "It's all my fault. It's always the girl's fault." Bud does not disagree.

Instead, worried that her pregnancy will mess up his plans for the future, he sets out to kill her. After he's tricked her into taking poison capsules, he's surprised to find her still alive the next day. She didn't take the pills—not because she thought he was trying to kill her (that thought, sadly, never occurs to her) but because she thought he was trying to get rid of the child. "I know how you felt about the baby," she tells him.

While *A Kiss Before Dying* still performs the function of punishing the young mother-to-be, it regards her more as a victim than as a woman of loose morals. Instead, the film reserves its disdain for the callow young man who is willing to use sex, and to resort to murder, to get what he wants.

In other films dealing with the same subject, however, the young woman in trouble was sometimes painted in an unsympathetic fashion. In *Mystery Street* (1950), Jan Sterling stars as a pregnant B-girl named Vivian who tries to blackmail her married lover, (Edmon Ryan) into leaving his wife. When he refuses to see her, she goes to a bar and picks up a drunk young man (Marshall Thompson) who is distraught because his wife (Sally Forrest) has suffered a miscarriage. Vivian loads him into her car and then drives out to confront her lover. She thinks maybe he'll bring some money. He brings a gun instead, kills her and dumps her naked body on the beach.

The juxtaposition of Sterling and Forrest is interesting here. Forrest is married and wants to keep her baby. Her reaction to her miscarriage is a strong contrast to Sterling, who apparently regards her pregnancy as little more than a way to shakedown her rich, married lover. The irony, of course, is that the charismatic Sterling steals all her scenes. We're sorry to see her go, since she's basically the engine of the movie's opening. Forrest, though delivering a solid performance, never really comes into focus as a character. Bad girls really are more fun.

In *A Place In The Sun* (1951), Shelley Winters is not really a bad girl, just a poor young woman who gets involved with a poor young man played by Montgomery Clift. She discovers she's carrying his baby at about the same time he falls in love with the gorgeous and rich Elizabeth Taylor. The moral conundrum here is serious, and has its roots in Drieser's *An American Tragedy*, but since this is a tragic Hollywood romance featuring Clift and Taylor (perhaps cinema's most beautiful onscreen couple) there is added weight to our conflicted desire to see Winters gotten rid of. *A Place In The Sun* works a strange magic. In setting up the unfortunately pregnant Winters as an obstacle to the protagonists' love affair, we're made to feel sorry for her on one hand and to root for her death on the other. After all, the movie seems to ask, who wouldn't rather be rich with Elizabeth Taylor than poor with Shelley Winters?

Rescuing the Woman in Trouble

Perhaps the most entertaining of the "woman in trouble" pictures was Mitchell Leisen's atmospheric *No Man Of Her Own* (1950). In the first few minutes of the film we see Helen Ferguson (Barbara Stanwyck) crying at the apartment door of a coldly indifferent bastard named Steve Morley (Lyle Bettger). She begs him to let her in, but Morley just wordlessly slips her a train ticket and five bucks under the door.

Helen gets on the train, unsure of where she's going or what she'll do. She meets a charming couple named Hugh and Patrice Harkness. They're newlyweds just back from Europe. Patrice is pregnant with their first child, and they're on their way to his hometown where his family is eager to meet the young mother-to-be. In the first of many twists to come, the train is involved in a terrible accident and both of the Harknesses are killed. Then, through a mix up, it is assumed that Helen is Patrice. When she's embraced by Hugh's bereaved parents—who want to take care of the young woman and newborn baby they believe to be their daughter-in-law and grandchild—Helen is faced with a terrible choice. Disgraced by a no-good man, with no money and nowhere to go, she assumes Patrice's identity.

This is undiluted melodrama. There's a plot development every ten minutes or so, but the central conflict is actually quite simple: will Helen be able to keep living a lie? The plot comes from the novel *I Married A Dead Man* by Cornell Woolrich (writing as William Irish), and the film retains both Woolrich's air of mystery and his sympathy for his protagonist. Helen is more than a victim, she's someone who for much of the film is doing the wrong things for the right reasons. Though Stanwyck is probably twenty years too old for the part (in the book her character is nineteen, while the actor was forty-three when the film was released), she brings the weight of her screen persona to the role. When that creep Steve Morely shows up at the end to try and blackmail her, Stanwyck makes the kind of choice that you damn well know Barbara Stanwyck will make.

As Helen's tormenter Steve Morely, Lyle Bettger offers up a scathing portrait of the deadbeat dad. Though known better today as a villain in Westerns, Bettger got his start in noir. He excelled at these kinds of pitiless roles (his ruthless kidnapper is the best thing about Mate's *Union Station*), and he makes a perfect foil to Stanwyck. No less than Wagoner in *A Kiss Before Dying*, Bettger is a nightmare vision of the Baby Daddy from hell.

No Man Of Her Own is the film noir which most clearly positions its young mother's plight as a failure of judgment (bad taste in men) rather than a failure of character (a lack of virtue). She's in need of rescue, a rescue that comes in the form of a warm, embracing family—as well as a lot of last minute plot manipulations which rewrite the utter hopelessness of Woolrich's original ending.

Maxwell Shane's 1955 *The Naked Street* presents the same subject from a different point of view. In the film Anthony Quinn plays a gangster named Phil Regal. When we meet him he's going back to the old neighborhood to see his mother (Elsie Neft) and his sister, Rosalie (Anne Bancroft). When he learns that his sister is pregnant, Regal leaps into a fury. He demands to know the identity of the father, only to find out that the boy in question is a hotshot kid named Nicky Bradna (Farley Granger) who is currently sitting on death row for the murder of an elderly storeowner. Regal pulls a lot of strings to get the kid released—intimidating eyewitnesses to the murder and buying the kid an alibi—and then demands that the boy marry his sister. His attempts to rescue his sister from disgrace, however, tell us more about Regal than they do about Rosalie.

The screenplay by Leo Katcher and director Maxwell Shane is a tough piece of work. At the center of the movie is the weird relationship between Phil, Rosalie and their mother. The image of the New York tough guy who loves his devoted immigrant mother was a cliché even in 1955, but there's something else going on here.

In an early scene, Phil's pretty blonde girlfriend complains that he's never taken her to see the family. Family, he tells her, is something separate. What he really means is that he operates in two spheres. In one, he's a gangster with sexy dames he can buy off with minks. In the other sphere, he has his mother and sister, both of whom must remain desexualized because Phil, on some level, thinks sex cheapens a woman (which, as a man, paradoxically makes him an agent of that cheapness). There's a fascinating scene in the movie in which Rosalie asks Phil if he thinks Nicky is innocent of the murder. He replies, "Would I want you to marry him if I didn't?" In fact, Phil doesn't care one way or the other if Nicky is innocent. He just wants his sister to get married to lift their family out of some perceived disgrace.

There's another angle on this material, and the key to it is in noticing how Phil touches his sister. There's something going on with this guy. When he finds out she's pregnant, he nearly beats her up. He buys her a husband. When the baby dies, he wants to get rid of the husband. When she rejects him and tells him she's sick of being defined as only his sister, he looks as crushed as a spurned lover. Either a latent incest theme is sitting right below the surface of things here or Phil is just really, *really* interested in his little sister's sex life.

Anthony Quinn seemed to sweat testosterone, and this role put that quality to good use. Phil is a man of passion but the passions seem to emanate from some place buried too deep for him to ever understand. He's matched perfectly with Anne Bancroft, who manages the difficult task of portraying a character who moves from a guilt-ridden innocent to a woman strong enough to stand up to her gangster brother. With these two strong performances, *The Naked Street* offers a sharp critique of the male response to the "woman in trouble." After all, Phil's desire to possess and somehow redeem his sister is, in its way, as dehumanizing toward her as the indifference shown by the deadbeat dads in other noirs.

The Option That Dare Not Speak Its Name

Abortion had essentially been a verboten topic in movies for as long as the medium had existed. "Essentially" is a key word here, though, because as the rate of abortions rose during the Depression, so too did "vice films" dealing with the subject, films such as the 1934 *The Road To Ruin*, 1937's *Race Suicide* or 1939's *Unborn Souls*. Though ostensibly educational in intent, these were attempts at exploitation along the line of "sex hygiene" pictures. As the scholar Eric Schaefer points out in his book *Bold! Daring! Shocking! True!: A History of Exploitation Films, 1919-1959*, however, abortion dramas "did not fare especially well with the audiences for exploitation pictures." The subject might have appealed to a certain curiosity, but as Schaefer notes, it lacked the necessary "titillating quality."

Following World War II, abortion was back as a possible cinematic subject. *Street Corner* (1948) was a low rent "sex hygiene" picture that took some cues from noir. It tells the story of seventeen year old Lois March (Marcia Mae Jones) who has sex with her boyfriend Bob after a school dance. She discovers she's pregnant about the same time Bob dies in a car crash. Unsure of what to do, she turns to an abortionist.

Street Corner has all the dramatic drawbacks that one should expect from what is essentially a 73-minute public service announcement. Told in flashback as a cautionary tale by Lois's family physician, Dr. Fenton (Joseph Crehan), it's a wheezing production full of stiff acting and unending speeches curiosity of the good Dr. Fenton. It kicks off with an opening message to the viewer that reads in part: "To those who appreciate the seriousness of the matter treated here—remember! It could happen to someone you love—it could happen to *you*." The film's highlight comes about an hour in when Dr. Fenton shows a graphic hygiene film. This film-within-the-film is a real documentary with explicit footage of a live birth, a caesarian section, and several venereal infections on male and female genitalia. Curiously, however, abortion is not mentioned in the hygiene film.

For all its shortcomings as a drama, *Street Corner* does present the sex drive of its teenage protagonist without moral judgment. Lois isn't a victim here, nor is she a "bad girl." She is, the film takes pains to point out, an average girl with a natural sexual drive. Bob does not seduce her into having sex. She has sex with him because she's being pulled along the same current of biological urges.

The villain of the piece is the unnamed abortionist (Gretl Dupont), who is presented in all ways as The Other, the dangerous outside influence. A butch, hatchet-faced woman of indeterminate Eastern European descent, she lives on the ominously intoned "other side of town" and performs abortions in the parlor of a dank little house. When she's finished with Lois, she shoves her into the street with a warning to keep her mouth shut about what's happened.

At the end the abortionist is sentenced to ten years in prison (the maximum penalty for performing an abortion at the time), but the film passes around the guilt. Dr. Fenton tells us that Lois's parents have been "most bitterly repaid for their negligence." And of Lois he sighs, "The girl must be punished, heaven help us. If she wasn't, the social order would break down." This last point isn't expanded upon, and Lois isn't heard from again, disappearing, it would seem, to protect the social order.

Though abortion was kept mostly out of the mainstream, it was hinted at from time to time. In *Leave Her To Heaven* (1945), psychotic Gene Tierney will do anything to possess Cornel Wilde. Even after they get married and she becomes pregnant, she refuses to share him with anyone—including their baby. The scene of her pitching herself down a flight of stairs still elicits shocked gasps from audiences.

While Tierney's self-induced miscarriage is the deranged act of one of noir's coldest villains, in Max Ophüls's 1949 *Caught* we have a situation of a group of filmmakers painting themselves into a corner and reverting to a de facto abortion to get themselves out of it. In the film, Barbara Bel Geddes plays an naïve young woman who marries a cruel Hughes-esque millionaire played by Robert Ryan. She falls in love with nice guy doctor James Mason at about the same time she realizes she's pregnant with Ryan's baby. This plot complication is changed from the source novel, *Wild Calendar* by Libbie Block (indeed, the movie as a whole is a radical departure from Block's novel), and it presents a conundrum. How can Bel Geddes remove herself from the clutches of the movie's villain? The filmmakers perform an abortion via *deus ex machina* and have her lose the baby in a standoff with Ryan, thus giving *Caught* the distinction of being perhaps the only movie in cinematic history to have a happy ending based on a miscarriage.

Some notion of the actual realities of out-of-wedlock pregnancies finally made their way into the mainstream with William Wyler's 1951 *Detective Story*. Certain words are never used: pregnancy, sex, abortion. Characters still avoid naming these things, but there is no ambiguity about what is being discussed.

Detective Story starts out as an efficient, if standard, police procedural. Based on a play by Sidney Kingsley, it covers one flatly photographed day in the life of New York's 21st Precinct. At the start, we meet a cast of hardworking cops and the criminals they spend their days with. Then, once this milieu is set up, in strides Detective James McLeod.

As played by a fiery Kirk Douglas, McLeod is the NYPD's answer to Inspector Javert. The product of a degenerate father and an abused mother, McLeod detests crime and *hates* criminals. His life is dedicated to imposing order on a world full of thieves, rapists, and murderers. Even his brothers-in-arms on the force think he's too much of a hardass. The only person he reserves any human feeling for is his delicate young wife, Mary (Eleanor Parker). We learn at the beginning of the film that they've been trying to have a baby with no success. It doesn't matter, McLeod assures her. They still have each other.

But their happy idyll is about to be shattered by Karl Schneider (slimy George Macready), an abortionist who offers to "help" young women who are in trouble. Many of his patients have died, and McLeod has been hunting him for a year, closing in on this man he calls a butcher of young women. All of this information is presented like silhouettes against a window shade. The film never comes out and identifies Schneider as a back alley abortionist, but the point clearly comes across. It comes across even stronger when Schneider implies that McLeod's young wife Mary is one of his former patients.

Detective Story is a fascinating piece of work. While it once again presents abortion as an unnamable evil and the abortionist as a remorseless ghoul, it is also sensitive to the plight of pregnant, unmarried women in 1950s America. The core of its drama is not the practice of abortion but rather the way a young woman has to deal with a man who can only love her if he thinks she's "pure." McLeod is not disturbed that Mary had an abortion as much as he is destroyed by the notion she had sex before she was with him. "At an autopsy the other day I watched the medical examiner saw off the top of a man's skull, take out the brain and hold it in his hand," he tells her. "I'd give my soul to take out my brain, hold it under the faucet and wash away the dirty pictures you put there tonight." For McLeod, Mary's sexuality can only exist within the purifying context of their marriage. For her to have ever been with someone else, to have found herself pregnant as a teenager, invalidates their entire relationship.

To different degrees, virtually all the noir films dealing with the "woman in trouble" have at their core a similar unease with the sexual life of their female protagonist. Some films present her as a conniving tramp, others as a fallen woman, and still others as an innocent victim. As is always the case, these different interpretations of the character reveal conflicting views in society—a competition of ideas that included the influence of religious orthodoxy, concerns over public health, and good old fashioned sexism.

The dividing line between these ideas was not always clear. In 1949, the same year that saw the release of *Abandoned*, the writer Howard Whitman wrote a widely syndicated newspaper article detailing the work of the Psychiatric Service of the San Francisco City Clinic, a "laboratory" for the treatment of promiscuity in teenage girls. After stating with alarm that "68 per cent [*sic*] of our brides are not virgins" the article goes on to warn that "The girl who is well integrated into a social group, who goes to community parties and club dances is rarely the girl who gets into trouble." These sentiments are not merely blasts from the past, though.

One need only look at the recent debates over contraception and mandatory ultrasounds, as well the ensuing controversy over radio host Rush Limbaugh's misogynist attack on Georgetown Law School student Sandra Fluke, to see that women's bodies are still an arena of public contention. Looking back then, the "woman in trouble" noirs of the forties and fifties were more than simple crime stories, they were early harbingers of the growing complexities of modern American life.

HEARING VOICES
THE VARIETIES OF FILM NOIR NARRATION

One of the telltale signs of a true film noir obsession is the belief that filmmaking has gone downhill. Once you've savored the elegance of a long take by Preminger or Farrow, it becomes increasingly difficult to tolerate a movie that looks like it was shot on top of a paint-mixer and edited by strobe light. As much as this is a matter of taste, it's also a matter of film literacy. A Siodmak film simply employs the grammar of film language with greater depth and daring than a Michael Bay CGI-a-thon. Noir geeks feel this deep down: we know what good filmmaking looks like. We do have to admit, however, that the classic age wasn't perfect. Not everything about noir has aged well, and even good films have their share of goofy devices. Exhibit A: the voiceover.

Used skillfully, the voiceover can be a great asset to a film, helping to create atmosphere and reveal character. Used with less care, however, it can sink the whole endeavor. Any discussion of this sort should begin by noting that most voiceovers are forms of narration, and as such, they run the gamut from interior monologues to omniscient narrators. Most narration breaks down along familiar literary lines: the first person (I), the third person (he/she), and the rarely employed second person (you).

We can dispense with second person narration rather quickly. While it was by and large a postmodern phenomenon, its literary roots go further back. Nathaniel Hawthorne deployed the device first in his story "The Haunted Mind" ("You sink down and muffle your head in your clothes…"), and it was picked up later by others, including mystery writer Rex Stout who used it in his book *How Like a God* (1929). It's an ungainly device, and its appearances in film are rare, and rarer still in noir. The best example is Allen Baron's 1961 *Blast of Silence*. Here the raspy voice of Lionel Stander provides a running commentary on the last days of a hit man: "You're alone. But you don't mind that…You've always been alone." A little of this goes a long way, as is often the case with voiceovers, but its function here is fascinating. Who is this narrator? This seems to be an internal monologue but one which is disengaged from the main character. He's not talking to himself and he's not talking to us (it's not his voice, after all). The voice seems to be his *unconscious* talking *to him*, even in death: "You're alone now…The scream is dead. There's no pain. You're home again, back in the cold black silence." While the second person works here, it was always too much of a gimmick to really catch on.

The narration that helped define noir was the hardboiled first-person dialog originated by Chandler and Cain. Film adaptations of their works often juggle plotlines in order to establish the main story as a protracted flashback and thus set up the protagonist as the storyteller. In *Murder, My Sweet,* Philip Marlowe narrates his story to a room full of cops, while *Double Indemnity* is rearranged so we can see a dying Walter Neff confess his sins into his boss's Dictaphone. This narrative device allows a film to keep up a running commentary on the action, as when Neff stops in the middle of the film to confide, "Suddenly it came over me that everything would go wrong. It sounds crazy, but it's true…I couldn't hear my own footsteps. It was the walk of a dead man."

When this is done well, it adds another dimension to a film and allows us access to important emotional shifts in characters. In *Raw Deal* (1948), one of the few noirs narrated by a woman, Pat Cameron (Claire Trevor) tells her story in a voice and manner that work quite differently from her outward performance. On the outside, Pat is a sassy, steely-eyed dame ready to help her man bust out of the joint. As she narrates the story to the strains of Paul Sawtell's haunting Theremin score, however, she reveals the bruised heart of the film: "This is the day… the last time I shall drive up to these iron bars which keep the man I love locked away from me." There is no disjunction between Pat's rather gruff exterior and her heartbroken internal monologue, though, because Trevor and Anthony Mann do the visual work of building those connections into her performance. Trevor was always good at hinting at a slowly building desperation beneath a facade of cheer and bluster. Mann uses this quality to great effect while enhancing it with Pat's narration, which seems to exist somewhere just outside the reach of her own consciousness. In this respect, *Raw Deal* uses the first person narration in much the same way William Faulkner employs it in stories like "Barn Burning." It's as if we're hearing Pat's feelings rather than her thoughts, her subconscious rather than her conscious. Sawtell's Theremin works as an auditory trigger each time we're about to go below the surface. By the time we reach the end of the film, we are witness to a tragedy that only we and Pat fully understand.

Noir played with many different forms of first person narrators, from the unreliable narrator in *Laura,* to the questionable narrator in *Detour*, to the narration from a dead man in *Sunset Blvd*. Many of the these experiments were fun and artistically successful, but they actually represent a minority of noir voiceovers. The majority of voiceovers fall into two camps, both of them annoying.

The first kind of bad voiceover is the First Person Voice of Authority. These narrators are tangential characters—often authority figures such as cops or doctors—who comment on the action of the plot. In another Anthony Mann film, his 1950 *Side Street*, we're given a narrator in the form of Captain Anderson (Paul Kelly) who begins the film in a typical manner: "New York City: an architectural jungle where fabulous wealth and the deepest squalor live side by side. New York is the busiest, the loneliest, the kindest, and the cruelest of cities—a murder a day, every day of the year, and each murder will wind up on my desk." This wouldn't be so bad if Capt. Anderson didn't keep talking like an annoying theatergoer, essentially describing the action onscreen to us. Even in the film's big moment—Farley Granger's fateful decision to steal some money—Capt. Anderson's narration is there to make sure we get the point.

Cops were often the authority figures in these scenarios, but once Hollywood discovered Freud a boring kind of hell broke loose. Films like Rudolph Maté's *The Dark Past* (1950) or Gurney and Lerner's *Edge of Fury* (1958) subjected audiences to tedious character analysis from learned psychiatric professionals. If cops were most often presented as moral authorities who preached the film's message, the shrink was there to operate as a disinterested, amoral authority—the man of science teaching his classroom of doltish theatergoers to let go of their simpleminded notions of character and embrace his diagnosis of the problem. Whether the First Person Authoritarian is a cop or a shrink, the device reveals a reluctance on the part of either the filmmakers or the studio to trust the audience to interpret the material on their own. This is especially galling in good films like *Side Street* or *Edge of Fury*, films that have already done the hard dramatic work of revealing character through action. This kind of preaching violates one of the cardinal rules of drama: show, don't tell.

The First Person Voice of Authority finally hit its nadir in another good film, *City That Never Sleeps* (1953). Here the film is narrated by no less than the city of Chicago itself, personified later in the film in the figure of "Sgt. Joe" (Chill Willis), a mysterious cop who shows up to accompany our protagonist on his long dark night of the soul. There is a strong dose of Clarence the Angel from *It's A Wonderful Life* in the character of Sgt. Joe. The problem with this, besides its pure cheesiness, is that it is fundamentally dishonest. It's one thing to tell us that angels in heaven care about us, it's another thing to tell us that Chicago does.

Perhaps the only thing worse than the First Person Voice of Authority is the Third Person Voice of Authority. This disembodied voice is prevalent in docu-noirs like *The Street With No Name, House on 92nd Street*, and *Call Northside 777*. It arrives with bombast at the beginning of a film and makes sure you understand that the story you are about to see is good for you. The voice has the feel of insurance. Noirs, like the gangster films that preceded them, were often at pains to justify their existence on the grounds that they were performing a civic function. The Third Person Voice of Authority was there as a kind of public service announcement, letting you know that the tale of theft, adultery, and murder that you were about to watch was made for your edification. This cliché inoculated the filmmakers against charges that they were trolling the bad side of town for the purposes of sleazy entertainment.

What is interesting about noir, however, is how often it uses this trope against itself. A film like *He Walked By Night* (credited to Alfred Wexler but mostly made by Anthony Mann), begins with obligatory narration (by actor Reed Hadley, a frequent noir voiceover man) praising the security provided by the LAPD. The rest of the story, however, undermines that very sense of equilibrium. For most of the film we stay with the disturbed figure of a police killer named Roy Morgan

The Blind Alley

(Richard Basehart). Since the film doesn't provide us with a strong protagonist on the police side to follow, we're more or less stuck with the nutjob. Basehart's fearless performance, mixed with John Alton's minimalist lighting, gives the film a perverse center. The Third Person Voice of Authority, then, seems to be trying to convince us of something the film doesn't really believe, and this tension only gives the film power.

Stanley Kubrick tried to pare down the third person narration to the thinnest kind of narrative thread in *The Killing* (1956). Gone was the moralizing and instead the narrator (actor Art Gilmore) is there to rattle off dates and locations, situating us in time to make sure we're not lost. This device mars what is an otherwise excellent film, however, because we don't need the voice. Kubrick hasn't lost us, so by having Gilmore there to bark out information like a track announcer the director only reveals his insecurity.

The voiceover hasn't aged well over the years. The hardboiled first person voiceover transformed from a popular device to a cliché, and now it exists somewhere in the land of parody. On occasion, it can still be done well—*After Dark, My Sweet*, for example—but it's a risky endeavor. With some exceptions—i.e. the ubiquitous use of Morgan Freeman as a wise old sage—most films have abandoned first person voiceovers altogether.

As for the Third Person Voice of Authority voiceover, it had become an antique before the fifties had even come to an end. The kind of righteous booming voices that used to assure us we were watching glorified civics lessons seemed increasingly like goofy fragments of the past. Knox Manning's narration at the beginning of Mann's superior 1949 *Border Incident* was simply too close in nature to the laughable narration he provided for the campy anti-reefer *Wild Weed* that same year. The device itself—superfluous at best, condescending and embarrassing at worst—simply ceased to exist. Now it's a film noir artifact, the sound of a brief, nervous era when movies had to conceal themselves behind a big blustering voice.

THROUGH THE CAMERA'S I
NOIR'S EXPERIMENTS WITH THE SUBJECTIVE CAMERA

In 1939, Orson Welles rolled into Hollywood promising to revolutionize the art of filmmaking. One of his first ideas was to shoot an adaptation of Joseph Conrad's *Heart of Darkness* entirely from the point of view of the main character, Marlow, as he travels up the Congo. In other words, Welles explained, we would never see Marlow because we would be looking through his eyes. The camera, in effect, would be the main character, thus reflecting the first-person narrative of the novel. While the director eventually abandoned the plan as unworkable and moved on to *Citizen Kane*, the idea of an entire movie told with a subjective camera was just crazy enough to keep floating around Hollywood.

Of course, the subjective camera shot itself (or POV shot) had been around for years. Deployed sparingly in films like Murnau's *The Last Laugh* (1924) and Mamoulian's *Dr. Jekyll and Mr. Hyde* (1931), it helped add emphasis and shift the emotion of sequences, acting in writer J.P Telotte's phrase as a form of "narrative punctuation." Alfred Hitchcock was particularly a fan of the technique, using it to great effect in his 1927 silent film *The Lodger* and famously using it to frame a suicide in *Spellbound* (1945). Used by these and other directors, the POV shot was just another tool in the kit. In 1947, however, the subjective camera achieved that most fleeting form of Hollywood glory: it became a fad.

Adapting Raymond Chandler's fourth Philip Marlowe mystery *The Lady In The Lake*, director/star Robert Montgomery started with an audacious idea: he would adopt the novel's first person narrative as his visual scheme. Not only would Marlowe (played by Montgomery) introduce the movie, we would see it through his eyes. Aside from a few quick sequences when he is onscreen addressing the audience directly (at the beginning of the film, near the middle, and then again at the end), we would see Marlowe only in fleeting glimpses in mirrors. Since the primary pleasure of a Marlowe novel was the private eye's first person narration, the concept of telling his story visually from his point of view might have seemed like a stroke of offbeat brilliance.

In practice, however, the resulting film *Lady In The Lake* pulls off the trick of being both experimentally bold and crushingly boring at the same time. By shooting an entire feature film with a subjective camera, Montgomery managed to prove only that shooting an entire feature film with a subjective camera is a bad idea.

The technique turned out to have several drawbacks. For one thing, it actually robs us of a main character. Noir scholars Alain Silver and James Ursini have pointed out that Marlowe doesn't really narrate *Lady In The Lake*. Since we hear his voice in dialog, the narration is kept to a minimum to avoid confusion. Without a visual representation of Marlowe for 95% of the film, and lacking a voiceover that allows us entry into his mind, there's really nothing to the character except some brusque dialogue and the stodgy movement of the camera. The irony here is that in trying to situate the film's narrative from Philip Marlowe's point of view, the film ends up quashing the voice of perhaps the most iconic first person narrator in all of crime literature. Montgomery's experiment ended up disproving the theory that a subjective camera would allow viewers more access to the interior life of a protagonist.

It also disproved the theory that by supposedly looking through the eyes of the character we would then assume the character's identity. At the beginning of the film, Montgomery promises that we the audience will investigate the clues and solve the case. We will be Marlowe, in effect. The usual process by which we identify with a protagonist onscreen will be intensified.

What actually happens, however, is that since Philip Marlowe isn't onscreen, we seem to float through the air, our focus eventually settling on the other characters in the plot. This explains why the screenwriters—a bitter Chandler (who quit the movie after thirteen weeks), and novelist/screenwriter Steve Fisher—greatly expanded the role of Adrienne Fromsett (Audrey Totter), the editor of a crime magazine who hires Marlowe to find a missing woman. This is a fundamental mistake in adapting a Marlowe novel because Chandler rarely wrote particularly compelling supporting characters, and never wrote a fully believable woman. Even with her role beefed up, Ms. Fromsett makes for a less than compelling protagonist.

Part of the problem here is connected to another drawback of the subjective camera: the actors in the film are forced to do their scenes with the camera rather than each other. The actors in this movie rarely look at one another. This stifles the performances of people like Totter and Lloyd Nolan, actors who are *always* good but who here, without any way to develop a rhythm in the scene, are reduced to histrionics. As our de facto main character, Totter gets the worst of it, having to do her big love scenes opposite a lens. A shot of her leaning in to kiss the camera gets a bad laugh, as do her overactive facial muscles in many of her endless reaction shots. This noir goddess, a beautiful and intelligent actor, has to keep finding new ways to arch her eyebrows in shocked disbelief.

One last problem with the subjective camera here is that it constricts the action onscreen. The *mise en scene* of this movie is dreadfully dull. Actors are constantly pinned to the center foreground so they can talk at the camera. Occasionally, Montgomery breaks free of this and manages an interesting image (Marlowe crawling on the ground after a car wreck or peering through a cracked door to spy on a meeting), but the bulk of the film is the same monotonous set-up of an actor standing a few feet from the camera trying to act with Montgomery's disembodied voice.

The argument could be made that the problem with *Lady In The Lake* is Montgomery's deployment of the subjective camera technique, not the technique itself.

A director of greater skill might have pulled it off. Perhaps this is true, but watching this film one gets the distinct sense that Welles was smart to abandon *Heart Of Darkness*.

While the idea for an entire POV movie didn't live past Montgomery's failed experiment, the technique itself kept making its way into noir that year. In 1947 alone, director Curtis Bernhardt employed the POV shot in two superior films, *Possessed* and *High Wall*, to reflect the disoriented perspectives of his protagonists. Used in isolated sequences, the technique is arresting and quite effective (particularly in the hospital scenes in *Possessed* where poor Joan Crawford is wheeled into the psych ward). Score two points for the POV shot.

Later that same year, director Delmer Daves thought the subjective camera might be put to interesting effect on *Dark Passage*, his adaptation of David Goodis's novel *The Dark Road*.

In the film, Humphrey Bogart plays Vincent Parry, a convict who has just busted out of prison when the film starts. He's picked up by a strange woman, Irene Jansen (Lauren Bacall), and surprisingly she already knows who Parry is and wants to help him. Turns out that Parry was wrongfully convicted of killing his wife, and Irene followed his trial in the papers, convinced of his innocence. With Irene's help, Parry undergoes a facelift and sets out to track down his wife's killer.

Because the story involves plastic surgery, Daves had to come up with a way to handle Parry's transition from one face to another. His solution was to have the pre-facelift sections of the movie told from Parry's subjective point of view. Studio head Jack Warner was reluctant to embrace such an avant-garde camera technique, especially for a new pairing of the lucrative Bogart and Bacall team—to say nothing of paying Bogart top wages to sit out half the movie while the camera essentially plays his part—but the subjective camera had the virtue of solving the problem presented by the facelift plot. Moreover, Daves was a talented craftsman eager to utilize the new AERO-FLEX handheld camera which allowed him the freedom to keep shots from becoming static. Warner capitulated.

The subjective camera work here is about as effective as Daves could have hoped. It builds suspense, for instance, in the scenes just after Parry has escaped from prison. This is not surprising since the POV shot is typically enlisted to help create suspense. It is, by its very definition, a technique which restricts the audience's knowledge of a scene, creating anxiety about what might jump out from the margins of the shot. A little later in the film, Daves uses the camera to replicate Parry's nervous state as he rushes down the sidewalk to his 3 am appointment with a shady plastic surgeon. As he passes a man on the street and the fellow catches his eye to ask if they know each other, the camera drifts just a bit as if Parry is trying to break eye contact. Later, the creepy surgeon (played with sleazy glee by Houseley Stevenson) looms over Parry, cackling about "botched plastic jobs" while fingering a straight razor. Here, and elsewhere, the subjective camera enhances the scene exactly as intended, by placing us in head of the nervous protagonist.

Having said that, however, the limitations with the POV shot are also on display. For one thing, the technique puts added burden on the actors. Because Bogart isn't onscreen, Bacall has to carry the first half of the movie by herself, essentially creating the emotional core of their relationship while staring into a lens. She carries off this task by skillfully underplaying these scenes, but there can be no doubt that the movie suddenly snaps to life once Bogie actually shows up onscreen. He's in his noir prime here, weary and scared, and his last few scenes with Bacall have a fragile emotionalism unlike anything else in their work together. The last shot of the film might be the sweetest one they ever shared. While all this material is terrific, however, it has the unintended effect of drawing attention to the limitations of the film's first half. It should also be noted that while much of the first forty minutes of the film is done subjectively, not all of it is. Daves alternates between Parry's point of view and a more conventional point of view that includes establishing shots, over the shoulder shots, and two-shots. While *Dark Passage* is stylistically daring, it did little to keep the subjective camera fad from going out of style.

Since noir directors often utilized odd camera set-ups to reflect discombobulated protagonists, the POV shot naturally stayed on as a valuable, if judiciously employed, technique. Director Rudolph Mate` was able to inject a little style into the otherwise talk heavy psychobabble noir *The Dark Past* (1950) with some striking POV work. He began the film with a lengthy first-person subjective shot (the camera functioning as the eyes of psychologist Lee J. Cobb on his way to work). Later in the film, as escaped con William Holden recounts a childhood trauma to Cobb, we assume his POV as a child. Tying together these two shots is a clever way to link the doctor with the hood, and both shots are deftly handled, particularly the Expressionistic flashback.

The POV kept popping up from time to time. Henry Hathaway framed some shots from the perspective of a distraught Richard Basehart as he threatens to jump off the ledge of a high rise in *Fourteen Hours* (1951). In Orson Welles's *Touch Of Evil* (1958) the camera assumes Janet Leigh's drugged POV as she awakens in bed to find Akim Tamiroff's bug-eyed corpse slung over the bed post above her. In 1964, Sam Fuller used it for one of the best openings in all of noir: as the wobbly POV of a man being beaten by a bald prostitute in *The Naked Kiss*. And Alfred Hitchcock never lost his enthusiasm for it, using it in his hymns to voyeurism, *Rear Window* (1954) and *Vertigo* (1958); on television in the *Alfred Hitchcock Presents* episode "Breakdown" with Joseph Cotton; and in late films like *Psycho* and *Frenzy*.

While some non-noir films employed the technique—Welles would use it, for instance, to reflect an epileptic seizure in his 1952 production of Shakespeare's *Othello*—its brief heyday in 1947 tells us something important about film noir. 1947 was a pivotal year for the genre, a year that saw the release of no less than thirty noirs, a year of benchmarks like *Body And Soul* and *Brute Force* and *Out of the Past*. The subjective camera experiments taking place in crime films during this same period reflect the larger aesthetic movement that only later would be recognized as *film noir*. Because the subjective camera worked best when used to convey the disoriented or worried perspective of a particular character, most often a bewildered protagonist in over his head, it makes sense that it should get so much usage in a genre devoted to chronicling the cracks in the human psyche. Indeed, one of the main reasons that Montgomery's *Lady In The Lake* failed artistically is that the camerawork was too stolid. It plodded along stoically from scene to scene. The subjective camera worked best when, in its weird way, it drew attention to the frightening limitations of our own perception.

GOD'S MURDEROUS MEN

THE FILM NOIR CRITIQUE OF AMERICAN RELIGION

The brilliant 1950 noir *The Sound of Fury* begins with a blind street preacher warning passersby that "Whatsoever a man soweth, that shall he also reap." This verse from the Apostle Paul's letter to the Galatians could work as an epigraph for all of film noir. It certainly works to set up *The Sound of Fury*, a film that tells the story of the downfall of a struggling family man named Howard Tyler (Frank Lovejoy). One day Howard meets a hood named Jerry Slocum (Lloyd Bridges) who offers him a job as a getaway driver for a string of robberies. At first Howard says no, but when he thinks it over and finally accepts Jerry's offer, you can smell the sulfur burning. After Jerry upgrades their criminal enterprise to kidnapping and murder, the film becomes a slow boiling nightmare fueled by Howard's deepening guilt. "I keep thinking God is coming after me," he tells his wife. *The Sound of Fury*, inspired by true events, was written by novelist Jo Pagano as an indictment of lynch mobs and journalistic cravenness, but the power of its narrative comes from the way it marries Howard's downfall to the street preacher's warning about sin and its terrible consequences.

That theme reverberates throughout film noir. Noir City might be one godless little town, a place of perpetual night, populated by men and women bleary-eyed with booze and bad judgment, but underneath the tales of lust and larceny, there beats a moralistic heart. After all, most noir boils down to the preacher's warning: you pay for your sins.

What makes this doubly interesting, however, is that noir rarely affords us a positive view of the clergy. The men of god we find in Noir City are of a piece with the town's other denizens: they're weak, wicked, or both. In noir, everybody's a sinner, and everybody is going to hell. That includes god's mouthpieces. In fact, they might be the biggest sinners of all.

Mark Robson's little seen 1950 *Edge of Doom* concerns a young man named Martin Lynn (Farley Granger) who develops a grudge against the church when his parish priest refuses to bury Lynn's father after he's committed suicide. Later, when Lynn's mother dies, he confronts the elderly priest to demand a fancy funeral for her. The indignant priest refuses, and Lynn kills him in a rage.

The above description should come as a shock to anyone familiar with movies of the time. Mainstream Hollywood movies in 1950 simply did not feature unsympathetic clergymen. They did not show young men who were ever mad at the church for anything. Religion in those days was a protected institution, especially during the time of the Red Scare, and the sinful denizens of Hollywood were all too happy to portray any and all religious authorities as unquestionably good. In most Hollywood films of the forties and fifties, God existed and he was an American.

Edge of Doom is a fascinating film because it shows the first strains in this façade. The movie still has to make several concessions to the production code (Dana Andrews plays a good priest trying to help Granger, and the church is, of course, ultimately absolved of any wrongdoing), but for most of its playing time it is a tough look at religion. The priest murdered by Granger may not be the pedophilic monster of today's headlines, but he is dogmatic, unforgiving, and entitled. We're shocked to see him murdered, but we're more shocked to see him portrayed as a self-righteous old fool hiding behind his collar. While he does not deserve to die, his murder flows out of Granger's understandable anger at him. In other words, we in the audience are asked to identify with the murderer of a priest. And, damn it all, we do.

Of course, the old Catholic priest can't hold a church candle to the crazy Protestants. Lewis R. Foster's tough-as-nails 1955 jailbreak flick *Crashout* gives us a motley group of escaped convicts on the run from the cops. Among their number is the always great William Talman (*The Hitch-Hiker*), in one of his best parts, as a knife-throwing Jesus freak named Luther Remsen AKA "Reverend Remington" who is in jail for the "celebrated soul-saving murder" of a church organist.

Crashout is no masterpiece—it starts to drift toward incomprehensibility in the closing scenes—but it is a deeply subversive piece of work. Star Arthur Kennedy is given a speech that pretty much sums up the noir ethos: "There's no road back. There're no yesterdays. There's no tomorrow. There's only today. Everyday you live is a day before you die." With this in mind, how much sense could one make of the promise of life everlasting? Especially when the only preacher on hand is crazy Reverend Remington? The film seems to answer this question by giving us what might be the most grotesque religious ritual in all noir when Reverend Remington baptizes a wounded man in a muddy drainage pool and tries to drown the guy in the process. The moment is still shocking. *Crashout* perverts Protestant Christianity's most sacred ritual—the immersion baptism which symbolizes the believer's death and resurrection in Christ—into a wickedly profane murder attempt.

In 1950, the character of Reverend Remington reflected a deep skepticism of new mass-media-mongering evangelists like Will Stidger and J. Frank Norris, Bible-thumpers given to greed, hedonism, or violence (Stidger inspired *Elmer Gantry*, and Norris once shot a man dead in his own church). New technologies, and shifts in political fortunes, were pushing religious snakeoil salesmen into the media spotlight. Someone like Billy Graham—of whom Harry S Truman disdainfully said, "All he's interested in is getting his name in the paper"—might have matured into a statesman and winner of the Presidential Medal of Freedom, but to a great many people in the fifties the pulpit-pounders still seemed like charismatic phonies.

While Catholic priests and Protestant preachers are the only religious leaders allowed on display in most noirs (you don't find many rabbis or imams in dark city), you can still find a great deal of fly-by-night conmen posing as spiritualists. Films like *The Amazing Mr. X, Fallen Angel, Night Has A Thousand Eyes,* and *Nightmare Alley* reveal a distinctly American obsession with occultist hucksters and trendy spiritualism. *Nightmare Alley*, in particular, observes how ready Americans seem to be to find new ways of contacting the Great Beyond. America is the land of new religion, of course, and beneath the calm Protestant face of officialdom, the country has always harbored a bubbling sense of spiritual curiosity. From Mormonism to Scientology, America has always been fertile ground for prophets and/or charlatans, and *Nightmare Alley* demonstrates how easily parlor tricks and intuition can be passed off as the newest revelation from on high.

Of course, the suspicion of religious authorities found its clearest expression in the most notorious clergyman in all noir: the Reverend Harry Powell (Robert Mitchum), the woman-murdering preacher who occupies the center of Charles Laughton's *The Night of the Hunter*. With HATE tattooed on one hand and LOVE on the other, the slick-talking Powell is like a Flannery O'Connor character wandering a weird landscape of bucolic Expressionism. His tattooed knuckles and his parable of the "story of good and evil" are symbols foreshadowing his ultimate showdown with a shotgun-and-Bible wielding old lady named Rachel Cooper (Lillian Gish).

It says something about noir's view of organized religion that Harry Powell is its most notable representative. Powered by Mitchum's mesmerizing turn, Powell embodies every criticism ever leveled at

American Christianity: greed, hypocrisy, misogyny, murderous self-righteousness. Of course, at the time of its release, the film was controversial in some corners for its depiction of the killer preacher, but it was mostly shunned, disappearing from public view, kept alive only by cinephiles and crime fans. That it has survived and flourished to the point that it is now widely considered a classic, is a testament not only to Laughton and his cast and crew, but to the enduring power of film noir's uniquely subversive critique of religion.

While noir paints a critical picture of American religion, it does lend some weight to the spiritual searching of ordinary people. One thing all religious authorities—from good priests to sham spiritualists—have in common is that they provide desperate people an answer to life's most vexing problem: death.

"The Cold Black Silence"

While theologians and philosophers have debated death and the possibility of an afterlife for millennia without coming to a definitive conclusion, the sprawling corpus of film noir seems to deliver a firm rejection of the hereafter. While it's true that many of the talents behind noir were believers, you don't have to be an existentialist to hit upon the genre's cumulative response to the issue of the afterlife: there's nothing after the end.

You can see this idea work itself out in film after film. In Tay Garnett's *The Postman Always Rings Twice*, John Garfield sits on death row talking to a priest. Is he talking about god? The great beyond? No, he's talking about Lana Turner. In Rudolph Mate's *DOA*,

The Blind Alley

when Frank Bigelow (Edmond O'Brien) discovers he has been fatally poisoned, he sets out to find his killer. Since he has no chance of being cured, the natural denial of death is wiped out, and yet with the sober reality of his death fast approaching, Bigelow doesn't give a moment's thought to the possibility of anything after it. *DOA* is often a goofy movie, but its worldview is purely fatalistic.

It is surpassed in this regard only by Allen Baron's *Blast Of Silence*, a film which follows the final days of a hit man named Frank Bono. The film is told in an odd second person narration (which might be the pulp equivalent of the voice of god). When Bono is gunned down at the end, the narration closes things out for him, "You're alone now, all alone. The scream is dead. There's no pain. You're home again, back in the cold black silence."

So much for heaven and hell. When a noir ends with the words The End, it's not kidding.

"Fate or some mysterious force"

For noir's remaining theological implications, one must look to its view of life. Doing this, one can argue that noir alternates between two theological ideas: predestination and free-will.

In essence, the idea of predestination is the idea that God intends some people to go to heaven and some to go to hell. In this view, there's nothing the individual can do to change his destiny. This idea may get its clearest expression in John Farrow's *Night Has A Thousand Eyes*. Edward G. Robinson plays a fraud spiritualist who discovers to his horror one day that he can actually see the future. He finds this power more a curse than a gift when he begins to foresee the deaths of those around him. When he receives a vision of his own death, he tries to use his few remaining days to save the life of a young woman played by Gail Russell. He succeeds and the film, ending with his death, is wearily optimistic that some meaning can be found even in death's creeping shadow.

That meaning can't always be found in a predestination noir, however. Perhaps the most famous line in all film noir is Al Robert's resignation at the end of the ultimate predestination film, *Detour*: "Fate, or some mysterious force, can put the finger on you or me for no good reason at all." (It's worth noting that Martin Goldsmith's original novel read, "*God* or fate") Robert's predicament is usually described as a kind of existential freefall representing the randomness of violence and doom. Interestingly enough, however, if we view it through the lens of predestination we don't come to a radically different conclusion. Does this indicate some point of contact between existentialist nihilism and Calvinist predestination? Perhaps. After all, for the characters experiencing an unearned destruction, there's not much difference between being destroyed for no reason at all and being destroyed because of God's unexplained whim. (Lorenzo Dow, one of the key figures in the Second Great Awakening, once mocked Calvinist predestination as "damned if you do and damned if you don't.")

Of course, poor Al Roberts is a born loser—perhaps the biggest born loser in all of Noir City, but many characters in noir aren't just victims of god or fate.

Some people deserve what they get. For some people, character is destiny.

Hell on Earth

Which brings us to the idea of free-will. In theological terms, free-will refers to the idea that the sinner can accept God's forgiveness and turn away from his or her sin. This, to say the least, does not happen very often in the dark city.

Perhaps the only literal example of this choice occurs in John Farrow's supernatural *Alias Nick Beale*, in which Satan (Ray Milland) comes to earth to tempt a politician (Thomas Mitchell) toward destruction. The ending of the film finds a way to reconfirm Farrow's belief in forgiveness and redemption (the director was a devout Catholic who wrote books of religious history and was honored by Pope Pious XI for his service to the Church). The film, however, is a dark piece of work and gives Nick Beal some parting words that sound like catechism in the Noir Book of Prayers: "You saved yourself just in time, didn't you? But there'll be others who won't. A lot of others. And I'll tell you why. In everyone there's a seed of destruction, a fatal weakness."

The movie critic Roger Ebert once described noir as "a movie where an ordinary guy indulges the weak side of his character, and hell opens up beneath his feet." The important word there is *indulges*, implying as it does the contravention of some established moral law. In this view, hell on earth is a punishment for sin.

Hell is a popular concept in noir. The idea of an afterlife may not seem to count for much in dark city, but *hell on earth* is the closest thing to a theological doctrine the town ever developed. This is because the twin obsessions of noir—transgression and ruination—are inextricably linked. If the First Church of Dark City has one guiding precept it is this: you pay for your sins.

That overarching sense of dread—the sense that a character's transgressions will be followed by his or her subsequent ruination—is at the heart of noir. Is there some lingering religious notion at the heart of that guilt-ridden fear? Or to put it another way, is god still watching and passing judgment? Noir provides about as clear an answer to that question as life does. In his essay "Nietzsche and the Meaning and Definition of Noir" scholar Mark T. Conrad suggests that noir's sense of doom comes from a post-Nietzschean anxiety over the death of God. That's certainly possible, but even if god is dead, the people of dark city still fear his judgment.

CHILDREN OF THE NIGHT

Representations of childhood from the classic period of American films tend to be chipper and upbeat. In the thirties, child stars like Mickey Rooney and Judy Garland were industrious, hyperactive, and—most vitally—happy. Happiness was the key. During the Depression, Shirley Temple giggled her way into superstardom by giving anxious Americans a vision of a healthy and relatively worry-free childhood. Films that did present children in thorny situations needed an aura of remove, and prestige pictures like John Ford's *How Green was My Valley* (1941) or social message pictures like William Wellman's *Wild Boys of the Road* (1933) were exceptions to a fairly stringent rule. Throughout the Depression and the war years, most films about children were celebrations of innocence rather than lamentations about its loss.

The rise of film noir did little to challenge this trend. By and large, Dark City was no place for kids. The average plot kicked in long past bedtime, and the tawdry emphasis on lust and murder made crime stories the mainstream adult entertainment of their day. The relative scarcity of children in noir, however, only served to make their occasional appearances all the more significant. These narratives directly involving children, including a handful of titles that actually centered around child protagonists, demonstrate a striking break with the established Hollywood image of carefree youth. Just as noir reveals the shifting currents and undercurrents of class, race, and gender in the forties and fifties, it also tells us something about the era's increasing anxiety about childhood and parenting.

Ignorance Isn't Bliss: The Child as Witness

In most noirs, kids function as little more than props. Incidental to the main plot, they are the domestic accoutrement, most of the time, of the married male protagonist. Yet even when they are serving this function, their presence can have a destabilizing effect.

Fritz Lang's *The Big Heat* (1953) has many virtues but an ease with children is not one of them. In the story of Dave Bannion (Glenn Ford), a cop out to avenge the murder of his wife, Bannion's daughter (Linda Bennett) functions as little more than familial decoration. Even after her mother is incinerated in the family car right outside her bedroom window, plunging her father into a near-psychotic rage, the girl is completely unfazed, jumping into her daddy's arms and asking for bedtime stories. Bannion tells someone that the little girl thinks her mother is "away on a trip." Even by the standards of most movie children, Bannion's daughter is oblivious. In a film like *The Big Heat,* the kid is there to function largely as a prop, a symbol of the protagonist's most fragile emotions, a visual representation of the threatened purity he is trying to protect. The tension that arises from this function is that Bannion, in his righteous fury, is disconnected from his daughter. In a sense, childhood is an impenetrable shell of innocence, wholly impervious to the troubles of the adult world, but it is also a barrier between father and daughter. The daughter cannot participate in her father's troubles; she is not even allowed to witness them.

Sometimes, though, children get closer to the truth without quite realizing it. Consider the role of Tommy Forbes (Jimmy Hunt) in the Andre De Toth masterpiece *Pitfall* (1948). Disgruntled family man John Forbes (Dick Powell), fed-up with married life, begins an affair with sexy Mona Stevens (Lizabeth Scott), but when Mona's obsessed stalker (Raymond Burr) finds out about the relationship he gives Forbes a viscous beating one night. The low point of Forbes's ordeal is lying to his son about the attack.

The boy, accepting a bogus story about multiple attackers, explains the situation to the doctor treating Forbes's wounds. "There were two of 'em or he could have handled 'em," the little boy says. "Couldn't you, Dad?"

Forbes's mumbled "Yeah, I suppose so" is swamped in the self-hatred of a man who has successfully lied to his child.

The façade is reinforced in a later scene, played for laughs, when Forbes misleads the boy about his service during the war. The audience understands that Forbes is being ironic in touting his humble military service—he won the Good Conduct medal while stationed in Denver, CO—but the child doesn't pick up on the irony. Though played for laughs, the scene serves to underline the deepest aspect of Forbes's personal crisis: he isn't the man his son thinks he is.

Occasionally, children do come to bear full witness to the troubles of their parents. In Cy Endfield's The *Sound of Fury* (1950), a financially-strapped family man named Howard Tyler (Frank Lovejoy) takes a job as the wheelman for Jerry Slocum, a low-rent stickup artist played by Lloyd Bridges. When this sloppy criminal enterprise descends into murder, Tyler's life starts to unravel with horrific speed.

The real locus of that life is, of course, his family. For most of the film, Tyler's son, Tommy (Donald Smelick) seems to be on hand mostly to ask his father for money that his father hasn't got. His first appearance in the film comes just after a low angled shot of a river of rambunctious children rushing to a baseball game. Howard wades through these children to his home where he finds Tommy bitterly complaining that his mother won't give him the quarter needed to get into the game.

Howard gives the boy his last fifty cent piece, a move that angers the boy's mother, Judy (Kathleen Ryan). "What'd you do that for?" she demands incredulously.

"My kid can go to a baseball game, can't he?" Howard snaps back.

In the immediate postwar economy, the problem isn't just feeding your children, it's giving them everything the culture says they now deserve. After coming home flush with cash from the first night's robbery, Tyler springs for baked ham and potato chips, and promises Tommy a bicycle and a television set.

"It's so expensive," Judy worries.

"So what?" Howard replies. "We got a right to live a little, too."

Tommy functions here not so much as a symbol of innocence but rather as a force of pressure weighing on his father. Raised in the turbulent postwar economy which saw America emerge as the world's dominant economy but which also endured two separate recessions between 1945 and 1949, Tommy is saddled with heightened material expectations at the same time that his family is consigned to the struggling working class. His father cannot meet Tommy's expectations without resorting to crime, but the real tragedy is that the father is at least partially responsible for setting those expectations. Throughout the film, Tyler's main motivation seems to be a desire not to be seen as a failure by his son.

By the end of the film, though, this desire has been reduced to ashes. When the cops finally catch up to Howard Tyler, they surround him in a shed behind his home, with his neighbors and his family massed behind a police barricade. Tommy, there to witness his father's arrest, speaks his last lines in the film, tearfully imploring his mother, "Mommy, what did Daddy do?" It is precisely the child's presence at this humiliation—witnessing his father as he is rather than as he would like to be—that gives the humiliation its agony.

Life Ain't Easy For A Prop: The Child as Victim

One aspect of life must have sucked for the average film noir kid: you had a good chance of being threatened, at some point, by a full tilt psycho. In Joseph Losey's brilliant 1951 remake of *M*, David Wayne plays a tormented child killer who stalks the streets of Los Angeles strangling little girls. As with the original German M, Losey's film is more about the hysterical reaction of society than it is about the killer himself, and the transition of the story to America is seamless. In one scene, a man stops to help a little girl who has fallen down and sprained her ankle, and he is quickly set upon by a violent mob. The anxiety on display here—the gut-wrenching fear of violence toward children—is universal. Placing the story in a noir context, and setting it in the most noir of all cities, renders it all the more powerful.

M was maybe the best, and the most serious, film to use child-endangerment as a hook, but the practice became fairly widespread. Phil Karlson's 1955 Alabama corruption drama *The Phenix City Story* captured some of the turmoil of the Civil Rights movement in a sequence that features the brutal murder of a young black girl. Tossed from a moving car, the child lands in the yard of a crusading district attorney as the man's own children play in front of the house. A note pinned to the little girl's dress reads: THIS WILL HAPPEN TO YOUR KIDS TOO. It's a chilling scene, all the more disturbing for the casual racism of the murderers who care so little for the life of a black child that they murder her a warning to a white man.

Despite the seriousness with which both *M* and *The Phenix City Story* treat violence toward children, it should be noted that most of the time child-endangerment was little more than a particularly underrated piece of B-movie existentialism featuring a terrifically bitter performance by Zachary Scott as an alcoholic ex-cop roused from a blackout binge by his desperate ex-wife who is frantic because their young son has gone missing. Though the film has many selling points, including a script crackling with good dialog, it uses the child abduction angle as nothing more than a way to kick start the plot. In a rather offhand manner, it turns child endangerment into a MacGuffin. The same is true of *Shadow on the Wall* (1950), based on the novel *Death in the Doll's House* by Hannah Lees and Lawrence Bachmann. Zachary Scott plays a man accused of murdering his wife, and the only person who can clear him is his amnesiac daughter played by Gigi Perreau. The child's presence here does little more than move the plot along.

Far worse is something like the 1959 cut-rate union drama *The Big Operator*—a failed attempt to cast Steve Cochran as an honest everyguy and Mickey Rooney as a heavy—which features a sadistic scene of thugs threatening to kill Cochran's young son. The scene is notable mostly for its inclusion in an otherwise lightweight entertainment. By this point, a piece of junk like *The Big Operator* could trot out a scene of a little boy being manhandled by killers for cheap thrills because it simply wasn't taboo to threaten kids with violence on screen anymore. The cinematic illusion of a danger-free childhood was gone.

Which isn't to say that films were suddenly interested in the inner lives of victimized kids. Even Samuel Fuller's *The Naked Kiss* (1964), one of the first films to deal openly with the issue of child molestation, is unable to deal with the psychological impact on children. Part of this is Fuller's trademark lack of subtlety—the children in his movie must be sickeningly sweet in order that their violation be all the more repulsive. In some ways, though, Fuller's representation of the children themselves adheres to the Hollywood norm. While he's willing to deal with the presence of the pederast, he is unwilling to deal with the psyches—damaged or otherwise—of children themselves. The mind of a child, even for a tough guy like Fuller, was a scary place to go.

The Kid From Dark City:
The Child as Protagonist

Occasionally, though, a few filmmakers dared to use children as more than props and put them at the center of dark crime plots. Ted Tezlaff's *The Window* (1949) is based on a Cornell Woolrich story in which a young boy witnesses his upstairs neighbors murdering a man. He tries to tell his parents what has happened, but because of his habit of telling sensational lies, no one will believe him. Featuring a restrained and winning performance by Bobby Driscoll, *The Window* is the rare noir that manages to give us a plausible image of the world from the point of view of a child. Driscoll's main obstacle in the film, after all, isn't the killer upstairs, it's the fact that, as a child, he has no standing in the adult world. Noir, which is so often about powerlessness, is the perfect vehicle for this story.

This is a good place to observe that that the noir era was kicking into gear at about the same time the golden era of the child star—a period when the box office had been dominated by Temple, Garland, and Rooney—was coming to an end. Sadly, Bobby Driscoll would go on to become the shambling embodiment of the lost Hollywood kid. After a short successful run in his youth (which included providing the voice of the title character in Disney's 1953 *Peter Pan*), Driscoll found himself unemployable. A heroin addict from his teenage years, he lived in a downward spiral of drugs and poverty for a decade until two children found his body in an abandoned building in Greenwich Village in 1968. It was a sad end to a heartbreaking story, but given Hollywood's propensity to destroy its child stars (Exhibit A: Garland, Judy) it is hardly shocking. In fact, *The Window* is a strangely fitting noir tribute to Driscoll, enshrining him forever as a scrappy little boy just trying to survive the cruelty and indifference of adults.

Perhaps noir's most powerful expression of childhood is Charles Laughton's *The Night of the Hunter* (1955). Here the children are protagonists in a stylized nightmare that unfolds like a twisted fairy tale: two young siblings, John and Pearl, are left fatherless outcasts after their bank-robber dad is executed for his crimes. Their mother (Shelley Winters), lonely and sad, marries the first man she meets after her husband's death, a hillbilly preacher named Harry Powell (Robert Mitchum). Once Powell moves into the house, however, he shifts his attention from the mother to the children. Every time their mother is away, he sneaks up to their bedroom. He interrogates them in different ways. He puts the little girl on his lap, flirts with her almost. He makes the boy stand in the center of the room while he hurls abuse at him. He warns them not to tell their mother. This is our secret, he tells them. She wouldn't believe you anyway.

We know that Powell is simply after some money from their father's final bank heist, but in positioning him as the tormentor of the two young children—and having him hide behind his privilege as an adult, as well as his position as both their stepfather and as a man of God— *The Night of the Hunter* gives us one of the first portraits of a child molester in American cinema. More than David Wayne's disturbing turn as the child murderer in Losey's *M,* Mitchum's performance is unrepentantly evil. Director Charles Laughton, hewing closely to the excellent novel by Davis Grubb, creates an image of childhood that is fraught with danger— danger that springs most often from the weakness or selfishness of adults. Since neither of the child stars, Billy Chapin and Sally Jane Bruce, is conventionally cute the film seems immune to the clichéd tone of most children's movies. The tone here is much closer to the hard-edged vision of Grimm's original fairy tales, replete with the very real possibility of harm and death.

In fact, both *The Window* and *The Night of the Hunter* are variations on much older stories. The former is clearly a retelling of "The Boy Who Cried Wolf" (Woolrich's original story was called "The Boy Who Cried Murder"), while the latter is reminiscent of "Hansel and Gretel." These origins point to a certain severity regarding childhood that existed prior to the Hollywood model of the cheerful American youngster, and it also points to the modern whitewashing of those gruesome old fairy tales. So while both *The Window* and *The Night of the Hunter* were groundbreaking in terms of representation of children onscreen, in reality they really harkened back to a much earlier kind of storytelling.

We Need To Talk About Veda: The Child as Villain

The recent film *We Need to Talk About Kevin* (2011) is a chilling look at the slow development of that most harrowing of modern inventions, the school shooter. Perhaps nothing else in our society is as confounding, as profoundly disturbing, as the news that yet another adolescent has taken a gun to school and opened fire on teachers and fellow students. It is precisely the mesh of innocence and psychopathic rage that we find so deeply troubling.

Though representations of the child-gone-wrong would find early expression in horror films like *The Bad Seed* (1956) and *Village of the Damned* (1960), noir had already laid the groundwork years before. The great child villain of noir is undoubtedly Veda Pierce, daughter of the longsuffering Mildred Pierce. Michael Curitz's *Mildred Pierce* (1945) is the story of the abusive relationship between these two women, and although the movie is named after the mother, it really belongs to the daughter. Which, after all, is exactly how the little brat would want it.

Veda is a teenager with an obsessive attraction to money and high society. From the beginning of the film her interactions with her mother have an edge. It's almost as if Veda were the parent—and a bad parent at that. She seems to look down on most people, and her beleaguered, hardworking mother most of all.

At the center of the film is the simply amazing turn by young Ann Blyth as Veda. Surely one of cinema's greatest villains, Veda is every parent's worst nightmare, the child who consumes love and support as thoughtlessly as a termite chewing through wood. Veda is a bottomless narcissistic pit whose only joys in life are spending money and berating her mother. This role sabotaged the rest of Blyth's career, seriously curtailing the kinds of parts she was offered. She was simply Veda. And everyone loves to hate Veda.

A lesser known but in some ways even more disturbing example of the child-villain appears in the odd 1952 *Talk About a Stranger,* an unlikely, and uneasy, blend of film noir and children's movie. At first glance it has all the trappings of a kiddie potboiler from the early fifties: produced at MGM, it stars George Murphy, Billy Gray, and Nancy Davis (who just prior to the release of the film had become Mrs. Nancy Reagan). That's about as wholesome a cast as you could ask for, and the storyline is closer to Franklin W. Dixon than James M. Cain. And yet, the film is a very good example of how style—particularly visual style—transforms material.

Written by Margaret Fitts from a short story by Charlotte Armstrong, the film is set in sunny Citrus City, a friendly little Southern California town where Bobby Fontaine (Billy Gray), a precocious nine year old, sells newspaper subscriptions, helps his dad (George Murphy) in the orange groves, and plays with a mutt he simply calls Boy. When the dog turns up dead one day, Bobby blames the strange man (Kurt Kasznar) who has just moved into the ramshackle old mansion next door. This next door neighbor is surly and keeps to himself, but the film doesn't try very hard to make us suspicious of him. Instead, our concern is directed more and more at Bobby, whose behavior toward his neighbor becomes ever more irrational. At the end of the film, everything is explained and everything is resolved, sort of, but the part of the film that lingers is the boy's descent into suspicion, fear, and rage.

The film's secret weapon is noir master John Alton. Consider the cinematographer's best sequence, toward the end of the film. The boy has become progressively more unhinged, fixated on exposing and punishing the man next door. Finally, crazy with anger, he smashes the man's oil tank, spilling thousands of gallons of fuel. Later, having discovered that this fuel is vital to the survival of the orange groves during a hard winter frost, the boy runs back to the tank, only to find his father and the other farmers gathered around it. Using an unsteady handheld camera, Alton puts us in the point of view of the boy as he looks up at the furious men, each backlit like a potential murderer as they hover above him. At this moment, it doesn't matter that the plot is goofy. These images have a stark power all their own.

Talk About a Stranger may not be the best of the film noirs about children (that honor clearly goes to *The Night of the Hunter),* but in some ways it's the most subversive. The kids in *Hunter* and *Window* are more or less conventional protagonists, but in this film Bobby is the main culprit. He's a true noir antihero:

self-absorbed, unwise, and neurotic. In the scene where he vandalizes the oil tank, there's a shot of his face that is maybe the most disturbing image of a child in all of noir. The camera, looking up at him, is extremely close to his face as a hard white light reveals a sweaty, almost sensual delight in destruction. It's one thing to photograph some thug like Neville Brand this way as he's working over a guy for information, but to shoot a kid this way is shocking. The whole movie, in its weird, off-kilter kind of way, is shocking. Like so many of the noirs that involve children, it is striking proof that behind the benign presentation of 50s era childhood lay a roiling sense of unease.

III

FACES FROM THE SHADOW GALLERY:

PROFILES

THE GIRL THEY LOVED TO KILL

THE MANY DEATHS OF PEGGIE CASTLE

In Hollywood's Golden Age, beauty was turned into a commodity, one found in abundance and renewed with each out-of-town bus. Thousands of lovely young women cycled through the studio system, had their physical attributes capitalized upon, and wound up back on the street with little more than the handful of cash it would take to get back home. Of these unlucky multitudes only a few lived long enough to see themselves become a new kind of star: the rediscovered film noir icon, the object of scholarly study and geek adoration.

All scholarship and trivia aside, film noir is, in large part, a cult devoted to rescuing forgotten women from the obscurity that once seemed to be their final destiny. Because noir preserves these women primarily as symbols of sex, their onscreen legacy is lit with an especially erotic flame. This is certainly true of Peggie Castle, who came into the business as an 18-year old starlet, achieved moderate success as a *femme fatale*, and then found herself out work by the age of 35. As a result, the images we have of her comprise a largely sexualized picture of a woman in her early twenties. What makes her legacy problematic, and fascinating, is the frequency with which this pretty picture is darkened by images of punishment and violence. Even in the fragile immortality granted by film, Peggie goes on dying, martyred again and again in misogynist fantasies of eroticized sadism.

You may not remember her. Most people don't. She was never really a star, not even in the insular world of film noir, where she was usually cast as an easily disposable sex object. In her most famous scene, she was shot to death while doing a striptease. It was that kind of career.

Though a lot of women played the doomed bad girl, Peggie Castle seemed to embody the ethos somehow. Something about her seemed dangerous—which is another way of saying, perhaps, that something about her threatened men. With her low, smoky voice and skeptical green eyes, she wasn't hot, she was cool. She never seemed to lose control. Her sensuality always seemed to be hers to do with as she pleased, a tool to get what she wanted. If this was her innate quality as an actor, then she was made to suffer for it in film after film.

That cool quality seemed to reflect the real woman as well. Well-educated and ambitious, she had a caustic wit about most things, and she evinced few romantic illusions about the business she'd chosen for herself.

"The difference between an old fashioned kiss and a movie kiss," she said once, "is about 1500 feet of film."

She lived a disconnected life from the beginning. Born Peggy (with a Y) Thomas Blair on December 22, 1927 in Appalachia, Virginia, she was the daughter of an industrial efficiency expert named Doyle Blair and his wife Elizabeth "Betty" Guntner. Doyle's job kept the Blairs on the road with their only child. "The harder an efficiency expert works the sooner he's out of a job," she would later observe. "I attended 22 different schools while traveling from city to city with my father…so I've got a 'home town' story for dozens of reporters."

All this moving around seemed to give young Peggy a thoughtful, inward quality. Yet it was during this same period that the quiet girl found her love of the spotlight. While living in Pittsburg as a child, she attended the Linden School in upscale Squirrel Hill where she studied French and ballet. At the age of eight, she danced and acted in a school play staged at the Pittsburg Playhouse. She seemed to know, even then, that she wanted to be an actor.

It must have felt like fate when the Blairs settled in Los Angeles around the time Peggy turned 14. She attended Hollywood High School, and lying about her age, got a job as a photographer's model.

After high school, she enrolled in the theater arts program at Mills College where she studied acting under Madaleine Mihaud, then a refuge from Europe. In 1945, a still few months shy of turning 18, she married a 24-year old serviceman named Revis T. Call.

It was to be the first of many name changes. Over the years, through various marriages and professional rebrandings, in movie credits and news publications and government documents, she was listed under as many names as a CIA operative: Peggy T. Blair, Peggy Call, Peggy Castle, Peggie Castle, Peggie C. Blair, Peggie C. McGarry, Peggie S. Morgenstern. (She once quipped that a name-dropper in Hollywood "is an actress who's been married six times.")

She did well in school but dropped out after only a year to work on the radio soap opera *Today's Children* at $375 a week. Still, her time in school seems to have shaped her perceptions of the world. "The college girl has more tolerance [than the average girl]," she would explain once she'd become a working actor. For an actor who would spend much of her time playing morally dubious women, it was important to her not to judge her characters. Later in her career she would muse to a reporter, "Most of our suspicions of others are aroused by our knowledge of ourselves."

The account of her "discovery" by a talent scout while she ate lunch in Beverly Hills is probably one of those too-good-to-be-true Hollywood stories. She'd already been acting and modeling for years by 1947, when she made her debut, billed as Peggy Call, in the Adele Jergins comedy *When A Girl's Beautiful* at Columbia.

It is certain that her second film had a bigger impact on her career. *Mr. Belvedere Goes To College* (1949) was the sequel to the hit comedy *Sitting Pretty*, with star Clifton Webb reprising his role as the wryly funny Lynn Belvedere. When Webb got snippy with Peggy on the set one day, Peggy—no one's doormat despite being only an uncredited bit player on the picture—got snippy right back. The director liked the exchange so much it stayed in the picture and caught the eye of super agent Charles Feldman. "I've always had a temper as long as I can remember," she later noted. "If I hadn't had a temper, I might not have come to Mr. Feldman's attention at all."

1950 was to be a big year for her. With Feldman's help, she signed a seven-year contract with Universal and changed her screen name to Peggie Castle. She also divorced Revis Call, bringing their brief marriage to a quick close. Not long after, she was linked to war hero turned movie star Audie Murphy. Finding herself in the tabloids only sharpened her sense of humor. "In Hollywood," she sighed, "gossip goes in one ear and out the mouth."

In those early days at Universal, she entered into the studio's drama school under the tutelage of Universal's acting coach, Sophie Rosenstein. Her peers in the school included up-and-comers like Rock Hudson, Peggy Dow, James Best, Ann Pearce, and Piper Laurie.

She didn't get along with one of her peers, ladies man Tony Curtis (who would later recall Peggie as "a girl I didn't particularly like"), which led to an altercation between Curtis and Audie Murphy. Though he'd been widely celebrated as America's most decorated enlisted man during World War II, Murphy suffered from a particularly rage-filled version of post-traumatic stress disorder. One day in the studio hallway he grabbed Curtis and growled, "Peggie says you've been talking bad about her."

While Curtis calmed Murphy down that afternoon, Peggie decided the troubled war hero was too violent and called off their relationship. "Audie is impossible to understand," she told a friend. "You make every concession, then if you can't help him, it's better to say goodbye."

In a pattern that would repeat itself the rest of her life, she didn't stay single long. Shortly, she started seeing one of the junior executives at Universal, Bob Rains. They would elope in Juarez, Mexico in January the next year.

For all of the initial excitement of landing the job at Universal, the work itself amounted to little more than bit roles, mostly in small fry productions: a waitress in Crane Wilbur's *Outside The Wall*, another waitress in the Ida Lupino vehicle *Woman In Hiding*, a telephone operator in *I Was A Shoplifter*, a hat check girl in *Shakedown*. She did her best "playing the roles Yvonne De Carlo turned down" and hoped for better.

More demeaning than the roles, however, were the endless scantly-clad publicity photos for which Peggie now found herself contractually obligated to pose. As the first signatory of Universal's new "cheesecake clause" she got a lot of press, though not really the sort an aspiring actor wanted. A brief hue and cry arose when Shirley Temple, who was just a year younger than Peggie, denounced the new mandated photos—which the press built up as something of an attack on young players like Castle. Asked for her comment, Peggie was characteristically blunt, explaining that for an up and comer it was a matter of economics: "A lot of gals who won't pose for cheesecake won't be eating cheesecake, either."

Still, the photos had their drawbacks. Perhaps an actor as beautiful as Peggie was always bound to be judged for her looks, but the "controversy" seemed to establish her as little more than a pretty girl in a swimsuit. "Soon enough I'll be too old to be a starlet," she said hopefully, "thank goodness."

Among her fellow actors in Rosenstein's drama school, she held herself aloof. Years later, the actor Donna Martell would remember Peggie as "a living doll and a beautiful girl" but she also sensed a deep sadness underneath Peggie's beauty. "There was something missing in that girl's personality," Martell told writer Tom Weaver. "She was very lonely, and she was not a happy person. I felt that right away."

Peggie's time at Universal seemed to slog on, with the roles getting a little bigger but no better. After a run of exotic princess-types in cheesy budget-epics like 1951's *The Prince Who Was A Thief* and *The Golden Horde*, she complained to a reporter, "It's good to get some clothes on again and not have to wiggle to the tune of a snake charmer's pipe."

She was hopeful when the studio loaned her out to RKO for a small role in *Payment on Demand* with Bette Davis. It was an A-picture, at last, but after shooting had wrapped, studio head Howard Hughes demanded recuts and a tacked-on happy ending which pushed the release date back. By the time the film came out, it was overshadowed by Davis's triumph in *All About Eve*, and Peggie was already back on the Universal lot.

If she wasn't waiting around the studio for another nothing part, she was on the road doing thankless publicity tours. "All I did was travel 56,000 miles [promoting] four pictures I wasn't in and had never seen," she lamented of her time there. "It was embarrassing when people asked me what I thought of the pictures."

In 1952, her option with Universal expired and she and the studio parted ways. It was a bitter end to what had seemed, only a couple of years before, like a dream job. Echoing the sentiments of many talented B-listers, she wondered aloud why the studio never found a place for her. "I used to watch wonderful parts go to outsiders while a lot of us gathered dust," she remarked later. "It seems odd that so many of the studios keep their young talent in the deep freeze instead of turning them out early…I wish I could figure it all out."

At the smaller studios and independent production companies, Peggie moved up to lead roles, though the pictures were of dubious quality: the Monogram western *Wagon's West*, Columbia's redbaiter *Invasion USA*, Allied Artists' *Cow Country* with Edmond O'Brien. Her career seemed stuck.

Then her savior arrived in the unlikely form of Mickey Spillane. The pulp writer *cum* publishing phenomenon had launched his Mike Hammer series in 1947 and kicked off a juggernaut of sex, violence, and astronomical sales that reconfigured the literary landscape. It was only a matter of time before his grisly vision found its way to the screen. Spillane talked of starting his own studio and teaching the Hollywood sissies a thing or two about the movie business. ("I told him," Peggie recalled, "'I hope you have lots of money.' And he said, 'I have two million!'"). In the meantime, the rights to his works were snapped up by producer Victor Saville.

Saville's first film was an adaptation of the debut Hammer novel *I, the Jury* (1953). In the lead role he cast a little known television actor named Biff Elliot, and as the film's villain, the sexy psychologist Charlotte Manning, he picked Peggie.

With her usual biting wit, she summed up the macho Spillane. "If you saw a picture of three guys, he'd be the little guy in the middle." She did acknowledge that playing the female lead in a Mike Hammer movie would at least get her recognized. "You seldom become famous playing good girls. I appeared in 20 pictures, mostly as a wide-eyed ingénue and nobody ever heard of me. Then I did *I, The Jury*. It wasn't exactly the greatest picture ever made. But now people know who I am."

The movie begins with a pre-credits murder and then Mike Hammer shows up to swear bloody revenge (the *ur*-plot of the entire Hammer canon). The story consists of Hammer going from one place to the next grilling potential suspects. His interactions with men invariably end in violence, while his interactions with women invariably end in sexual innuendo. At the end, he suddenly figures out Manning is the killer and carries out the execution.

The film's big selling point, aside from the gimmick of being a 3-D crime flick, was the showdown between

Hammer and Manning. At the end of Spillane's novel, she strips naked in an unsuccessful attempt to dissuade Hammer from carrying out his execution. The poster for the film featured a graphic of Peggie unbuttoning her blouse—which seemed to promise the notorious striptease but, of course, the film itself had to work purely through innuendo. Peggie slips off only her rain coat and her shoes before Hammer guns her down. Her last words are, "How could you?" To which he replies, "It was easy."

What's notable here is that Peggie gives, pretty much by unanimous agreement, the best performance in the film. Whereas Biff Elliot's strained performance as Hammer consists mostly of petulant barks, Peggie has the exact combination of aloof beauty and devious intelligence that her role calls for, and one wonders what she might have done opposite a decent actor in the lead role. Her final scene in the film might be a distinctly puritanical form of misogynist fantasy—male stoicism obliterating the threat posed by female sexuality—but Peggie's mesmerizing in it. Captured in John Alton's shimmering black and white cinematography as Franz Waxman's sultry jazz score does everything it can to push us toward the bedroom, Peggie's palpable sensuality is the driving force in one of the most sexual scenes in classic noir.

That same year, she made her best film noir, Phil Karlson's *99 River Street*, where she plays Pauline Driscoll, the cheating wife of ex-boxer turned cabbie Ernie Driscoll (John Payne). At the beginning of the film, she leaves Ernie for a hood named Victor Rawlins, played by cold-eyed Brad Dexter. This initiates a long dark night of the soul for Ernie, who crisscrosses nighttime New York City, dodging cops and gangsters, while he mends his broken heart with a chipper actor named Linda (Evelyn Keyes).

Noir doesn't get any better than *99 River Street*. It's marvelously acted and shot, and the cast is uniformly excellent. Payne was never better as a leading man, and Keyes is almost stunningly good, rocking two her big scenes (one recounting a murder and one seducing Dexter) like she's auditioning for greatness.

Allow me to suggest, however, that it is Peggie Castle's performance which ultimately makes *99 River Street* fascinating because it hints at a counter-narrative that complicates the main story. Peggie doesn't play Pauline as a type, as the rotten wife wooing her man to his doom for the sheer hell of it. Pauline seems truly disappointed in her life with Ernie. When she asks him to turn off a television rebroadcast of his last losing bout, she does it with a note of pained weariness. Their marriage is an old story: she married him on the way up when the future seemed full of parties and fur coats, but now that he's driving a cab, she feels like she made a mistake. She's not thrilled by Ernie's promises that maybe one day they'll be able to open a filling station. Well, hell, who can blame her?

Something else is troubling, something never explicitly stated in the film, but which, upon repeated viewings, becomes unmistakable: Pauline is terrified of her husband. After Ernie finds out that she's been cheating on him, she trembles as she tells Dexter, "He'll kill me. You don't know what he's like. He broods about things, and suddenly he explodes." Take Pauline's fear along with the fact that Ernie twice gets physical with nice girl Linda—lifting his hand to strike her in one scene and shoving her across a room in another—and it becomes clear that the Driscoll marriage isn't the simple story of a sweet guy and a rotten dame. Like all great femme fatales, Pauline has her reasons.

Our sympathy for Pauline only increases as her attempt to escape her marriage goes horribly wrong. Victor turns out to be very bad news indeed. He takes her to meet the fence for some stolen jewels (Jay Adler) and then lets a thug (Jack Lambert) slap her around. When Adler calls off the deal for the jewels because of Pauline's presence ("I don't do business with women!") Victor makes a coldblooded business decision. He takes Pauline back to his apartment, kissing her while he tightens a scarf around her throat. As the camera moves past her face to his, she purrs "Victor, don't…" The next time we see her, she's been strangled and left in Ernie's cab.

In a disturbing trend, this marked the second time Peggie was murdered in an eroticized way in a film noir. As with her death in *I, The Jury* her murder here has the effect of punishing her character in a sexualized manner. *This*, both films seemed to be saying, *is what happens to bad girls*. This message is suffused with a deep sexism, of course, but it also contains the integral ingredients of noir: transgression and ruin.

Consider something else. At the end of *99 River Street*, we find that good girl Linda has abandoned her lifelong dreams of being a Broadway star so she can have babies and man the front desk at Ernie's filling station. Thus, Linda gets a happy ending complete with the socially sanctioned dreams of motherhood and middle class prosperity. Pauline, on the other hand, is destroyed because her dissatisfaction with her marriage and her attraction to a l'homme fatale lead to her downfall. Though Pauline is discarded at the end, it is her story and Castle's haunting performance that give *99 River Street* its true noir heart.

By this point, she was known primarily for playing the bad girls in crime pictures. Putting a good face on it, Peggie asked a reporter, "Well, doesn't every girl want to be a *femme fatale*?"

Sometimes, though, she admitted that being the bad girl had one redundant aspect. "I have yet to live through a picture," she joked in an interview. "There I am on the set reading the script, feeling just wonderful. I'm going to come out alive for a change. Then I turn the page and three bullet holes appear in my back. Peggie Castle bites the dust again."

What an odd thing, dying for a living. "I've been shot, knifed, clubbed, strangled, poisoned and hanged. I'm beginning to feel like the girl everybody hates."

What was it about her that made her, as one headline put it "The Girl They Love To Kill"? Was it the cool reserve, the green eyes that always seemed to be doing some inner calculations? Tall, voluptuous, and palpably intelligent—everything about her read as strength. In westerns, she was a surprisingly violent leading lady, often butched up in pants and six-shooters with ad copy like "No Man Could Tame Her!" The bitter irony, of course, was that she was forever being tamed, usually by force.

Her next noir utilized her dangerous vixen reputation to a different end. *The Long Wait* (1954) was another Spillane adaptation, though it wasn't a Hammer story. The movie stars Anthony Quinn as a tough amnesia victim named Johnny McBride who discovers that he's wanted for murder. He sets out to clear his name and the film follows the usual amnesia plot pretty much to the letter. McBride comes into contact with people who know more about him than he knows about himself—including the cops who want to bust him for murder, the crooks who seem to be after him for secret reasons, and a parade of beautiful women, one of whom may or may not hold the key to the mystery of McBride's past.

The film was again produced by Victor Saville, who also directed—and his direction is rather lacking, particularly in the performance that he gets out of his leading man. Anthony Quinn could be a dynamic performer in the right role, but here he mostly seems like a grumpy lunkhead. He kisses every woman in the picture like he's trying to wring information out of her face. There's not a single moment of genuine eroticism, and no one has any chemistry with anyone else, which might be the effect of Saville's particularly awkward reverse shots.

The picture has redeeming features, though, and chief among them is Peggie. Though her role is little more than a sexy red herring—turns out she's not the mystery woman with all the answers—she's still the most dynamic performer in the film. With her shimmering blonde locks and her air of quiet mystery, she handily gives the best performance in the movie, and every time she shows up on screen, *The Long Wait* perks up.

She also features in the film's strangest—and best—scene: an almost impressionistic little number in which Castle and Quinn are kidnapped by a gangster and taken to an abandoned warehouse. In the middle of a huge pool of white light, bordered by complete darkness, Quinn is tied to a chair and Castle is bound-up on the floor. In a montage of askew camera angles that stands out stylistically from the rest of the film, Castle crawls over to Quinn as the psychotic gangster throws obstacles in her path.

The scene was designed by the great art director Boris Leven, who drew a series of sketches for the director. Saville recalled using 87 different set-ups to match Leven's drawings, shot for shot. It's the big set-piece of the film, the one scene that everyone remembers. It also has the added benefit of summing up Peggie Castle's essential position in noir—bound and crawling across a floor, tortured by a man.

The sequence ends with Peggie retrieving a hidden gun, shooting the gangster, and getting shot in return. For once, she lives, but although she takes a bullet for the hero, she still doesn't wind up with him in the end. Another dame gets him. Peggie gets a ride to the hospital.

For better and for worse, her screen image as the sexy-but-suspect woman of the world was set. To an extent, she accepted this fate. "Let's face it," she said. "Nobody likes nice women on the screen. Nice women are dull."

But there were other things she would have liked to have done. Given her quick wit, it's a pity no one ever put her in a comedy, something she longed for. "Not the slapstick type," she said, "but the kind of comedy that Carole Lombard used to do. I think I could do very well in that sort of role, the tongue-in-cheek kind."

The comedy roles never came, though.

In 1955, she gave perhaps her most nuanced noir performance in Harold Schuster's *Finger Man*. Frank Lovejoy plays a hood named Casey Martin, who at the behest of the feds, is trying to infiltrate a gang led by Dutch Becker (Forest Tucker). He enlists the help of a reformed prostitute named Gladys, played by Castle. As she helps him work his way into the gangster's good graces, Gladys and Casey fall in love.

"You're two people aren't you, Casey?" she asks him.
"Who isn't?" he replies.
"That's right," she says with a soft smile. "Who isn't?"

The best thing about the movie is the relationship between Gladys and Casey. Their scenes together have a deep, natural chemistry. Part of what made Castle an interesting actor is that although she had an beautifully expressive face, her impulse was always toward restraint.

Lovejoy, one of the great unsung actors of the fifties, similarly held himself in check. Together they do a subtle duet, moving haltingly, cautiously toward love.

Here Peggie, at the end of her noir career, plays a slightly older, more roughed up version of her usual vixen role. Gladys, a past-her-prime beauty who's had some hard breaks, fears she maybe coming to the end of things. Peggie still looks stunning, but at only 28 she can already do world weariness like she means it. When he asks her "Where'd you get that halo all the sudden?" she just chuckles and says, "Me? That's funny."

Unfortunately, Gladys doesn't make it to the end of the picture. Her time runs out when Becker's psycho henchman, played by Timothy Carey, decides to kill her.

We don't see Peggie's demise. In her last scene, she simply says goodbye to Lovejoy. Then she crosses Hope Street and disappears into the night.

With *Finger Man* she closed out her noir career—and with it, the roles that somehow best suited her. She found herself in increasingly inferior material. Something like the western *Two-Gun Lady* ("Every Man Was Her Target!") assembles a great cast including Peggie, Marie Windsor, and William Talman, and then wastes them in a shoddily produced mess of boring exposition and sloppy action. "It was lightweight," Marie Windsor later judged, "and done in a hurry!"

Peggie kept working: supporting Randolph Scott and Dorothy Malone in the western *Tall Man Riding*; starring opposite Richard Conte in *Target Zero*; headlining a no-budget western called *The Oklahoma Woman*, one of the first productions of the young Roger Corman. In 1957, she headed to England to star opposite Zachary Scott in the tepid Anglo Amalgamated production *The Counterfeit Plan*—one of those transcontinental crime pictures that often signaled the death knell of a fading Hollywood career in the late 1950s.

That same year she had a good role in an interesting horror film, *Back From The Dead*, written by the novelist and screenwriter Catherine Turney. Peggie plays a woman possessed by the ghost of her husband's first wife, an evil spirit who has returned from the dead to rejoin a Satanic cult leader. Part *Rebecca* and part *Rosemary's Baby*, the small production paired Peggie with the talented, but blacklisted, Marsha Hunt and gave her some juicy scenes to play, including a sequence where she gasses Hunt and takes a scythe to her dog. Her co-star was impressed with both Peggie and her performance in the film. "I had not known her or even her name prior to that," Hunt later recalled. "But she was professional and *very* good."

Back From The Dead might have been the highlight of 1957, but Peggie also hit her career nadir that year in the aptly titled *Beginning Of The End*, a bargain-budget creature feature that found her teaming up with Peter Graves to fight giant killer grasshoppers. Graves remembered her as "a wonderful actress" who "always looked appealing" no matter what, but viewers are more likely to notice that she looks bored in a movie that could only signal the demise of her career in features.

She'd already started doing more and more television. This transition, of course, happened to the entire generation of second-tier stars in the fifties. As the B-movie market dried up (due to the decrease in studio output and the dissolution of the double feature), television work expanded. It was a living, but like many others, Peggie saw it as a step down.

"I hate television," she announced with her usual bluntness. "I don't like to watch it and I don't like to act in it. They make those half-hour shows so fast, you can't possibly do a good acting job. And they pay you shoe buttons."

But once the giant grasshoppers eat what's left of your movie career, what's a gal to do?

Befitting someone with noir cred, she did plenty of crime show work. She played the murder suspect in "The Case of the Negligent Nymph" an episode of *Perry Mason*. On a *77 Sunset Strip* episode called "The Well-Selected Frame" she played a woman convinced that her husband is trying to kill her. And she waded back into Spillane territory one last time for an episode of *Mike Hammer* called "The Big Drop" in which she hires Hammer to find the man who killed her father.

Her longest gig in television, and very nearly her last, was for the western series *Lawman*. At first, she turned down the role of Lily Merrill. "They wanted me to be a regular on the series," she said, "but they wanted me to run the local café. I had a vision of myself serving coffee in an apron for 38 weeks so I said no." Besides, she had never bought into the mythos of the western. She suspected, she once said, that "the strange irresistible force which drives some men out into the wilderness is known as house cleaning."

Anyway, the job came with a hitch. They wanted her to sing. "I'd never sung in my life," she told reporters. "Not even in the bathtub."

But in the end, the job was steady work in the most popular genre of the day. The show's producers changed her character to a saloon owner and hired a voice coach to get her in shape for the singing. When they floated the idea of putting together a record, Peggie joked, "Well, I don't have the greatest voice in the world. Maybe I can record an album titled 'Songs To Groom Horses By.'"

Unfortunately, *Lawman* itself was little more than a poor man's *Gunsmoke* starring stone-faced John Russell. The series added Peggie at the start of the second season to be a spunkier, sassier version of Miss Kitty (one headline read "Blonde Comes to Laramie to Defrost TV's *Lawman*"), but while she quickly became one of the best things about the show, the show itself remained a fairly pedestrian oater.

During her run on the program, Peggie started drinking more heavily. She still looked good, but the old sheen had disappeared. When *Lawman* surrendered its badge after three more seasons Peggie decided she'd had enough and effectively retired from acting.

She had divorced second husband Bob Rains back in 1954, claiming cruelty and general boorishness. A few months later she married assistant director William McGarry, who was twenty-two years her senior. "At least I'm glad I didn't marry an actor," she said. "That's one form of insanity I didn't indulge." In 1963, the year after *Lawman* was cancelled, she and McGarry had a daughter named Erin.

Their marriage outlived her career (she notched a final television appearance on an episode of *The Virginian* in 1966), but in 1970 she and McGarry divorced. Writer David J. Hogan reports that Castle's drinking had developed into a full-blown crisis by this time, hastening the end of her third marriage. "Her appearance changed for the worse," Hogan wrote in "Green Eyes Crying" a 1992 article about Castle, "and she gradually slipped away from reality. Her situation was made worse by increasingly unhappy relationships with her father and daughter."

After her divorce from McGarry, she moved into a two-room apartment over a garage in East Hollywood. She stayed inside for days on end, drinking alone and listening to records. Just before Christmas, the landlord went to check on her. She answered the door in tears. When he inquired what was wrong, she told him, "Today's my birthday. Nobody remembered."

The model and actor turned Hollywood oral chronicler William Ramage was friends with Peggie's landlord at the time and later recalled his stories about the famous guest above the garage:

She only left her apartment to buy groceries, Rainier Ale malt liquor, and gallon jugs of Almaden Chablis. Her car was a Ford convertible which was about twelve years old and in poor condition. Since the battery on the car was frequently dead, Lee, the landlord, had to use his jumper cables to help her get it started. Her speech was rarely slurred, but when she was drinking the malt liquor her language would turn profane and vulgar. Lee was afraid she would fall down the stairs drunk someday, so at the end of the six month lease, he asked her to move.

Not long after her move she met and married a businessman named Arthur Morgenstern in October of 1970, but the hasty fourth marriage did little to stop Peggie's alcoholic descent. In 1973, two events unraveled what was left of her life. On February 17th her mother, Betty, died. Then, just two months later, Morgenstern suddenly died.

Peggie plummeted into alcoholic despair. In a final attempt to save herself, that summer she checked into the Camarillo State Hospital. When she got out, however, she went back to drinking. She holed up by herself in a cheap room at the Hollywood Hawaiian Hotel and Apartments, just up the hill from Hollywood Boulevard where her star on the Walk Of Fame lay all but forgotten.

On the night of Friday, August 10th, William McGarry, worried about Peggie, went to check on her. He found her sitting on the couch in her living room, dead. Authorities said she'd been drinking just before her death. An autopsy revealed what anyone could have guessed: cirrhosis. She was 45.

The next day, her passing rated a perfunctory write up in the newspapers. Most mentioned *Lawman* and the grasshopper movie. They all mentioned the drinking and the divorces. They couldn't agree on the spelling of her name.

Hardly any of the obituaries recalled the noirs. Yet it is those films which have lasted; and, as rough a time as she got in them—perhaps *because* she got such a rough time in them—it seems only fitting that the noirs should be the films to safeguard her memory.

After all, to save a film is to save images haunted by the mystery of brief, ineffable human lives. The film doesn't have to be an artistic masterpiece, either. It can

The Blind Alley

be a cheap little B-movie, something like *Finger Man*, where Peggie plays a tragic ex-bad girl attempting to redeem herself. If you know her other films, and if you feel the weight of her real life behind them, then one scene in the film takes on a particular resonance. She has a short monologue in which she explains herself to Frank Lovejoy. As her eyes well with tears, Peggie beautifully delivers this, her noir epitaph:

"All my life, I've had dreams. Not big ones, just my share of the little things—that someone would like me, really like me, maybe even respect me…I know I'm no bargain. I've been around, plenty. I don't feel sorry for myself. Only, sometimes, I get the feeling there isn't any more time, like there isn't going to be any tomorrow. Be nice to me. Please."

THE BROKEN MAN

He is, in many ways, the forgotten man of film noir. Although he is the star of one of the most heralded films in American cinema, he has been overshadowed by his costar and his director. While *Detour* has been proclaimed a cinematic masterpiece, and Ann Savage christened a noir icon, and Edgar G. Ulmer canonized as a Poverty Row genius, poor Tom Neal still can't catch a break. To the extent that he's remembered, he's remembered for the ruin he made of his life. Even his posthumous glory is swamped in failure and disgrace.

It could have been so different. He started out life with the advantage of a good home. His father, Thomas Carroll Neal, originally hailed from a prominent family of bankers in Dover, Arkansas. After spending thirteen successful years in the banking industry in West Virginia, Thomas married Mayme Martin and had two daughters, Mary and Dorothy. The Neals moved to Illinois in 1909 when Thomas took a job as the vice president at Monroe National Bank (soon to become the Central Trust Company of Illinois). The family settled in Evanston, a wealthy suburb of Chicago, and it was there on January 28th, 1914, that Mayme gave birth to a son they named Thomas Carroll Neal Jr.

The young Tom Neal had a privileged life. With a family in the social register—his father sat on hospital boards, presided over Free Mason meetings, and belonged to the Westmoreland Country Club—Neal grew up in a ten bedroom house and attended prep school at Lake Forest Academy. When he graduated, he went to Northwestern University to major in mathematics.

Neal had discovered other interests besides math, however. He did quite a bit of boxing (and though his brief amateur career was largely successful he was never the boxing champ that studio publicity would later claim). He was far more interested in the drama club, which he originally joined to meet women, and in 1933 he left Northwestern after only a year to pursue an acting career in Chicago and then New York. His father was reportedly not happy that his son had dropped out of college to chase dreams of stardom.

He was even less happy with what came next. In New York, the freewheeling younger Neal fell in love with notorious ex-showgirl Inez Norton. Originally from Jacksonville, Florida, Norton had gotten her start as the swimsuit double for Betty Compson in the 1924 film *Miami* and then made her way to New York to be a model. She'd become infamous in 1928 when it was revealed that the will of murdered gangster Arnold Rothstein divided his estate between Norton and his wife. Norton had fought a highly publicized, and semi-successful, legal battle to get her piece of the Rothstein cash (she won a settlement for twenty grand) and then further capitalized on the scandal by publishing syndicated articles about Rothstein and headlining a trashy, short-lived play about his murder called *Room 349*.

What Norton lacked in class, she made up for in excitement, and 21-year-old Tom Neal was smitten by the worldly woman thirteen years his senior. In September 1935, he excitedly announced his imminent marriage to Norton, telling the press that they were going to tie the knot "as soon as father arrives." When his father arrived, however, he threatened to disinherit the young man and told him to call off the wedding. Rebuked, Neal did as he was told. All of this drama played out in the pages of the New York Times and in papers across the country. Tom Neal didn't know it, but he'd just had his initiation into a lifetime of bad publicity.

After the Norton affair, his career seemed to be stuck. He got small parts in plays but nothing really seemed to catch fire. He worked on *Spring Dance* opposite Jose Ferrer, but the show closed after 24 performances. Later that same year, he worked with up-and-coming actors Edmond O'Brien and Cornel Wilde on *Daughters of Atreus*, but that show tanked after only13 performances.

Then his luck turned around. While vacationing down in Florida, the handsome and charming young man was spotted by an MGM talent scout. Seemingly overnight, he was moving to Hollywood to sign a contact with the most important film studio in the world.

He made his screen debut in one of MGM's most important franchises, the Andy Hardy series, with 1938's *Out West With the Hardys*. He followed it up with *The Great Heart*, a one-reeler which cast Neal as Father Damien, a heroic priest. The film was nominated for Best Short Subject Oscar. Neal was starting to get noticed.

The next year he starred in a two-reeler called *They All Come Out*. In the film Neal plays an out-of-work drifter lured by sexy Rita Johnson into driving the getaway car for a bank heist. Directed by a young Jacques Tourneur and written by John C. Higgins, *They All Come Out* proved far better than the studio had expected, so Louis B. Mayer ordered it expanded into a full length feature. Tourneur's first American feature became Neal's first starring role.

Then just as Neal's career seemed to be on the rise, he managed to screw it up. Exactly what led him to argue openly with Louis B. Mayer is still unclear. Some reports say he insulted Joan Crawford. Others say that he was sleeping with a studio executive's wife. What seems certain, though, is that when Mayer proceed to dress down the young actor in public, Neal responded in kind—learning too late that a) it's a bad idea to cuss out the boss, and b) in Hollywood, handsome young men are a buyer's market.

And just like that, things went into reverse. To get fired from MGM in 1940 was to lose the best job Hollywood had to offer a working actor. Neal quickly found employment at other studios, but things were never the same again. He played a handful of roles in A-list feature films (*The Pride of the Yankees* with

Gary Cooper, *Air Force* with John Garfield), but they were tiny parts, often uncredited. No one quite knew what to do with him, and his featured roles at the smaller studios seemed random—posing shirtless as a lovesick boxer in PRC's *The Miracle Kid*, glowering as Bela Lugosi's coldblooded henchman in Monogram's *Bowery At Midnight*, donning "yellowface" to play a fanatical Japanese soldier in Edward Dmytryk's *Behind The Rising Sun* for RKO. The lowest rung on the ladder was the 15-episode serial *Jungle Girl* opposite Frances Gifford at Republic where, as a Z-grade Errol Flynn, Neal spent most of 1941 running around cardboard jungles fighting African tribesman with Brooklyn accents. The bloom was off the Hollywood rose.

Still, it was a living. Moreover, compared to what most working stiffs earned in the war years it was a good living and a relatively easy one. Neal bought a two-acre Bel-Air estate and spent most of his off-time chasing starlets.

And the work itself wasn't all bad. In 1943, he settled down for a while at Columbia Pictures. His first film there was the Horace McCoy-penned war drama *There's Something About A Solider* opposite Evelyn Keyes. It wasn't a masterpiece, but he was working with a gifted co-star and he wasn't swinging from vines or duking it out with natives.

Later that year, he made a Western called *Klondike Kate*. The film had a decent budget and a talented director in William Castle (*When Strangers Marry*), but more importantly it starred the actor Ann Savage. While *Klondike Kate* showed some promise, Neal made a horrible impression on his no-nonsense leading lady.

As she would recount it years later to writer Mike Fitzgerald:

> *I was standing there as they were lighting me for the next scene. [Neal] came into the scene, saying he had something to tell me. I leaned over and he stuck his tongue in my ear. I hit him as hard as I could! I slapped him with my hand open! I was a tough little kid and could take care of myself...He staggered back, and I immediately left the set, so I didn't see his reaction, be it anger or whatever. Later...there was no talk at all—we just did our scenes together and that was it. We stayed apart and never spoke.*

Over time, things settled down between the two actors. And although *Klondike Kate* wasn't the hit that its makers had hoped for, Neal and Savage were noticeably good together, and Columbia rushed to pair them again. Their next project was a cheapie war flick *Two-Man Submarine*. Unfortunately, Neal again ruined the atmosphere on the set by making, in the words of Savage biographers Lisa Morton and Kent Adamson, a "direct and crude" sexual overture to her just before filming commenced. "The most difficult part of dealing with Tom was that I liked him," Savage would remark later. "He could be lots of fun and very charming, but he had a devil inside him, and was also capable of the worst behavior."

Sulking because of Savage's rejection, Neal turned the making of *Two-Man Submarine*—already a less than inspiring piece of work—into something of a chore. According to Savage, Neal would feed her the wrong lines on purpose and try to trip her up:

"Tom gave me a rough time all the way through." To complicate matters, Savage got pneumonia during the water-logged production. It was hard for her to say in later years which was worse: Neal or the pneumonia.

By the time of their third Columbia film together, *The Unwritten Code*, all the heat around the actors had cooled down. It had become obvious that the Neal/Savage duo was never going to strike box office gold (or silver, for that matter), but Columbia paired them together one last time to squeeze out another quickie war drama.

At least relations had finally improved between Neal and Savage. He still acted like an ass and teased her, but he had mellowed. One major reason for the change was his relationship with a 16-year-old aspiring actor named Vicky Lane. Born in Dublin, the black-haired, green-eyed Lane had started in movies when director Cy Enfield cast her as Satan's secretary (because, she said, "I looked like the devil") in the short film 1942 *Inflation*. While her roles had not improved beyond a handful of bit parts in small pictures, Lane and Neal were happy together and tied the knot in Las Vegas on May 27th, 1944, just around the time he started production on *The Unwritten Code*.

While filming went smoothly on the picture, the result was lackluster. Neither Neal nor Savage had much to do in a plot that centered around a Nazi spy played by Roland Varno. While Varno got to play the only scenes with any tension or spark, the ostensible leads just exchanged romantic clichés and waited for the plot to wind down.

Though the film is forgettable, there is an interesting moment about halfway through. At one point, Neal gets unreasonably jealous of Savage's relationship with Varno. It's a brief moment—little more than a flash of his eyes and a whine in his voice—but it's instructive. His knee-jerk petulance in this scene is the only moment in the movie where the actor seems to come alive. When playing heroes, Neal always attempted the same unconvincing impersonation of stoicism, and it's easy to see why he never made it as a leading man. Something insubstantial about him was revealed every time he tried to play bravery and fortitude. But watch him flare up at Savage in self-pitying jealousy and for a brief instant he seems completely real. It's an example of a harsh fact of screen acting: an actor has only limited control over how he is perceived; the camera reveals what it will.

When nothing came from *The Unwritten Code*, Columbia finally booted Neal and Savage. Both turned back to freelancing at smaller studios, and Neal finally signed on to work at Producers Releasing Corporation (PRC), where his first picture was the entertaining musical/mystery mash-up *Club Havana* with Edgar G. Ulmer.

While they were still making *Club Havana*, both Neal and Ulmer agreed to make an odd little crime story called *Detour*. Neal read the script by Martin Goldsmith (adapted from his own 1938 novel) and liked the role of Al Roberts, a hapless nightclub pianist who tries to steal a dead man's identity, only to be discovered by a misanthropic hitchhiker named Vera. He immediately thought Savage would be perfect for the scene-stealing part of the maneating Vera (maybe that slap she gave him was still ringing in his ear), and when he showed Savage the script, she agreed.

The making of the film went off without a hitch. Working quickly and on the cheap, Ulmer fashioned a harrowing nightmare out of Goldsmith's diamond-hard screenplay. What the film lacks in polish—and it lacks all polish—it makes up for in the minimalist perfection of its style and a total commitment to its moral vision. Writing about the film years later the scholar James Naremore would observe, "*Detour* is so far down the economic and cultural scale of things that it virtually escapes commodification, and can be viewed as a kind of subversive or vanguard art." It's not just that Ulmer was able to use avant-garde techniques (such as the surreal close-up of an oversized coffee cup, or the way the picture goes in and out of focus as the befuddled protagonist realizes he's doomed), he was able to adapt the story without compromising its bleak message. *Detour* is this one of the very few noirs that lacks both the tacked on obligatory happy ending and the code-approved punishment of evil at the end. The film's message is unadulterated existential hopelessness. In later years, various scholars and film lovers would come to see *Detour* as the purest expression of the noir ethos.

What has been almost consistently undervalued in the sixty-seven years since the film's release, however, is the performance of its star. While Ulmer and Savage have gotten their well-deserved due, Neal has often been disparaged (Roger Ebert called him "a man who can only pout") or simply overlooked entirely.

Yet it is Neal who appears in every scene of the film. If Savage gives *Detour* its high notes, it's Neal who gives it its steady rhythm. His voiceover is pleading, insistent, angry—the voice of a man depleted of hope but still tortured by its memory. The more one watches the film, the more impressive Neal's performance becomes. Notice the restraint in his scenes with the ill-fated motorist Charles Haskell (Edmund MacDonald)—the watchful way Al Roberts listens as "the big blowhard" goes on a misogynist rant about Vera, and the clipped nature of his responses to Haskell's questions. In contrast, notice how Neal plays his scenes with Savage. Always a physical actor, he's never still, never calmly accepting of her control. As Roberts exhausts the dwindling options for dealing with Vera—friendliness, sarcasm, anger, threats—Neal drives it all with an undertone of desperation. Though he's probably the most emasculated protagonist in all of film noir, he never stops fighting her. It's just that the fighting does no good. By the end, Roberts is just a rat scurrying around in Vera's cage.

Ulmer uses Neal's face to great effect—which no other director ever did—in *Detour*'s two most iconic shots. The first is the illuminated close-up of Roberts at the Nevada Diner, as he sits in total darkness except for a light on his eyes. It's the signature visual of the film and owes everything to the innately mournful quality of Neal's deep set brown eyes. The second is the decisive turn in the story when Haskell dies in the car and Roberts carries his body through the rainstorm and leaves it in a muddy gulch. As the rain whips his face, Roberts runs his hand over his forehead and decides to steal the man's identity. Neal's acting here is suburb—restrained and frantic at the same time, doing all that is needed, and no more, to convey Roberts's realization that he has entered a world where there are only bad options left. This shot of Tom Neal's face is the best shot in the film and one of the key images in all of film noir.

Whether the actor realized it or not, the role of Al Roberts bore an eerie resemblance to Tom Neal himself. It wasn't simply that, like Roberts, he'd begun as a man with great promise only to find himself slumming at the low end of his chosen profession; it was that the real trouble had only just begun.

After *Detour* came and went at the box office, Neal was back at it in increasingly bad material. In trash like 1946's *Blonde Alibi*, he's a total nonentity as the romantic lead, blown off the screen by a supporting cast including Elisha Cook and John Berkes. Lacking the charisma to be a leading man, and lacking the quirkiness to be a character actor, he just seemed small and instantly dismissible.

In 1948, he signed on to do another 15-part serial called *Bruce Gentry*. The work was humiliating—Neal fighting cartoon flying saucers—and his home life wasn't much better. Vicky Lane's career had bottomed out with a role as a killer "Ape Woman" in the 1945 cheesefest *Jungle Captive*, and she'd given up acting to be a torch singer. Worse than playing a monster lady, apparently, was being married to Tom Neal.

After leaving him on the Fourth of July, she filed for divorce, citing his "unreasoning jealousy." During the divorce proceedings in 1949—which were dutifully reported by the *Los Angles Times*—she told the court that "I couldn't go down to the corner to get a package of cigarettes without being accused." Meanwhile, she testified, Neal often left her at home while he went out on the town. "We never went out evenings together," she said, but when she did have friends her own age over to visit, Neal would "storm out" of the house in a huff. The stress of living with him, she said, had caused her to lose fifteen pounds. In August, Lane won her decree on the grounds of mental cruelty.

After the divorce, Neal spent most of his time chasing starlets and cocktail waitresses in between notching screen credits in dreck like *Amazon Quest* and *Radar Secret Service*. Then in 1951, at a pool party at the Sunset Plaza Apartments, he met the woman who would drive the final nail into the coffin of his Hollywood career.

Like Neal, Barbara Payton had started at the top in Hollywood and was working her way down. After making a nice impression opposite Lloyd Bridges in the 1949 Richard Fleischer noir *Trapped*, she'd been tapped to be James Cagney's leading lady in *Kiss Tomorrow Goodbye* (1950). That was higher than Neal had ever climbed, but Payton had also descended faster. Due to a tabloid nightlife that included copious amounts of booze, dope, and shady underworld characters, she had blacklisted herself with the major studios in little more than a year and a half. When they met, she was still seeing actor Franchot Tone (himself on the downward slope of a classy A-list career), but when she saw Neal at the pool, "It was," she said "love at first sight." He felt the same, later telling reporters "Four minutes after we met, we decided to get married."

Though it must have seemed like fate was on their side, fate had its own ideas. The Neal/Payton romance would irreparably shatter both of their careers and plunge their lives into chaos. Each one brought out the most self-destructive tendencies in the other. Payton was needy and sexually impulsive—deciding to marry Neal one day, going back to Tone the next, only to return to Neal soon after—which only made the emotionally insecure Neal more volatile and jealous.

They set the wedding date for September 14th, 1951, but on the 13th Payton made some vague excuses about attending to business in town and then disappeared. Later in the day, with no word yet from Payton, the phone rang and Neal overheard the maid taking orders. Payton had asked to have her mink coat and an overnight bag sent to the Beverly Hills Hotel. "I knew," he later grumbled to a reporter, "that Tone was back in her life again."

While Neal holed up at her apartment and got drunk, Payton and Tone spent the afternoon at the hotel and then went out for a night of carousing. Around the same time, Neal, in the words of Payton's biographer John O'Dowd, "called some friends[…]and threw a raucous pity party."

About 1:30 in the morning Payton and Tone showed up at the apartment to find it full of drunken revelers. Tone asked the belligerent Neal to step outside. Payton followed. As Neal would later tell reporters, "At this point Barbara kissed Tone[…]and the old adrenaline in me started to boil. I saw red. He swung on me, but

I crossed my right and his punch never reached me. I knocked him ten feet and was on him like a cat, and I gave him the old left and right, and left and right…"

One witness told reporters, "It sounded like a prizefighter in a gym beating the bags."

Neal blamed Tone for throwing the first punch (which both Tone and Payton denied), but in an unintentional slip of honesty, he blamed the ferocity of his attack on a deeper need to impress Payton. Claiming that she kept egging him on, he said, "She digs that blood and guts stuff."

Neal had nearly killed Tone. With a cerebral concussion, and a broken nose and cheek bone, Tone was rushed to California Lutheran Hospital where he spent the next day in critical condition. Neal, asked for a comment, muttered, "I'm sorry to hear the guy's in the hospital. I hope he's not hurt bad."

Tone eventually made a full recovery, and after some tough talk about suing Neal, backed down. He'd lost the fight, but he'd won Payton and soon they were married.

Within a matter of weeks, however, Payton and Neal had resumed their affair. Tone, finally having had enough, sued her for divorce on the grounds of adultery. If she wanted Tom Neal, Tone had decided, she could have him.

Hollywood agreed. For the next few years, Payton and Neal scraped together what work they could, but no one wanted to hire them. (One of the last jobs Neal could find was a role on a 1952 episode of the cop show *Gang Busters* called "The Red Dress Case" which paired him for a final time with Ann Savage.)

The Blind Alley

Neal came up with the idea that they should cash in on their notoriety by starring in a touring stage production of *The Postman Always Rings Twice*. By this point, Payton, depressed over the state of her career (and life), was drinking more heavily than ever. During a performance at the Drury Lane Summer Theater in Chicago she was so smashed she passed out on stage. So much for the theater.

When Neal and Payton finally parted ways not long after, he hustled a couple of television gigs, but nothing remained of his career. He gave his final performance on an episode of Darren McGavin's *Mike Hammer*. Then he called it quits.

In his book *Kiss Tomorrow Goodbye: The Barbara Payton Story*, John O'Dowd reveals that Neal moved to Palm Springs in 1955 and found work as a bouncer at a cocktail lounge called The Doll House. According to O'Dowd, Neal left after six months to become part owner in an Italian restaurant. Not long after, the restaurant went bust.

In 1956, Neal married his second wife, a pretty Pan-Am stewardess named Patty Fenton, and began a new phase of his life. He started a landscaping business—a skill he claimed to have learned from the Japanese gardeners who'd worked on his long lost Bel-Air estate. He proved to be an excellent landscape architect, and his business flourished (including work on an apartment complex financed by Poverty Row producer Robert L. Lippert, for whom Neal had worked as an actor just a few short years before). In 1957, with things going strong, Patty gave birth to their son Patrick Thomas Neal.

Then fate stuck out its foot once more. In 1958, Patty died of cancer. Distraught, and not knowing what to do with an infant, Neal sent his son to live with his sister Mary in Chicago. O'Dowd reports that over the next few years as Tom traveled back and forth between California and Illinois to see his son the business began to suffer.

In 1961, at the age of 47, he married a 25-year-old receptionist at the Palm Springs Racquet Club named Gail Evatt (the ex-wife of boxer Buddy Evatt, she'd been born Gail Kloke). In an echo from his marriage to the much younger Vicky Lane, he and Gail were married in Las Vegas. It would prove to be a catastrophic union. Neal, always given to violent insecurity and distrust, made life difficult for the vivacious young woman 21 years his junior. He was particularly jealous that she'd once dated Art Modell, the millionaire owner of the Cleveland Browns. As he struggled to keep his business afloat, Neal tortured himself with the possibility that she would leave him for a younger or more successful man.

Amid accusations that Neal had become violent with her, the couple separated in January of 1965. With Neal spending much of his time in Chicago to see his son, Gail quietly filed for divorce in March. Then, less than a month later, on April 1st, Neal walked into a Palm Springs restaurant owned by friends, sat down and told them that he'd shot Gail in the head that afternoon as she was taking a nap.

The next morning Neal surrendered himself to the Palm Springs police at his home. As writer Arthur Lyons would record the events:

Heading to the location, Patrolman Joe Jones was flagged down by [Neal's] attorney, James Kellam, who led him into the house. The body of Gail Neal was lying on the couch, partially covered by a bedspread. She had been shot behind the right ear with a .45 automatic. The spent cartridge was found four feet away.

In the trial that followed, prosecutors charged Neal with first degree murder and sought the death penalty. Near the end of the trial, Neal took the stand. His story of shooting Gail as she slept had changed. In his telling now, the two were discussing the state of their marriage in a "soul bearing talk."

When he had accused her of sleeping with his friends, "I felt her body tense and the next thing I knew, I heard her yell at me, 'I'll kill you, you bastard! I looked up from where I was—and what I faced was the .45 automatic in her hand."

Claiming to pray as he wrestled with her, Neal told the court, "I shoved the gun with both hands from the position I was in and the gun went off."

As a rebuttal witness, the prosecution called the pathologist who'd performed the autopsy on Gail Neal who would testify that the direction of the wound made Neal's story highly dubious. (It didn't help that Neal could not explain why the gun had disappeared before the police arrived.) Also called to the stand were three of Gail's coworkers from the tennis club who testified that she had planned to leave town because she feared for her life.

The jury deliberated for ten hours and found Tom Neal guilty of involuntary man-slaughter. In some respects, of course, it was good luck. Despite the findings of the jury, it seemed (and still seems) to most observers that Neal had gotten away with murder.

No one was sure how much time he would have to serve on the manslaughter rap. As he waited to find out, Barbara Payton made her last appearance in Neal's life when she showed up to his sentencing. Though he was a convicted killer very likely on this way to jail, in some respects she was in worse shape. Alcoholic and strung out on drugs, she was now a bloated skid row prostitute with missing teeth and nowhere to go but down. In less than two years, sanitation workers would find her unconscious beside a dumpster in a grocery store parking lot. A few weeks later, she would be dead from liver failure. That day at the Indio Superior Court, Neal and Payton exchanged waves. Then the judge walked in and sentenced him to fifteen years in state prison.

He went away protesting his innocence, but few people believed him.

He served six years, starting out at Soledad State Prison before being transferred to the minimum-security facility at Chino. He spent his time reading, laboring on the work furlough program, and writing to his son. He was released on parole on December 7th, 1971. The press was there to report on the white-haired 58-year-old ex-con. Neal simply told reporters that prison was a "bad scene."

Prison had aged him. Though pushing sixty, he looked at least a decade older. Reunited with his son Patrick, now 15 years old, he moved into a cheap apartment in Studio City and tried to rebuild his life. He'd become a devout Christian Scientist and made a daily study of the bible and various books on metaphysics. "The Gideons gave me a bible to read in jail," he told reporters "and when they did they gave me enlightenment and a means of atonement."

Then, just a few months after being released from prison, on August 7th 1972, Neal died unexpectedly of congestive heart failure. His son found him in bed. "I picked up his hand to wake him," Patrick Neal told the writer David Houston. "It was cold. I let go of it, and it dropped like lead."

Tom Neal's final bit of bad luck was that he did not live to see *Detour* become recognized as a classic. Without him knowing it, its rediscovery had already begun in his lifetime, and in the years after his death, with the flourishing of noir studies and the increasingly easy dissemination of the film itself, its reputation only grew. Of course, in his own horrible way, Neal had helped its myth take shape by destroying his life like a noir antihero. Over time, Tom Neal and Al Roberts simply merged—actor and role folding into one dusty, broken man wandering the desert at night, cursing his fate and wondering just how much of it was his own damn fault.

WHAT SHOWS AND WHAT DOESN'T
FRANK LOVEJOY
AND THE CRISIS OF MASCULINITY

He had a face that always seemed braced for bad news. You could see it in that grim, lipless mouth and in dark eyes so deep-set he seemed to be glaring even when he was simply listening to someone else talk. Among film noir's leading men and assorted supporting characters—a pretty reticent bunch, generally speaking— perhaps only Dana Andrews could match his quiet, worried reserve. Frank Lovejoy just seemed like a man expecting the worst.

He usually got the worst, too. He only worked in feature films for about ten years, but a sizable portion of that body of work was hardcore noir. He watched Bogart go over the edge in Ray's *In A Lonely Place*. He went to hell and back in Lupino's *The Hitch-Hiker*. And in his best film, *The Sound Of Fury*, he went to hell to stay, and in doing so created one of noir's great doomed protagonists.

It was an impressive film career, all the more striking for its brevity. Born Frank Lovejoy Jr. in the Bronx in 1912, he didn't get started in movies until the last leg of his career (in what would turn out to be the final years of his life). Although his father worked as a salesman for Pathe Films, as a young man growing up in Woodbridge, New Jersey, Lovejoy originally aimed to go Wall Street, working there as a runner until the crash of 1929. That experience soured him on the idea of a career in finance and gave him a front row seat to the swift ruin that could befall ostentatious hotshots. It was a lesson he would not forget, remarking later that he learned "how people react, what shows on their faces and what doesn't."

He put these early observations of human behavior to work when he turned to the theater after college. Quickly finding work in stock theater companies like the Virginia Barter Theater, he learned his craft and made his Broadway debut in 1934's *Judgment Day*. The play wasn't a hit, but he knew he'd found a career.

As a journeyman actor he traveled the country, and while on tour with the ill-fated play *The Pursuit of Happiness* he discovered a second medium for his talent. When the production unexpectedly folded in Cincinnati, Lovejoy nabbed a job as an actor and announcer at the radio station WLW. His craggy baritone—which would play a large part of his success in film—was enough of a hit with audiences that Lovejoy could make his way back to New York, this time in radio.

The work came fast and constant. Given the sometimes spotty record keeping of radio at the time, and considering that he did a lot of uncredited work, an exact estimate of Lovejoy's radio appearances is hard to come by. Lovejoy himself put the number somewhere around the 4,000 broadcast mark. He did a little bit of everything, but his rugged voice lent itself to mystery and adventure programs. He worked on *The Adventures of Jungle Jim* and *Columbia Workshop*, *Superman* and *Gang Busters*. He played the title character in the superhero show *The Blue Beetle*. And after World War II started, he worked on the Peabody-winning series *The Man Behind The Gun*.

His favorite of his radio jobs was probably *This Day Is Ours* because it was there he met a pretty young actor named Joan Banks. By this time Lovejoy had married torch singer Frances Williams (who was eleven years his senior), but his tenure as her fourth husband was short-lived. Three months after his seven-month marriage to Williams was legally dissolved, he married Banks.

For the next decade, they acted on stage and on the radio and had children—a daughter Judy, followed by a son named Steve. It was a nice life, one that seemed to content Lovejoy. Later, by way of explaining his down to earth reputation, he would tell an interviewer, "I didn't start making motion pictures until 1948, and by then I'd been married quite a while and had two youngsters." He wasn't really yearning to go to Hollywood.

But Hollywood came to him in the form of producer Stanley Kramer. When Kramer saw Lovejoy appearing alongside Kirk Douglas and Mercedes McCambridge in the play *Woman Bites Dog*, he scooped up the actor and took him off to California. Lovejoy never gave up radio or theater, but he would be defined now by another medium.

His first film was supposed to be an adaptation of Taylor Caldwell's *This Side of Innocence*, but when the project was shelved at the last minute he was hustled into the western *Black Bart* (1948) opposite Dan Duryea and Yvonne De Carlo. The project didn't suit him, and though he would go on to make several more oaters, he was honest about his lack of enthusiasm for the genre. "Westerns aren't for me," he admitted. "I'm a city fella."

His next project was the war film *Home Of The Brave* (1949) opposite James Edwards, the first film (in the typically topical Kramer fashion) to deal with the 1948 desegregation of the armed forces. He made the most of his role as a crusty war vet, and he got to deliver the film's best lines when he tells a buddy:

I'll never forget the first letter I got from my wife. It started: 'Darling, I'll never again use the word love without thinking only of you.' And I remember the last one I got from her. It started: 'Dear T.J., this is the hardest letter I've ever had to write.'

Though only 37 years old, he already had the gravitas of an older man. He played a sergeant in the film. He would go on to play many military men, and while he played his share of captains and colonels, he was always best cast as a sergeant. He just looked liked a sergeant.

Or a cop. His next film was the masterpiece *In A Lonely Place* (1950), with Lovejoy playing Det. Sgt. Brub Nicolai, a cop investigating his old army buddy Dixon Steele (Humphrey Bogart) for murder. Though Steele's given an alibi by his sexy neighbor

Laurel Gray (Gloria Grahame), Brub isn't convinced that his pal hasn't turned into a psycho. While Bogart and Grahame play out a romance tortured by mutual suspicion, it falls on Lovejoy and sweet Jeff Donnell, playing his wife Sylvia, to give the picture some footing in the real world. After Steele creeps out Sylvia by lustily recounting a possible murder scenario, she tells her husband. "He's sick, Brub." When Brub defends his friend as exciting and gifted, Sylvia replies, "Well, I like the way you are: attractive and average."

It was Lovejoy's gift to be wholly believable as an average Joe. In a characteristically modest way he explained that, despite his new home in Hollywood, he was a normal family man. "I'm a middle class square," he told one interviewer. "I like to coach the Little League games. I like baseball and television."

This unpretentiousness was genuine—and it had the added benefit of making for good publicity—but it also undersold his skill as an actor. Circling Bogart in *In A Lonely Place* he never makes a false move. With very few lines of dialog he is able to convey Brub's affection for Steele while also tipping the audience to his suspicions. Always in the scene and of the moment, he's never caught acting. He simply *is*—quiet but watchful, troubled by thoughts which he gives subtle physical expression but no voice.

Although the film was a great artistic success for all involved, the production became strained as the troubled marriage between director Nicholas Ray and leading lady Gloria Grahame began its messy, and inevitable, descent. Lovejoy tried to keep out of the way of the sex-and-jealousy dynamics between the director and star, but Ray and Grahame together comprised a storm front that occasionally took its toll on innocent bystanders. According to Ray biographer Patrick McGilligan "Ray pointedly cut back on close-ups of Frank Lovejoy…after deciding that Lovejoy had been supporting Grahame with her alibis." Lovejoy and Ray would reportedly get into a drunken argument at a party some years later, though nothing much ever came of it.

His next project wasn't hampered by jealousy and backstabbing, but it was fraught in a different way. Director Cy Endfield was adapting novelist/screenwriter Jo Pagano's book *The Condemned* which was based on the 1933 lynchings of Thomas Harold Thurmond and John M. Holmes, two California men who had abducted and murdered a socialite named Brooke Hart.

In the film, re-titled *The Sound Of Fury*, Lovejoy plays Howard Tyler, an ex-serviceman who has recently relocated to California with his wife and young son. The economy is supposed to be humming in the sun-kissed promised land, but Tyler can't land a job ("Can I help it if a million other guys had the same idea?") and his wife's getting panicked. In frustration, he takes off one afternoon, stops by a bowling alley for a beer, and meets a guy named Jerry Slocum (Lloyd Bridges). Slocum's a fast-talking hoodlum with a business proposition for a man who's steady behind the steering wheel. At first, Tyler has some reservations about being a getaway driver, but Jerry spells out his options: stop being a sucker and go home with some cash in your wallet, or take your dignity and go home broke. Tyler thinks about it and calls his wife to tell her he's going to be late. By midnight, he's waiting outside a gas station while Jerry's inside pistol-whipping the attendant. It isn't long, though, before Jerry decides they need to upgrade their operation to kidnapping and murder.

Though its reputation has grown over the years, *The Sound Of Fury* remains one of the great unheralded films of the 1950s—an essential work of subversive American cinema and one of the truly indispensible noirs. Its portrait of post-war America is uncompromising and bleak. Pagano envisioned the film as an indictment of capitalist indifference, journalistic cravenness, and lynch mob justice. If at times his script pushes too hard (he and Endfield butted heads over sections of the script Endfield felt were too didactic), the power of its narrative comes from the way Endfield weaves these themes in with Howard's choice and its terrible consequences. Like all great noir, the power of the ideas here derive from their expression in human terms.

This is why the film owes so much to the performance of Lovejoy. He's everyman turned noir anti-hero. He's watchful and worried, masculine but weak—his normal reserve indicating not an absence of emotion, but rather anxieties held in check. As his world starts to crumble—literally, since Endfield positions the murder on a sliding mound of gravel—all of Lovejoy's usual defenses fall away, and he's left to tear himself apart. It's a brave and haunting performance, the best of his film career.

Alas, audiences didn't care for the film's acidic social commentary, and theater managers around the country caught hell for running such an "anti-American" picture at the outset of hostilities in Korea. Endfield, targeted by the House Committee on Un-American Activities, was blacklisted and fled the country. In an attempt to sidestep the controversy, producer Robert Stillman re-titled the film *Try And Get Me!* and re-packaged it as a straight genre piece. It quickly sank into obscurity.

History did not record Lovejoy's thoughts on the backlash against the film, but professionally he moved on quickly. His next film, after signing a contract with Warner Brothers might, in fact, be seen as a form of damage control.

I Was A Communist For The FBI (1951) was pure redbaiter material. Based on a "true story" it tells the tale of FBI agent Matt Cvetic (Lovejoy) who goes undercover as a Communist party organizer in order to work his way into the organization. Since no one knows that Cvetic is a double agent, he is rejected by his friends, neighbors, even his family. Cvetic is deep undercover for years before he's able to bust open a nefarious Commie plot to make the House Committee on Un-American Activities look like a bunch of opportunistic blowhards. At the end, the unassailably heroic House Committee swoops in to save the day, and there are tearful reunions with relieved family members.

The film is so stupid that it's funny for long stretches—a kind of redbaiting *Reefer Madness*—but it is also *the* prime example of what the anti-Communist crusaders were looking for from Hollywood (it received an Oscar nomination for, of all things, Best Documentary). In FBI files newly unearthed for his 2000 book *I Was a Communist for the FBI: The Unhappy*

Life and Times of Matt Cvetic, Professor Daniel J. Leab revealed that the real Cvetic was never really an "agent" for the FBI so much as a paid informant. According to Cvetic's own reports at the time, he never faced any danger or engaged in any of Lovejoy's hardboiled heroics in the film. His spilt with his family occurred because of his drinking, and it was only after he was dumped by the FBI for being an unreliable drunk (he had a habit of getting soused in public and bragging about his FBI connections) that he "surfaced" as a counterspy. As with *The Sound Of Fury*, history has not recorded Lovejoy's feelings about the film, but, politics aside, the script is shoddy and the actor goes at his poorly written role with the enthusiasm of a man doing court-mandated community service.

With the *Sound Of Fury* stink off him (removed by the historically longer lasting stink of *I Was A Communist For The FBI*), Lovejoy found himself, briefly, in A-lister territory, co-starring with Joan Crawford in *Goodbye, My Fancy*. The famously haughty Crawford reportedly found him crude, though, and sparks didn't exactly fly between them onscreen. Offscreen, Crawford was distracted by her troubled relationship with the film's director, Vincent Sherman. According to Crawford biographers Lawrence J. Quirk and William Schoell, Sherman was jealous of Lovejoy and—though there seems to have been no basis whatsoever for the jealousy—tried to have him removed from the film. At that point in shooting it was too late for a change in leading men, so Lovejoy stayed on the picture and managed to hold his own onscreen without making a particularly strong impression.

By this point, Lovejoy was an established commodity in Hollywood, a dependable supporting player and a plausible B-movie leading man. He backed up Doris Day in Michael Curtiz's *I'll See You In My Dreams* and fought the Korean War in Joseph H. Lewis's *Retreat, Hell!* In 1953, he took on Vincent Price in Andre De Toth's 3-D horror classic *House Of Wax*, and he was back riding the range in *The Charge At Feather River*.

His wife Joan had semi-retired to raise the kids (though she did occasional film work, such as 1951's *Cry Danger* with Dick Powell, as well as some radio gigs), and together they built a relatively normal middle-class life. "I have a wife and two children and two mothers to support," Lovejoy explained. "We have a nice, comfortable house and we keep two cars, but one is a 1948 model. This is a good living, and we've no complaints, but it isn't rich living. It's no Hollywood extravaganza."

1953 saw him team up with director Ida Lupino for one of his best films, *The Hitch-Hiker*. Lovejoy plays a draftsman named Gil Bowen who is on a fishing trip to Mexico with his buddy Roy Collins (Edmond O'Brien). They contemplate a stopover at a bar they used to frequent down on the border, and there is the implication that the old watering hole holds some rowdy memories. Collins would like to relive some of those memories, but Bowen, already missing his wife and kids, nixes the idea. They keep driving, and then outside of town they pick up Emmett Myers (William Talman) on the side of the road. He pulls a gun and tells them to drive south.

The Blind Alley

The Hitch-Hiker is a harrowing addition to the hitchhiker from hell sub-genre. While it's not ultimately as bleak as *Detour*, it is in many ways the harder, tougher picture—especially in its examination of three competing versions of masculinity under pressure. As these three men (interestingly, there's not a woman in sight) careen through the desert, seemingly headed nowhere, personalities burst to the surface. The hitchhiker is a raging nihilist, brutalized by life. "My folks were tough," he says at one point. "When I was born, they took one look at this puss of mine and told me to get lost." As a result Myers (played brilliantly by Talman) is a pure sadist whose only real interest seems to be the humiliation and emasculation of his captives. Collins soon starts to unravel (and nobody unraveled better than Edmond O'Brien), driven to desperation by the man with the gun in the backseat.

While Myers tortures Collins, Bowen manages (barely) to hold himself together. What's fascinating here, however, is that there is no heroism in either his survival or in his attempts to save his friend. Lovejoy never reaches for macho effect, never nods toward any stolid masculine exceptionalism. Bowen is just an ordinary man trying to endure the unendurable. Of the three performances, Lovejoy's is the least showy, yet it is his grounded presence that, in a manner of speaking, keeps the car from flying off the road. As Talman goads O'Brien closer to madness, Lovejoy keeps us tethered, however tenuously, to sanity—and it is that fraying connection which gives the film its essential tension.

After the ordeal in the desert, he was back to work: playing a soft-hearted crime boss in *The System*, fighting

World War II in *Beachhead* and the Korean War in *Men Of The Fighting Lady*, riding the range again in *The Americano* opposite Glenn Ford.

He also started in television—another new medium for him. For *Lux Video Theater* he played Walter Neff in a production of "Double Indemnity" opposite Laraine Day and Ray Collins (a performance that earned him an Emmy nomination), and Uncle Charlie in "Shadow Of A Doubt."

His most important television production, or at least the one with the longest lasting impact on his career, was an episode of *Four Star Playhouse* called "Meet McGraw" in which he played a private eye named McGraw hired to protect a sexy client (Audrey Totter, in full-on blonde vixen mode) from her violent husband. The show was a success and prompted the production company Sharpe-Lewis to bring the character back in an episode of *Stage 7* called "The Long Count." When that proved to be a success as well, Sharpe-Lewis started making plans to give Lovejoy his own series.

In the interim, Lovejoy made his first foray into series television when he took over Ralph Bellamy's starring role in *Man Against Crime*. The show was already dying, however, so Lovejoy only filmed nine episodes as private eye Mike Barnett before the production shut down. He took it in stride, calling his time on the show "Crime Against Man."

His noir work continued in film. Playing a corrupt war vet with a dark secret, he's the best thing about the otherwise tepid *The Crooked Web* (1955). That same year he made the weirdest film of his career, the redbaiting absurdity *Shack Out On 101*, a movie so atrocious it achieves a kind of low-rent absurdist grandeur. Its bargain budget production values, sloppy direction, gonzo acting, and horrible script all rise to the level of camp goodness. Lovejoy is nearly comatose as a (*cough, cough*) nuclear physicist battling Communist spy/short order cook Lee Marvin. Though this film is, in its goofball way, infinitely more fun than his previous anti-Commie work, Lovejoy looks about as thrilled to be here as he was in *I Was A Communist For The FBI*.

He was far more engaged in his best film of 1955, and his last important noir, Harold Schuster's *Finger Man*. In the film, Lovejoy plays a hood named Casey Martin. After he's pinched by the feds for sticking up a truck, Martin is offered the opportunity to stay out of jail by going undercover to nab a big time gangster named Dutch Becker (played icily by Forrest Tucker). Martin doesn't exactly jump at the chance. He doesn't want to be a snitch, but he doesn't want to spend his life in jail, either.

Ultimately, he decides to turn "finger man" and enlists the help of an ex-prostitute named Gladys (Peggie Castle). She knows Becker, vouches for Martin, and soon he's working his way into the gangster's good graces. Becker likes Martin right off, but his right hand man is a psycho named Lou Terpe, played by the king of the nutjobs, Timothy Carey. Terpe knows Martin from a stint in prison, and the two men butt heads. Meanwhile, Martin and Gladys begin a relationship—though interestingly he never tells her what he's up to for the feds. Maybe he should have told her what was going on because as soon Becker decides it's Gladys who represents a threat to his operation he sends Terpe around to straighten her out.

Finger Man is noir to its bones. Despite some obligatory nods to civic duty, Casey Martin is an interestingly unsympathetic protagonist, a man operating first and foremost out of self-preservation and fear. As he sums up his dilemma late in the film, "I had a choice: life in prison or…a bullet in the head. I had no future either way."

The best sections of the film involve his relationship with Gladys. She's played beautifully by Peggie Castle, who transforms the rather conventional role into a figure of tragedy, a lonely woman with her own dwindling set of options. Her duet with Lovejoy gives the film a undertow of real sadness, and these scenes would be the best Lovejoy ever played with a female co-star.

By the late fifties, it had become apparent that Lovejoy was never going to break out as a leading man in feature films. He kept making movies, but he turned increasingly to television for his bread and butter.

In 1957, he starred in *Meet McGraw* with the hopes that he could build a long running series around the character. He described McGraw as less hardboiled than Mike Hammer or Mike Barnett. "When someone pulls a gun on me," he said, "I dive for cover like any red-blooded American." He didn't even accept the term "private eye" for the character, preferring the term "trouble-shooter."

The production initially logged good ratings but never really found its audience. Shifted around on the schedule, mostly dismissed by critics, it died after 42 episodes. Lovejoy confessed to being disappointed and to being skeptical about the ratings. "I was a hero on Monday and a bum on Wednesday," he said.

All in all, he took the failure in stride—bowing, however sarcastically, to the superior knowledge of the executives and sponsors who controlled television. "I was a little emotional about it," he said, "but what can you do? You can quote Shakespeare but what's the point when this fellow points out that his company has been selling soap for 124 years and knows something about selling? When I'm dead 124 years, Proctor and Gamble will still be selling soap."

He seemed to keep his entire career in a kind of middle-class perspective. "I live in Beverly Hills. Celebrities aren't a dime a dozen there. They're a dime a gross." Explaining the cars sent around by the studios to pick him up for work, he told his children, "They'd send a car for a trained monkey if he sold enough tickets."

Given this attitude, it wasn't surprising that his co-stars mostly found him unpretentious and easy to work with. Phyllis Kirk, who worked with him on *House Of Wax*, called him "an adorable man, a very kind, warm human being and a generous actor." And Eddie Garrett, who became friends with Lovejoys in the fifties, called him "a kind, sensitive human being. Frank was just very caring and compassionate."

Some people admitted, though, that Lovejoy could be a little caustic at times. Mary Murphy, his co-star in *Beachhead*, confessed, "I hated Frank at the beginning of the production... When I first met him, he seemed cold and sarcastic." And Paul Picerni, who worked with him eight times, didn't like Lovejoy for many years. Recalling their first picture together (1950's *Breakthrough*) Picerni remembered, "My first scene on the picture was with Frank…We went through the rehearsal, and I had several big speeches in the scene. And Frank looked at me with a straight face and he said, 'Is *that* the way you're going to play it?' To this day I don't know if he was serious or if he was kidding."

Both Murphy and Picerni came to see a different side to Lovejoy, though. Murphy deeply admired his talent, recalling "he had one of these hideous abilities to read nine pages of a script and just know it! A photographic mind! Frank was simply phenomenal." Furthermore, when Murphy was harassed by a camera operator on *House Of Wax*, Lovejoy consoled her and helped her get the man tossed off the film. After that, she became friends with both of the Lovejoys. "By the end of filming" she said, "I adored him."

Picerni saw an even more human side while co-starring in an episode of *Meet McGraw* in the late fifties. One day on the set, Lovejoy

made a face and he sat down and he said, 'Paul…do me a favor, will you? In my dressing room…on top of my dresser…you'll find a little bottle of nitroglycerin pills. Go get 'em for me, will ya?' I looked at his face, and I could see he was in pain, so I rushed and got the nitroglycerin. He took a couple and said 'Thanks a lot…thanks…' And at that moment I suddenly liked Frank.

The Blind Alley

* * *

His health was a cause for concern as the fifties came to an end. He broke his leg jumping out a window for a stunt on *Meet McGraw* and on the 1958 western *Cole Younger, Gunfighter* (which would turn out to be his final film) his co-star Jan Merlin remembered that while he was "a joy to work with…and very much as you saw him," he also "seemed weary…feeling his age."

The sad irony is, of course, that he wasn't really that old. While there had always been some talk around town about his drinking (Mimi Gibson was a child actor on *I'll See You In My Dreams* and she later remembered Lovejoy as a heavy drinker with bloodshot eyes), he was part of a generation that tended to die young from too much booze, too many cigarettes, and too much cholesterol.

His last big success (in some ways, the biggest success of his career) was on stage originating the role of the closeted and unscrupulous senator Joe Cantwell in Gore Vidal's Broadway triumph *The Best Man*. Produced by the Playwrights' Company at the Morosco Theatre, the play ran from March 1960 to July 1961, with Lovejoy playing Cantwell over 500 times. The New York Times drama critic Brooks Atkinson raved, "Lovejoy gives an extraordinary portrait of a bigot and charlatan who believes his own propaganda. There is something horribly plausible in his ethical obtuseness."

Lovejoy was starring in and directing a production of *The Best Man* at the Playhouse on the Mall in Paramus, NJ when he died unexpectedly at the Warwick Hotel in New York on October 2, 1962. After watching the Dodgers and Giants play on television that night, he retired early, telling Joan he felt fatigued. When she tried to wake him at 6:15 the next morning, she found that he'd died in his sleep. The attending doctor diagnosed a coronary thrombosis.

His premature passing was met with condolences and regret, as well as nods to his work in film, television, radio, and theater—with special emphasis put on his great success with *The Best Man*. What was missing, however, and what is still yet to be fully appreciated was the way his work in film noir seemed to perfectly capture the post-war predicament of American masculinity.

Lovejoy's film career was confined to a ten year stretch from 1948 to 1958, making his work an ideal study in the male ego *in extremis* during the 1950s. Through a film career bookended by two routine westerns—a genre that more often than not presented an uncomplicated vision of male strength—and punctuated throughout the decade with triumphal war films (he was pretty much the B-movie face of the Korean War), he earned his stripes as a macho standard bearer. Which only makes it more interesting that his most compelling work, the work that has lasted and continues to fascinate, always subverted the masculine masquerade.

His three finest films—*In A Lonely Place, The Sound Of Fury, The Hitch-Hiker*—are all about the male ego in various states of disintegration. In *In A Lonely Place* he is the worried observer of his friend's psychic unraveling, while in *The Sound Of Fury* and *The Hitch-*

The Blind Alley

Hiker he is in the arena himself. In the latter, he barely escapes, a shattered victim of the random violence of a disturbed man. In the former, he is pulled under—consumed in the vortex created by economic hardship, familial responsibility, and societal indifference. Which is not to say that he was ever purely a victim. Part of what made Lovejoy great was his amazing interiority, the sense that behind that face of the fifties-era husband and father, behind the stolid face of the American man, there trembled a deep anxiety.

THE CROOKED ROAD OF RICHARD QUINE

Be warned: this story is a heartbreaker. Richard Quine might have spent most of his career making people laugh—first in front of the camera as a goofy sidekick to Mickey Rooney, and then later as a successful writer/director specializing in comedy—but behind that sunny veneer lay a man with a terrible knowledge of suffering and loss. That knowledge, in fact, proved in the end to be unbearable.

The tragedy at the heart of Richard Quine's story begins with a New Year's day hunting trip with friends in 1945. Barely 24-years old, Quine had already been in the film business since 1933. Having just returned from duty in the coast guard during World War II, he was newly married to the talented young actor Susan Peters and was looking forward to restarting his career. The young couple had only been married a little over a year, but they'd already endured the heartache of a miscarriage in 1944. As the new year began, they struck out to the Cuyamaca Mountains near San Diego to hunt duck with Quine's brother and sister-in-law.

After setting up camp and deciding to go for a walk, the group stashed their weapons under some brush for safekeeping from any passersby. It was the last walk Peters ever took. Upon returning to their camp, she pulled her .22 rifle muzzle-first from the brush and caught the trigger on a twig. The rifle fired and shot her in the stomach.

The bullet lodged in her spine. After she was rushed to a nearby hospital for an emergency operation, the doctor told her she had no chance to walk again. Quine, distraught, told reporters, "All my life I'll hear that shot."

In the press, Quine and Peters remained perky and upbeat. A headline in the *LA Times* declared, "Though doctors say that she may never walk again, Susan Peters is not letting the news change her future plans, her hopes or her smile" and news reports detailed Quine's devotion to his new wife, noting how he carried her places her new wheelchair couldn't go. When the couple adopted a 10-month old boy the following year, Peters told reporters, "We want to give him lots of brothers and sisters—children of our own, as soon as I am well. We want a big family." In 1948, Peters returned to the screen in *The Sign of the Ram* as a disabled young woman. Doing press for the film, she gave a cheerful interview to Gene Hansaker's "Hollywood Sight and Sounds" column, telling Hansaker, "The doctor told me that about six months after the accident…I'd probably have a terrific mental upset. Well, I'm still waiting for it." That same month, in an article she wrote trumpeting her inspirational story of perseverance, Peters said of her recovery, "[V]ery slowly it began to dawn on me that my husband and I still had a long life before us and that unless I wanted to make other people miserable I'd have to stop being miserable myself."

In private, things weren't so cheerful. Just two moths later publishing her inspirational article, Peters filed for divorce. That month, Quine told Hedda Hopper that Peters would be "happier alone." Peters herself declared as much in interviews, but after their divorce she grew increasingly reclusive. When Quine remarried, to Barbara Bushman in 1951, Peters took a turn for the worse. By 1952, she had grown gaunt and sickly, and it appeared to people who saw her, including her worried doctors, that Peters was starving herself to death. In October, she died of kidney failure. One of her doctors told the press, "She lost the will to live."

Quine didn't give interviews to the press about what had become of his ex-wife. After their troubled marriage, he seemed put it all behind him. He and Bushman had two children, and Quine began to enjoy great critical and commercial success as a director, mostly in the field of comedy where he worked successfully with writer Blake Edwards and star Jack Lemmon.

In the year following Peters's death, though, Quine made two small films that deserve more attention. Noir to the bone, they are films of striking power and sadness. Placed in the context of this period of his life, moreover, they seem to tell us something about Richard Quine, hinting at the tragedy still to come.

Pushover stars Fred MacMurray as an undercover cop named Paul Sheridan. Assigned to seduce a bank robber's girlfriend named Lona McLane (Kim Novak),

Sheridan instead finds himself falling in love. Lona, however, is no fool and has quickly pieced together the situation with the cops. She makes Sheridan a proposition: why don't they kill her bank robber boyfriend when he shows up at her apartment and keep the two hundred grand from bank score for themselves? This plan will require Sheridan to juggle his lover, his superior, his partners, the bank robber, and the neighbors all at once.

Pushover is 100% hardcore noir. Always good with actors, Quine keeps performances understated even when the material is heating up. For example, he deftly orchestrates the scenes between Sheridan and his hard-drinking but suspicious partner Paddy, each man warily circling the other as they head for a violent collision. Above all, Quine shows a flawless grasp of the bleak world of film noir. One spectacular crane shot follows three characters down a darkened city street, creeping along behind them as if to eavesdrop on their impending doom. Throughout the film, what is most impressive is Quine's handling of mood—at once perfectly controlled on the surface and turbulent underneath.

For over fifty years this film hasn't gotten its due. Perhaps because it stars Fred MacMurray as an antihero manipulated by a dangerous woman it was labeled a rip-off of *Double Indemnity*, but this label says more about the laziness of film critics than it does about the film itself. *Pushover* is a major achievement, a spectacular film noir that deserves reassessment.

The script was based on two novels—*Rafferty* by Bill Ballinger and *The Night Watch* by Thomas Walsh—

adapted by the enormously talented writer Roy Huggins. A novelist himself (*Too Late For Tears*), Huggins took the bulk of the bad cop story from *The Night Watch* and melded it with some of the cop-and-bad-girl material from *Rafferty*. The result is an ingeniously evolving plot, one that Quine shoots as much for its psychological possibilities as for its suspense.

MacMurray is perfect as Sheridan, giving us an amoral cop who is very nearly smart enough to pull off his master plan. Heresy alert! This, not *Double Indemnity*, is MacMurray's best noir performance. It's slower and meaner around the edges. Sheridan is less of a sap than Walter Neff, more of a man whose innate bad side has been given permission to get him into serious trouble.

And Kim Novak is stunning here. The filmmakers contrive to put her in so many sexy outfits it starts to get a little silly—one outfit is a sheer braless number that Quine goes out of his way to emphasize—but the essence of the character is, after all, her affect on men. She's the kept woman of a bank robber, and she's considering making the switch to being the kept woman of a crooked cop. She's a femme fatale for sure, but Novak sells the role in the same way that Lona is selling more than just the promise of the greatest sex in the world. There was always something a little sad about Novak. You see it in *Vertigo*, and you see it here. Her appeal isn't just sex, after all, it's need. *I'm sexy*, she seems to say, *and I need you to take care of me*. It's easy to see why a man might throw away his life trying to do just that. Before long, Quine would find this out the hard way.

* * *

Quine's other film noir of 1954 was *Drive a Crooked Road* starring Mickey Rooney as Eddie Shannon, a lonely racecar driver lured into a bank heist by a beautiful woman named Barbara Matthews (Dianne Foster). Quine and Rooney had been close friends since their early days hoofing it up in MGM musicals and had maintained a working relationship even as Rooney's box office fortunes had diminished. They'd done two comedies together earlier in the decade (*Sound Off* and *All Ashore*) but this film could scarcely have been different from their previous films. Rooney, an actor known for his ebullience, gives his most introspective performance, making the sad little racecar driver a man more in danger from love than the heist scheme hatching around him.

This makes his relationship with Barbara all the more interesting. What ratchets up the emotional stakes are Barbra's conflicted feelings. She seduces Eddie Shannon, but it's a seduction of the heart. The two don't even share a kiss. They talk, and she invites Shannon to dream big dreams for the first time in his life. He falls in love, not lust, and we get the sense this job would be easier on Barbara if it was only physical.

Drive a Crooked Road was written by Quine and his frequent collaborator Blake Edwards (from a story by James Benson Nablo). There is a wealth of snappy lines here—as when the smooth bank robber played Kevin McCarthy tells a drunk girl at a party, "Dear love, why don't you go somewhere and pass out like a lady?" Yet an aura of heartbreak hovers over the film. This is one of the saddest of noirs—the story of lonely man who's taken for a sucker by a gang of sharks. The final scenes, as Shannon confronts the woman he loves and finds out the awful truth about her and the handsome bank robber, turn the heist film into a tragedy.

The same year *Drive a Crooked Road* was released Quine and Edwards helped create a sitcom for Rooney, *The Mickey Rooney Show (aka Hey Mulligan!)*, but when it failed to catch fire, he segued back to directing comedies like *My Sister Eileen*, *Operation Mad Ball*, and *How to Murder Your Wife*—all successful showcases of star Jack Lemmon's manic energies. Another film he and Lemmon made together was the 1958 *Bell Book and Candle*, costarring Jimmy Stewart and Kim Novak.

The film reunited Novak and Quine, and by the end of the year the director had separated from his wife and announced plans to marry his leading lady. In this heated atmosphere—married to one woman and publically engaged to another—Quine made the searing adultery drama *Strangers When We Meet* (1960). The film, based on the novel by crime writer Evan Hunter, paired Novak with Kirk Douglas in the story of two neighbors, both married, who carry on a torrid affair that upends their lives. The film is an oddity, a Technicolor Cinemascope production about the sex lives of bored suburbanites, but is also a dark and brutally honest look at matrimony and infidelity. Novak is excellent—she was always good playing a woman perplexed by her own desires—but she and Douglas warred on the set because the strong-willed actor insisted on giving her direction. Quine sided with Novak, but he let her fight her own battles. Then, toward the end of filming, Novak abruptly announced that their engagement was off. Their affair would drag on—full of passionate reconciliations and public breakups—before they finally called it quits in 1962.

Quine's love life rebounded with a five year marriage to actor Fran Jefferies, and then to a final union with Diana Balfour , but by the 1980s his career had ground to a halt. Times and tastes had changed, and his brand of comedy seemed outdated and stale. Even though he was only in his sixties, poor health plagued him. Despondent over his failing career and failing body, on June 10, 1989 Quine committed suicide in his home in Beverly Hills. In a dark echo of the tragic shooting of Susan Peters, he shot himself with a rifle.

His obituaries made the connection between Quine's suicide and the Peters tragedy. Implicit in almost all the coverage of his death was the irony of a man known for comedy taking his own life. What went unmentioned were the two heartbreaking noirs he made in 1954, two films that serve as evidence that there was always more going on behind the laughter.

THE LONG WAIT OF NORMAN FOSTER

Consider now the strange case of Norman Foster. A footnote in cinematic history, he's best remembered as the hack director of a bad movie. Tapped by Orson Welles in 1941 to direct the producer/star's new thriller *Journey Into Fear*, Foster became a trusted member of the inner circle during Welles's stormy tenure at RKO. After Welles was fired from the studio, however, the film was edited into incomprehensibility and abandoned on the public's doorstep. Today, very nearly the only place Norman Foster is mentioned is in the footnotes of Welles biographies. (When asked by writer C. Jerry Kutner if Welles directed parts of *La Décade Prodigieuse*, Claude Charbol responded, "Who do they think I am, Norman Foster?") Sadly, this oversight neglects Foster's contributions to both film noir and world cinema, and it dismisses a life nearly as fascinating as that of Welles.

Born Norman Foster Hoeffer on December 13, 1903, he first wanted to be an actor. His good looks and charm gained him entry to the New York stage where he dropped his last name and made his Broadway debut in 1926 in John Bowie's *Just Life*. The following year he acted opposite Edward G. Robinson and future noir director John Cromwell in the successful *The Racket*. More important to Foster's life, however, was another play he did that same year, *The Barker*, costarring a lovely young French actor named Claudette Colbert.

Foster and Colbert married in March of 1928, the beginning of an odd seven year arrangement in which the two never lived together in the same residence. The ostensible reason was that Colbert's domineering mother, Jeanne, didn't like Foster. Mother and daughter lived together on Central Park West while Foster kept an apartment on West Forty-fourth street. When the couple moved to Hollywood in the late 20s to make a run at the movie business, Jeanne came along and Foster again set up a separate residence. Both husband and wife found steady work throughout the early 30s, but while Colbert shot to superstardom, Foster stayed a second-string player, the handsome lightweight wooing ingénues like Carole Lombard, Clare Trevor, and Loretta Young. As Colbert's fame grew, the public's interest in her unusual marriage grew along with it. Explaining that she and Foster had a "modern marriage," she laughed it off. "The most important requirements for a successful marriage" she said "are living apart and a lack of jealousy." Whether or not this signaled an open relationship, or whether it gave the ring of truth to the persistent rumors that Colbert was a lesbian, the modern marriage didn't last. On August 6, 1935, while still married to Colbert, Foster publically announced his plans to marry actor Sally Blane, Loretta Young's older sister. Colbert granted him a divorce sixteen days later. His marriage to Sally, far happier, would last the rest of his life.

While ending one marriage and beginning another, Foster attempted a similar switch professionally. In 1936, he made his directorial debut (and starred in) a low budget mystery for the Standard Photoplay Company , *I Cover Chinatown*. The next year he started cranking out the *Mr. Motto* mystery series starring Peter Lorre, writing and directing for producer Sol M. Wurtzel. He made six Motto films in all. These films were hardly the stuff of legend, but Foster established himself as a director who could work fast, cheap, and competently.

This quality attracted the young Orson Welles, newly arrived at RKO, when he assigned Foster to direct a segment of his anthology film, *It's All True*. Foster and novelist John Fante adapted Robert Flaherty's short story "Bonito the Bull" about the friendship between a young boy and a fighting bull, and he and Welles scouted locations together in Mexico. Foster and his crew started shooting the short film (retitled "My Friend Benito") in September of 1941, and by October Welles was so ecstatic about the footage Foster was sending back that he promised Foster co-directing credit on the film. By this time, however, Welles was in trouble at RKO and in December he recalled Foster to Hollywood and put him in charge of directing an adaptation of the thriller *Journey Into Fear*. Since Welles designed the film, some critics and historians give him de facto co-directing credit. In truth, though he did direct the final scene (in postproduction), for most of the shoot he functioned more like a producer in the

Selznick mode. He oversaw all aspects of production, but since he was in South America making *It's All True* during much of the shoot, Foster was the man standing next to the camera while the film was rolling.

Shooting on both projects was hampered by a variety of issues, none more pressing than the rapid disintegration of Welles's position at the studio. By the middle of 1942, shooting on the thriller was complete, but the studio, unhappy with the results (unhappy, in fact, with everything Welles had touched), hacked down the final cut without consultation with Foster or Welles.

Foster might have had some reason to be mad at Welles (in 1942, a great many people were), but the two had become fast friends on the project and maintained warm relations the rest of their lives. Moreover, Foster had fallen in love with Mexico. Furthermore, he had impressed enough people in the film business there (particularly at Producciones Mèxico), that he could return and make some films on his own.

He began with an adaptation of Federico Gamboa's gritty 1903 naturalist novel *Santa*. The story of a young woman's descent into prostitution, it was a project Welles had considered making at one time, but film historian Harry Waldman later noted that Foster's film "went beyond Welles" in depicting a "blind, indifferent, cruel world." For his leading man, Foster had cast an unknown young actor named Ricardo Montalban who proved to be a sensation in the film. The following year Foster and Montalban reteamed with *Santa*'s leading lady Ester Fernández for the tragic romance *La Fuga*. The script, written by Foster and Betty Cromwell, is an amalgamation of two stories by Guy de Maupassant, "Boule de Suif" and "Mademoiselle Fifi." As such it's something of a rewrite of Ford's *Stagecoach*—which was also based on "Boule de Suif"—but Foster's film is pointedly tragic rather than uplifting, more in keeping with the source material. Shot at Azteca studios, the film allowed Foster to work with the legendary Mexican cinematographer Gabriel Figueroa who gave the film an epic look to rival Ford's film. Foster and Montalban followed that hit with the bullfighting drama *La hora de verdad* in 1945. Their third tragic, star-crossed romance in a row, the film proved to be their biggest popular and artistic success—winning Montalban a Heraldo, the Mexican equivalent of the Oscar, for best actor, as well as offers to work in Hollywood. Foster liked Montalban so much he arranged a blind date between the handsome young actor and Sally Blane's younger sister, Georgina Young—a good bit of matchmaking that resulted in a lifelong marriage.

Foster's most impressive Mexican film is the fascinating *El ahijado de la muerte* (1946) starring Jorge Negrete. The story of a man who makes the colossal mistake of accepting Death's offer to be his son's Godparent, *El ahijado de la muerte* remains a potent cinematic example of the "magic realism" emergent in Mexican and South American literature in the forties. Foster co-wrote the screenplay with the husband and wife team of Luis and Janet Alcoriza (an actor and ballerina respectively, the Alcorizas were just embarking on a screenwriting career that would eventually lead them to a close collaboration with Luis Buñuel and, later, to work on their own films).

Working with veteran expat cinematographer Jack Draper, Foster gave the film a rich atmosphere: low-key lighting, chiaroscuro contrasts, subjective camera shots, and one magnificent pan that slowly tilts into a bizarre angle. By 1946, the Indiana-born Draper had spent most of a long career working in Mexico, but the visuals that he and Foster employed here were as exciting as anything being done in American noir at the same time. The film had the big musical numbers that were a requirement of Mexican films of the era, but the overall feeling was one of deep foreboding.

When Foster came back to the states it was to shoot a Western starring his sister-in-law Loretta Young, *Rachel and the Stranger* (1948). That same year, however, he made an impressive swing into noir territory with *Kiss The Blood Off My Hands*. The film was the first release from Norma Productions, a new company founded by star Burt Lancaster and his agent Harold Hecht (they would go on to make *Sweet Smell of Success*). Lancaster stars as an ex-serviceman who kills the bartender of a London pub one night and escapes into the foggy, bombed out remains of the city. With the cops in pursuit, he climbs into the window of a young nurse played by Joan Fontaine.

The mechanics of the plot grind a little as they maneuver Lancaster and Fontaine into a romance, but once the story is set up, things run smoothly. At heart, the film is a tale of doomed love, the kind of thing Foster had been doing down in Mexico with his Montalban films. The film was a different role for Lancaster, however. Usually cast as a chump who gets mixed up with a vixen, here he's *l'homme fatale*, the dangerous man who brings ruin on an unsuspecting woman. Since Lancaster was the rare performer who was equally convincing punching a guy in the face and telling a woman that she was the only thing that ever mattered, this film gives him plenty of opportunity to do both.

Foster and his team brought a rich visual style to the film. Lensed by veteran cinematographer Russell Metty, the look of the film recalls Joseph August's work on John Ford's *The Informer* without simply repeating it. Metty blends sharp blacks and whites with mysterious foggy backgrounds, and he's helped mightily by the lovely set design of Bernard Herzbrun and Nathan Juran. This is a shattered London just beginning to get to its feet after the war, a physical metaphor for what's going on with the characters. Foster combines these elements with precision and skill. The film's beginning combines long crane shots of Lancaster scurrying through the ruins of London trying to avoid capture. When he's captured after getting into another brawl, he's sentenced to a caning. This torture sequence is as intense a scene of violence as one will see in classic noir, but it's only by going back later and looking at it again that one realizes that Foster and his editor Milton Carruth accomplish this feat by alternating shots of Lancaster's face (each from a slightly closer, more askew angle) with shots of the flogger and onlookers. A later sequence, in which a blackmailer tries to sexually assault Fontaine and gets a pair of scissors in his liver for his trouble is a fabulous piece of suspense. Even better are the scenes that follow it. A later shot of a dead man sprawled out on a shattered aquarium, fish flapping on the soaked carpet, is as gruesomely funny as anything Hitchcock had put onscreen by 1948. And another scene of a disoriented Fontaine is captured with a terrific little tracking shot that tilts and stumbles like an unsettled guardian angel (and is reminiscent of the tilted pan in *El ahijado de la muerte*).

In 1950, Foster delivered one of the odder noirs on record, *Woman on the Run*. It stars Ann Sheridan as a woman trying to track down her husband when he disappears after witnessing a murder. The exact details of the murder plot are sketched on the fly—always a good indication that the plot is of trifling importance. Instead, the main thing that *Woman on the Run* has going for it is that it's weird. The combination of slanted angles and Arthur Lange's pounding score produces some of this effect, but most of the oddity here derives from a contrast between realism and artifice. While the film was shot on location in San Francisco, much of it was also clearly shot in the confines of a studio. This creates a disjointed effect for the viewer, but in a sense disjointed effects are what film noir is all about. Consider the final sequence, set in Whitney's Playland amusement park. For reasons too complicated (and, in the proud noir tradition, too convoluted) to explain here Sheridan winds up trapped on roller coaster ride while her husband and the killer wrestle near the tracks below. This sequence is rapidly edited with a mixture of location footage and studio effects, slanted angles and chiaroscuro lighting, all of it scored with thumping music, the roar of the roller coaster, and the cackling of a mechanical witch. In a word: weird. It's a fabulous sequence, though, and a perfect way to tie up the picture.

After his stint in noir, Foster made the quasi-documentary *Navajo* (1952) and the following year went back to Mexico to make the romance *Sombrero* with Montalban, Yvonne De Carlo, and Thomas Gomez. After that, he settled into a long, comfortable career in television, directing Fess Parker in the hugely successful Davy Crockett episodes of *Walt Disney's Wonderful World of Color* (later edited and released theatrically as *Davy Crockett King of The Wild Frontier*), as well as episodes of *The Loretta Young Show* and *Zorro*. He worked up until 1974, and then two years later on July 7, 1976, died in Santa Monica.

In the years since his death, Norman Foster has mostly been confined to the shadow of Orson Welles. Portions of "My Friend Benito," Foster's segment of *It's All True* were included in a 1993 documentary about the ill-fated project. Back in the seventies, Foster had played a supporting role Welles's long gestating *The Other Side of the Wind* opposite John Huston. The project, never finished and never released, still makes headlines as new rumors of its impending release come and go. And, of course, the mangled corpse of *Journey Into Fear* continues to limp on like a zombie reminder of Welles's last turbulent days at RKO.

Cinema is resilient, though, and Foster's best films are treasures awaiting rediscovery. In fact, this long overdue process may be finally underway. When Film Noir Foundation president Eddie Muller showed a copy of *Woman on the Run* during the "Art of Noir" series at the 2009 Grand Lyon film festival in France, the response was ecstatic. Following the showing, publications like *Le Monde* and *Telèrama* wrote rave appreciations of the film. Who knows? Norman Foster may yet find his way out of Welles's shadow.

JOURNEYMAN

Not everyone can be an artist. Despite the presence of a few Bohemians in the movie business, most film directors tend to be competent professionals hired to do a job. This was never more true than in the studio era when many—maybe even most—proficient directors never created an identifiable persona for their work. They simply made good movies on a consistent basis. It is always worth remembering that the classic era of cinema was, for most directors, factory work.

The poster boy for the solid cinematic workman may well have been Felix Ellison Feist. Without ever achieving widespread recognition, he toiled in every genre from science fiction to musicals and created a consistently entertaining body of films. Since some of his best work was as the hand behind a series of strong film noirs in the late forties and early fifties, his career serves as a reminder that noir, long the focus of auteurist studies, was not simply the domain of heralded geniuses like Siodmak and Wilder. Some directors, like Felix Feist, were merely professional storytellers who punched in, told their stories, and punched out when the job was done.

Born in 1910 in New York City, he was the son of Felix F. Feist, MGM's general sales manager. Since his father was, in essence, Louis B. Mayer's superior, Feist was able to land a job at the studio loading film for cameramen when he was nineteen. By the early thirties, however, the fiercely ambitious Feist had developed enough of a reputation at the studio that he was placed in charge of directing screen tests. He directed Maureen O'Sullivan's audition for the role of Jane in *Tarzan the Ape Man* (1932) and advised her to play the role with spunk rather than softness—a piece of direction that O'Sullivan later claimed landed her the job. He also directed the first screen tests for both Deanna Durbin and Judy Garland, and in 1936 he directed the young girls in their first film, an eleven-minute short called *Every Sunday*.

By that time, Feist had already made his feature film debut as the director of an independently financed disaster film called *Deluge* (1933). The film was a success, but strangely it didn't lead to any other directing jobs, perhaps because the real star of the film was the special effects crew. Even with a big budget success under his belt, Feist went back to being one of the many up and coming young directors toiling away in MGM's shorts department. Alongside future directors like Fred Zinnemann and Jacques Tourneur, he wrote and directed short films in a variety of series, including the *Pete Smith Specialty* comedies, John Nesbitt's historical *The Passing Parade*, and the popular *Crime Does Not Pay* micro-dramas. Working with screenwriters like Robert

The Blind Alley

Benchley and John C. Higgins, the shorts were a good training ground for a director to learn his craft, but for a man of Feist's ambition—a man eager to break out of the shadow of his successful but distant father—it must have seemed like a long road to nowhere. Years later, MGM producer Samuel Marx remembered Feist as a brash youngster always jockeying for a better position within the company.

It was during the contentious 1934 California governor's race that Feist had a chance to impress his bosses at MGM. That year, Upton Sinclair's socialist End Poverty In California campaign had become a political juggernaut, culminating with the author's clinching of the Democratic nomination for governor. With Sinclair steamrolling toward victory in the general election, the state's Republicans—many of them in the film industry—scrambled to fight back. Louis B. Mayer, who had served as the California Chairman of the Republican party in 1933, dispatched the young Feist and a Metrotone News crew out to make a shocking "newsreel" about the race. The film showed clean, upstanding citizens expressing their support for the Republican candidate, while all of Sinclair's supporters sported burly whiskers, thick accents, and spouted dialog like, "Eef eet works een Russia, eet can work here too!" Sinclair's campaign never recovered, and he lost in a landslide. Feist's doctored newsreel wasn't the only factor in Sinclair's defeat, of course, but there was no doubt that for the first time in American history, the medium of moving pictures had helped bring down a political movement.

Even doing Mayer's dirty work didn't get Feist a job on a feature at MGM, however. Despite his efforts, MGM never seemed to embrace the young man, and after his father died, Feist's pull at the company diminished. Still, his apprentice years working in shorts had taught him to work quickly and efficiently. He chipped in some uncredited help on Edward Dmytryk's boxing film *Golden Gloves* (1940), and he finally got his second feature with the comedy *All By Myself* (1943) at Universal. After that, he was a free agent, working in different genres at different studios.

1947 found Feist at RKO working on a tight little thrill ride called *The Devil Thumbs a Ride* with the wild man of noir, Lawrence Tierney. Clocking in at sixty-two minutes (five minutes shorter than *Detour*), the film is as fast, and about as subtle, as a freight train. Nutjob Tierney thumbs a ride with nice guy Ted North and then turns his life into an ever escalating nightmare. Feist, who wrote the script from a novel by Robert DuSoe, hammers down on a simple story arc: every scene makes things worse. Tierney, famously difficult to work with, seems to have behaved himself during filming in part because he liked the director. Moreover, Feist respected Tierney as an actor and had an instinctive sense of how to use him. Like Tierney, Feist was a natural born man's man, and the two played gin rummy on the set. The harmony paid off, with Tierney delivering perhaps his signature performance, and although Feist hated the upbeat ending mandated by the studio, he had good reason to be proud of the film itself. Alongside *Detour* and *The Hitch-Hiker*, *The*

Devil Thumbs a Ride deserves a place in the Hitchhiker from Hell Hall of Fame.

By 1949, Feist was back at RKO making the prison break thriller *The Threat*. Again working with miniscule screen time (66 minutes), Feist keeps things moving at a breakneck pace. Crime lord Charles McGraw busts out of Folsom Prison and kidnaps the cop who put him there. The film ostensibly stars Michael O'Shea as the cop, but Feist has the good sense to focus everything on the ferocious performance of McGraw who growls out his dialog and slaps around the rest of the cast.

The next year Feist made the red-baiting thriller *Guilty of Treason* (1950) with Charles Bickford. Feist was particularly proud of the film and, for a while at least, it turned him into a staunch anti-Communist. Still, he was far more preoccupied with a supporting actor on the film named Lisa Howard. The two had met sometime in the late forties and had become romantically involved around the time Feist directed the young woman (nearly twenty years his junior) in a Steve Fisher/Sloan Nibley play called *Angel Face*. A quick marriage and the birth of a daughter in 1947 were followed by a divorce in 1949. Just as suddenly, however, the two reconciled and remarried. Feist cast her in both *Guilty of Treason* and another 1950 noir, *The Man Who Cheated Himself*.

Starring Lee J. Cobb as an honest cop who agrees to help his girlfriend cover up the killing of her well-to-do husband, *The Man Who Cheated Himself* is an uneven but unjustly overlooked little gem. Cobb's beautifully restrained performance is a revelation from an actor who spent most of his career trying to outscream Rod

Steiger. While the film is hampered by Jane Wyatt's somewhat limp performance as the femme fatale, Feist's direction keeps things moving at such a clip that it hardly matters. The action culminates in a haunting sequence in San Francisco's Fort Point—some of the best location shooting in any noir of the era.

In 1951, Feist and Howard divorced for a second time, but that year also saw the release of his best film, *Tomorrow is Another Day*. Steve Cochran stars as a man recently paroled from prison who gets involved with a dancehall girl played by Ruth Roman. When he accidently kills her sugar daddy, they go on the lam.

Feist's direction here is superb. In contrast to the time constraints he usually worked under, Warner Brothers gave him a relatively epic ninety minutes, and Feist uses the time wisely. The movie is notable for the way it allows Cochran and Roman to get to know each other, to change, to fall in love and have that love tested. It's also notable for the way Feist uses silence, especially in the opening scenes, both to develop character and to build suspense. There's a tour de force sequence at about the halfway mark in which Cochran and Roman attempt to sneak into a car on top of an auto-transport truck. It's an excellent blend of acting, camerawork, and sound. The script by Guy Endore and Art Cohn is, for the most part, a smart piece of work, and Feist has a nice time with the scenes mounting toward the climax. As a series of mishaps start to squeeze Cochran and Roman, it's interesting to note that the tension derives from a further complicating of their relationship. She can take the pressure, but we're not so sure about him. Feist and the screenwriters have less success with the film's overly tidy resolution. Many noirs have weak finishes, but the finish here is notable in its forced attempt at uplift. Still, *Tomorrow is Another Day* is an excellent film waiting to be discovered by noir fans. It's a success for everyone involved, and it's especially something of a vindication for Felix Feist.

His last venture into noirish territory, *This Woman is Dangerous* (1952) was less successful. Starring Joan Crawford as a gangster who loses her eyesight but finds true love, it was a soppy melodrama with noir touches. Crawford hated the film, and Feist later told his son, sci-fi novelist Raymond E. Feist, that Warner Brothers was eager to ditch the notoriously irascible Crawford and encouraged him to "make her look bad." Feist, like most people who knew her, didn't particularly like Crawford, so he did as he was told. After three days of shooting, however, he called his producer Bob Sisk and told him, "Bob, you'll have to tell the studio guys to find another way to get her out of her contract. This woman can't give a bad performance."

Like many people in the business, Feist made the transition to television in the fifties. He directed a Cornell Woolrich adaptation, scripted by Steve Fisher and starring Agnes Moorhead, for the *Revlon Mirror Theater* in 1953, and did a stint on Dick Powell's *Zane Grey Theater* directing episodes starring Scott Brady, Jack Palance, and Robert Ryan. He directed the debut episode of *Sea Hunt* and multiple episodes of *Voyage to the Bottom of the Sea*.

By the mid-sixties, Feist had been in the business thirty-five years. Any hopes of breaking out had long since faded away, and he had established a well-deserved reputation among producers as a competent craftsman, a man who could get things done. His last job was as a line producer on the series *Peyton Place*, but in 1965, he took a leave of absence from the show in order to fight a losing battle with cancer. He died on September 2 at Encino Hospital at the age of 55. While it's unlikely that he'll be rediscovered as an auteur, Feist should get more respect. For noir fans, at least, he leaves behind the triple punch of *The Devil Thumbs a Ride*, *The Man Who Cheated Himself*, and *Tomorrow is Another Day*. Not bad for a hack.

NO ONE ESCAPES
THE FALL OF ART SMITH

As the Red Scare burned through Hollywood in the spring of 1952, it destroyed a lot of friendships and careers, but it might not have consumed a more idealistic man than Art Smith. At the time, he was a respected character actor specializing in dark crime dramas like *In A Lonely Place* and *The Sound Of Fury*, but in April of that year Smith would find himself publically betrayed by an old friend and forced out of the profession to which he had given much of his life.

Arthur Gordon Smith was born into a theatrical family on March 23, 1899. His father ran a traveling stock company, so the younger Smith lived a vagabond life on tour around the country. Tragedy struck him early, however, when his father died and fourteen year old Art was forced to go out into the world and make a living. He did hardscrabble work—as a dockworker in the east and a lumberjack in the west—building a sympathy for the working man that was soon to become a passion. By 1924, he'd found his way back into acting, working for a time at the Goodman Theatre in Chicago and living briefly as a bohemian in Paris. By the early thirties, he'd made his way into the New York theater world when he fell into the orbit of Harold Clurman, Lee Strasberg, and Cheryl Crawford. This trio was putting together a new kind of "collective theater" based in part on the Russian model established by Konstantin Stanislavski, and they asked Smith to join. The new Group Theater sought to redefine acting at the same time that it issued Leftist criticisms of society. Smith joined the Communist Party and was among the theater collective's most outspoken members in favor of making important social statements, particularly in regards to the disparity between the rich and the poor.

The Group Theater lasted nine years and included a roll call of some of the most important actors, playwrights, and directors of its day. In addition to Smith, the group included actors Julius (soon to be John) Garfield, Luther and Stella Adler, Franchot Tone, and Lee J. Cobb; playwright Clifford Odets; and a young director named Elia Kazan. Alongside this distinguished group, Smith acted and taught performance classes (where one of his first students was Charles McGraw). He assembled and directed an experimental pantomime mocking the petty bourgeoisie of Germany, which managed the unlikely task of incorporating the art of George Grosz, the Book of Psalms, and a recording of Marlene Dietrich. In 1935, he and Kazan co-wrote an anti-Nazi piece called *Dmitroff: A Play of Mass Pressure* about the Reichstag fire and the resultant trial of five Communists for arson.

Eventually, however, the collective fell apart, the result of ideological and personal differences. For a while, Smith worked as the director of Chicago's Federal Theater Project. Then in the summer of 1940, he taught acting classes in Rye Beach, New Hampshire and met an aspiring actor named Edith Hopkins with whom he began a relationship. He had been married for seven years by then—to a wealthy art student named Betty Upjohn—but his marriage was in trouble, the result of pressures with the Group and, perhaps, with Smith's own drinking. He went back to New York and starred on Broadway alongside Robert Ryan in the original production of *Clash By Night* in 1942. That same year Hollywood came calling.

Since Smith was diminutive and prematurely going gray, Hollywood quickly cast him as either an old man or a nebbish. Somehow, though, Smith seemed to be a good fit for the dark crime dramas beginning to slip out of the Dream Factory's graveyard shift. He had small roles at first—an uncredited bit in *T-Men*, a desk clerk in *Framed*—but he quickly began moving up. He had one poignant scene as his old friend John Garfield's doomed father in Rossen's *Body And Soul*, and he played the sad prison doctor in Dassin's *Brute Force*. In *Ride The Pink Horse*, he was an FBI man with an unconvincing Southern accent. That same year his director and costar in *Ride The Pink Horse*, Robert Montgomery, testified as a friendly witness before the House Un-American Activities Committee and encouraged them to root out subversives in the movie business. The anti-Communist fervor in Hollywood, and in the country at large, was starting to burn.

Still, Smith kept working. He did Ophüls's *Letter From An Unknown Woman*, Milestone's *Arch Of*

Triumph, and even the odd musical or western. His bread and butter, however, were the gritty crime films. He was in *A Double Life* with Ronald Coleman, *Caught* alongside Robert Ryan, *Manhandled* with Sterling Hayden and Dan Duryea, *Quicksand* with Mickey Rooney, and *The Killer That Stalked New York* with Evelyn Keyes. In 1950, he had two of his best roles: in Ray's *In A Lonely Place*, he's Bogart's faithful agent and occasional punching bag, and in *The Sound Of Fury* he's a newspaper man who's a horrified witness to a public lynching.

In 1952, Smith got his own helping of mob justice when his old friend and Group Theater writing partner Elia Kazan testified before the House Un-American Activities Committee. On April 10, Kazan took the stand and named Art Smith and fifteen others as Communists. When Kazan finished, the Committee's chairman, Francis Walter, thanked him for striking a blow against the "Communist conspiracy for world domination."

And like that, Smith's Hollywood career was incinerated. He fled back to New York and, after a year or so, managed to scrape together some stage work. He and his old flame Edith Hopkins (she'd since married, taken the named O'Hara, and had three children) started a summer theater in Bushkill, Pennsylvania. By 1957, he appeared on Broadway as Doc in the original production of *West Side Story*, and in 1958 he was in *A Touch Of The Poet*, a Eugene O'Neil production staged by his old Group Theater partner Harold Clurman.

Not long after appearing in a successful Broadway run of *All The Way Home*, Smith retired. When he died in a nursing home in West Babylon, New York in 1973, he got a nice write-up in the *New York Times*.

Times had changed. The Red Scare had subsided, and many of his friends had done great things. Edith O'Hara founded the Thirteenth Street Theater, which would become a New York institution. Stella Adler founded the Stella Adler Conservatory and helped redefine acting by mentoring trailblazers like Marlon Brando and Robert De Niro. Smith's own personal Judas, Elia Kazan, had become a director of undeniable accomplishment, his legacy a mixture of artistic success and personal betrayal.

And Art Smith would be all but forgotten, except, perhaps, to those film noir fans who kept noticing that little man with the large nose and the sad eyes. While he played sidekicks and the occasional bad guy, most of the time Smith played the haggard voice of moral authority. He always played an authority figure as someone haunted by a sense of moral failure, the kind of older man whose years and experiences have brought him closer to sadness than to wisdom. He's the voice of the lost and the hopeless who intones the brutal last lines of *Brute Force*: "No one escapes. No one ever escapes."

FATE SLAPS DOWN ANDY HARDY

MICKEY ROONEY AFTER MGM

It's easy to get in over your head when you're only five foot two. Mickey Rooney found that out the hard way in the fifties. After singing and dancing his way through most of the thirties and forties, he found his particular brand of sunshine out of fashion in postwar America. Potential career oblivion must have come as a shock to a man who, only a few years before, was the biggest (if also the shortest) male movie star in America. Up to that point, his career had been a rocket ride.

Born Joe Yule Jr. in Brooklyn on September 23, 1920, the son of vaudeville performers, he was hustled onstage in a tiny tuxedo at 17 months old. In a sense, he never left the spotlight. After his parents divorced in 1923, convinced her boy had the makings of a star, little Joe's mother hauled him out to Hollywood. He didn't make the cut for *Our Gang*, but he did land a part as a midget in the short *Not to Be Trusted* (1926). After he was cast as Mickey "Himself" McGuire in a series of popular comedy shorts, his mother legally changed his name to "Mickey McGuire" to cash in. A few years later, when he was ready to branch out into other roles (and following a lawsuit by the creator of the original Mickey McGuire comic strips on which the character was based), he was rechristened Mickey Rooney. In the 1937 B-movie *A Family Affair* he turned the supporting role of a spunky kid named Andy Hardy into a money-making powerhouse. Over the course of fourteen Andy Hardy films, he represented a worry-free American boyhood (a precursor to the precocious TV kids who would supplant him in the fifties). More successes followed: hit musicals like *Babes in Arms* and *Strike Up the Band* with Judy Garland, a critically acclaimed dramatic turn in *Boys Town* opposite Spencer Tracy, the smash hit *National Velvet* with Elizabeth Taylor. From 1939 to 1941, he was Hollywood's biggest box-office draw.

Then came Pearl Harbor. By the time the war was over, everything had changed—from Hollywood itself to the country it was trying to entertain. Rooney himself put in 21 months of service in the Army only to come back and find his career in serious trouble. No longer a kid, he faced darkening horizons. The country had taken a turn for the noir.

Like many a man faced with trouble, Rooney tuned to crime—at least on screen. In 1950, he teamed up with actor-turned-director Irving Pichel for the cautionary tale *Quicksand*. In the film, Rooney plays a cash-strapped mechanic named Dan Brady. In the opening scene, Dan's drinking at a greasy spoon diner with a couple of buddies when a beautiful woman (Jeanne Cagney) walks through the door. Her name is Vera, and like all women named Vera in film noir she seems to have wandered in from hell looking for a man to kill. Dan volunteers to take her out for a good time because he's too dense to see that all Vera really wants is a two-thousand dollar mink coat. Since he can't even afford to take her to the boardwalk, he borrows twenty bucks from the cash register at work. This one act of dishonesty sets into motion a nightmarish chain of events. Every move Dan makes only gets him into deeper trouble, and yet moment by moment his decisions seem to make sense. His mistakes are huge, but it's easy to see how and why he makes them.

Something of a film theorist, director Irving Pichel wrote for the leftist film journal *Hollywood Quarterly* (a forerunner to *Film Quarterly*) in which he expounded on camera technique and advocated an auteurist-like theory of filmmaking in articles with titles like "In Defense of Virtuosity." His work in noir gravitated toward weak-willed protagonists (as evidenced by the superior 1947 *They Won't Believe Me* featuring Robert Young, of all people, as a philandering husband). Written by the talented Robert Smith (*99 River Street*), *Quicksand* never feels like an object lesson. Like many noirs, it stumbles in the last few minutes with an unconvincing resolution, but the methodical death march to get there is thrilling.

The film owes a lot to Rooney's willingness to complicate his iconic optimism. In past roles, this quality had always been a plus, an all-American can-do assertiveness. Part of what he does in *Quicksand*, however, is to let that attribute curdle into a little man's insecurity and bluster. Dan's a dope and doesn't know it—and, this being film noir, that's exactly as it should be. Watching this film is like watching fate stick out its foot to trip Andy Hardy.

Fate wasn't done, either. In 1951, Rooney starred in the curious musical noir *The Strip*. The set-up is pretty standard stuff: he plays a Korean vet fresh out of the psyche ward who gets involved with a numbers-running gangster and an icily beautiful nightclub dancer played by Sally Forrest. The film alternates between this crime story love triangle and a series of musical numbers featuring people like Louis Armstrong, Vic Damone, and Monica Lewis. Forrest, a trained dancer, gets to hoof it up in a couple of numbers, and Mickey does a duet with William Demarest. The film is not for every taste, to be sure, but it's entertaining and well made. Moreover, it's a real noir, not just a musical with noir cinematography. The ending is curiously perfect. The plot has been resolved, and the only takeaway moral of the story is that sometimes life sucks. So, hell, why not strike up the band for one last song?

By the mid-fifties, Rooney must have felt like he was out of songs. He had become a national punchline. His movies flopped, and his attempts at television failed. Most damning in the public eye, he seemed to treat marriage like a hobby—notching up five marriages by 1958 including stormy, short-lived unions to noir goddesses Ava Gardner and Martha Vickers. This last point made him a dependable gossip rag headline, but it didn't seem to help him convince people that he was genuine noir material. The ultimate child star had become the ultimate washed-up child star. During this same period, though, he did make a truly extraordinary film.

Drive a Crooked Road (1954) tells the story of Eddie Shannon (Rooney), a mechanic and part time race car driver. Without knowing it, Eddie catches the attention of a group of bank robbers led by Steve Norris (Kevin McCarthy). Norris needs a wheel man for a job he's planning, a job which will require a driver of great skill. He dispatches his sexy girlfriend Barbara (Dianne Foster) to seduce the little guy and talk him into helping them pull the job. Eddie balks at first, but he's simply too in love with Barbara to resist for long.

What happens next is interesting. We might expect the bank job to go badly, or for Norris and his gang to stiff Eddie on the money, but the film makes a rather unexpected detour. The money (oddly enough for a film noir) isn't really the sticking point here. The fallout is really over matters of love.

While Rooney still had some spring in his step in *Quicksand*, in *Drive a Crooked Road* we find him playing a very different kind of role. For one thing, the film uses none of the usual tricks to lessen the impact of the actor's height. Everyone in the film, including Foster, towers over him, and the film uses his diminutive stature as a catalyst in the drama. Eddie Shannon is an odd little guy. He's quiet, even around his buddies at work (and Rooney's surprisingly effective as an introvert). He's a lonely man, and the gang picks him out *because* he's a lonely man.

As good as *Drive a Crooked Road* is it did little to staunch the bleeding of Rooney's career. He reteamed with Quine and Edwards to create the short-lived sitcom *The Mickey Rooney Show* (aka *Hey Mulligan!*), but the viewing audience didn't buy the 34-year old

Mick as a bumbling teenager. He blamed himself for the show's failure, telling a reporter years later that "I guess it was because of my unfortunate marriages." It was true that the private Mickey Rooney had never measured up to his MGM-created image. Being the onscreen embodiment of sweetness and light had financed decades worth of booze, hookers, and a particularly egregious gambling problem (reportedly causing Louis B. Mayer to once implore him, "You're the United States! You're a symbol! Behave yourself!"). By the fifties Rooney was showing up in the papers for ducking child support payments and getting into brawls, once duking it out with actor Fred Wayne over singer Mary Hatcher and bragging to the papers, "I don't need a bodyguard." Actor Ernie Kovacs would later bitterly tell an interviewer that Rooney had "a big chip on his miniature shoulder."

In the late fifties, Rooney decided to take his dark side out for a spin. In Don Siegel's 1957 *Baby Face Nelson*, he took on the role of psychotic Lester Gillis, the trigger-happy bank robber known to the world as George "Baby Face" Nelson. During the depression, the real Baby Face Nelson was a kidnapper, murderer, and thief who teamed up for a time with the famous John Dillinger. Baby Face never had Dillinger's flair—in part because unlike Dillinger Baby Face was a full-tilt nutjob—but after the more famous bank robber was gunned down by the FBI, Baby Face took Dillinger's spot as Public Enemy Number One. He didn't keep the title very long before he was killed in a shootout with the authorities.

Siegel's *Baby Face Nelson* doesn't depart too much from that basic narrative (though it rewrites some history in order to make Baby Face more important than he was). Always a trooper, Rooney is servable in the role without being dynamic in it. While he could dominate a screen as well as anyone in a musical or comedy, in drama he seemed to shrink. Good films like *Quicksand* and *Drive a Crooked Road* used this quality and played off Rooney's small stature. *Baby Face Nelson*, on the other hand, uses his smallness an explanation for the killer's psychological scars (Nelson was about 5'5). He's a psychopath because he's short, in other words. Beyond this very basic idea, the film doesn't see fit to go. Siegel apologists have turned the film into something of a cult classic, but aside from the fine performance of Carolyn Jones as Nelson's wife it is a rather drowsy affair.

Drowsier still was *The Big Operator* (1959), a bargain-basement *On the Waterfront* starring Rooney as 'Little' Joe Braun, a ruthless gangster who's the real power behind a labor union. Steve Cochran plays the honest everyman trying to stand up to the gangsters. Though indifferently shot and staged, the film is notably violent—including surprisingly vigorous threats against Cochran's young son. Ultimately the film is an uninvolving bore, but it does offer the unintentionally hilarious sight of a climatic fracas involving (among others) Rooney, Cochran, Mel Tormè, Mamie Van Doren, and future *Gilligan's Island* star Jim Backus.

At the time, the public wasn't buying Rooney's switch to gritty crime dramas. Of course, for a while there, the public wasn't buying anything Rooney was selling. By the sixties, he was doing supporting roles and working nightclubs while hacking through an ever-expanding thicket of divorce proceedings and bad press. In 1958 his fifth wife, Barbara Ann Thompson nearly died from an overdoes of sleeping pills. In 1966, she left Rooney for the actor Milos Milosevic, but when she and Rooney made plans to reconcile, Milosevic murdered her in Rooney's home and then shot himself. Rooney, despondent, fell into a deep depression. Later that same year, he married Thompson's best friend. Three months later, they divorced.

As the years went by, the actor found his equilibrium. In 1978, he married for an eighth and final time, to actor Jan Chamberlain. His career rebounded as well when Rooney transformed himself into a character actor. He appeared in Mike Hodges's neo-noir *Pulp* (alongside Lizebeth Scott). In 1978, he was nominated for Best Supporting actor playing a horse trainer in *The Black Stallion* (a role he reprised on television during the 1990s in *The New Adventures of the Black Stallion*). In 2006, he found himself in a box office smash when he played a supporting role in *Night at the Museum*.

Eighty-five years into his Hollywood career, Rooney is still making films. In a profession not known for shelf-life, his career stretches from silent one-reelers to CGI blockbusters. Outside of longevity, though, what will be his legacy? How will he be remembered? Unlike his frequent co-star Judy Garland, Rooney never made an enduring *Wizard of Oz*-sized phenomenon. And while Shirley Temple movies have had staying power, does anyone watch Andy Hardy movies anymore? If he is to be remembered as more than a song and dance man who peaked at the age of 21, Rooney's surprising work during the fifties might make for an excellent point of reevaluation. After all, if Louis B. Mayer was right, and Rooney was a symbol of a more innocent America, it's worth noting what happened to him as history pressed forward and left that idealized vision of America in the past.

IV

MUG SHOTS:

OVERDUE APPRECIATIONS

HARD LUCK LADIES
THELMA RITTER, BARBARA PAYTON, LINDA DARNELL, MARTHA VICKERS

I. The Old Clock: Thelma Ritter

God bless Thelma Ritter. She improved every movie she was ever in by providing an immediate jolt of plain-spoken authenticity. Usually cast as domestic help—the maid, the nanny, the cook—she seemed always to have wandered in from pulling a double shift in the real world.

She didn't make it onto the silver screen until she was well into her forties, which meant that when she arrived she brought the unmistakable air of a woman who had lived an actual life. The daughter of a Brooklyn shoe company office manager, she was born in either 1902 or 1905 (opinions vary, though most sources list '05), Ritter started acting as a child and worked her way through various stock companies during high school. After graduating, she attended the American Academy of Dramatic Arts but had to drop out after only year to find work. Throughout the Depression, she remained a struggling, albeit working, actor on stage (rarely Broadway) and on the radio. She married fellow stage actor Joseph Moran in 1927 and gave birth to two children.

Her big break came in 1947 when producer Daryl Zanuck noticed the wonderfully weary way she read a one-line bit part in *Miracle On 34th Street* and ordered her role expanded. He signed her to an exclusive contract and Ritter's film career as the embodiment of the working-class everywoman began.

She delivered stand-out performances in classics like *All About Eve*, *The Misfits,* and *Pillow Talk*, but her best roles came in crime films.

Her performance in Samuel Fuller's masterful *Pick-Up On South Street* (1953) is simply exquisite. As a fatalistic little stool pigeon trying to save up enough money for a decent plot of ground and a stone, Ritter infuses her role with such bone-weary street smarts—she is incapable of uttering an inauthentic syllable—that she steals every scene she's in. Seeing a film like *Pickup on South Street* makes you realize how star-centered films have become as budgets have increased and the quality of the screenwriting has decreased. Ritter doesn't just class up this picture, she is essential to creating its labyrinthine world of pickpockets and deadbeats, cops and commies.

In her last scene, staring down a killer, she gets to deliver a speech that sums up the Ritter ethos in this picture and so many others:

When I come in here tonight, you seen an old clock runnin' down. I'm tired. I'm through. Happens to everybody sometime. It'll happen to you too, someday. With me it's a little bit of everything. Backaches and headaches. I can't sleep nights. It's so hard to get up in the morning and get dressed and walk the streets. Climb the stairs. I go right on doin' it! Well, what am I gonna do, knock it? I have to go on makin' a livin'... so I can die.

Perhaps her best known role was as Stella, Jimmy Stewart's homecare nurse in Alfred Hitchcock's *Rear Window*. While Stewart peeks in his neighbors' windows and makes out with Grace Kelly, Ritter keeps tossing him verbal grenades like "We've become a race of Peeping Toms. What people ought to do is get outside their own house and look in for a change."

Or this gem:

You heard of that market crash in 1929? I predicted that. I was nursing a director of General Motors. Kidney ailment, they said. Nerves, I said. And I asked myself, 'What's General Motors got to be nervous about?' Overproduction, I says; collapse. When General Motors has to go to the bathroom ten times a day, the whole country's ready to let go.

Again, Ritter's presence helps to ground the whole story. When Stewart expresses his reservations about marrying Kelly, Ritter sums up her own marriage with lines so well delivered it's as if she making them up on the spot: "When I married Miles, we were both a couple of maladjusted misfits. We are still maladjusted misfits, and we have loved every minute of it."

On television she grabbed a rare starring role in a gruesomely funny episode of *Alfred Hitchcock Presents* called "The Baby Sitter." The episode positions her once again as the blunt working woman ("What is my precious time worth? Eighty-five cents an hour.") but gives her the opportunity to explore the dark side of that character. Ritter plays a babysitter who is thrilled when her employer's wife is murdered because she has dreams of marrying the dead woman's rich husband. In some ways the film is a mean joke—as so many episodes of the show were—because the humor derives from the older working-class woman's delusions. That makes it all problematic, of course, but Ritter is still strangely touching as a woman daring to dream of love and wealth—even though that dream turns into a nightmare by the end.

Over the course of her career, Ritter was nominated for six Academy Awards (*All About Eve, The Mating Season, With A Song In My Heart, Pick-Up On South Street, Pillow Talk, Birdman Of Alcatraz*) but never won—proof, if any is needed, that the Oscars are entirely pointless. Thelma Ritter was as fine an actor as ever worked in movies, but she was never flashy or fashionable, and never seemed to reach for effect. She just seemed real.

II. Bad Blonde: Barbara Payton

Bad Blonde (1953) is the kind of movie that exists on two levels. On one level it is an entertaining film noir about an up-and-coming boxer who is lured into a scheme to commit murder by the duplicitous wife of a boxing promoter. I've seen this plot referred to as *Body And Soul* meets *The Postman Always Rings Twice*—a fair description of a film that has no pretensions toward redesigning the wheel.

On the other level, it is a time capsule that captures a very troubled woman at a very troubled time in her life. The star of the film, Barbara Payton, was on a downward slope as she worked on this production, a slope that would only get steeper as the years progressed. The film is built around her bad girl image, an image that in many ways was all too real.

Bad Blonde is also an example of a fascinating subspecies of noir that emerged in the early fifties: the Anglo-American coproduction. In 1950, Hammer Films went into the crime movie business with the American B-movie producer Robert L. Lippert. Over the next few years Lippert would ship his English associates a long line of fading Hollywood stars, as well as once promising second-string players who'd failed to become stars. People like Dan Duryea (*Terror Street*), Zachary Scott (*Dead On Course*), Lizabeth Scott and Paul Henreid (*Stolen Face*), and Dane Clark (*Blackout*) made the transatlantic flight into darkness as their careers slowed down.

Barbara Payton was in worse shape than most. Born Barbara Lee Redfield in Cloquet, Minnesota, she'd come to Hollywood only a four short years before. Possessed of an incredible, and somehow hauntingly vacant beauty, she'd burned hard and bright for a about a year, grabbing attention as the good-girl-gone-bad in the Cagney noir *Kiss Tomorrow Goodbye*. Though it was a good start in the business, her personal life was already plagued by a drinking problem and a weakness for the wrong men. After being passed around as the Saturday night girl-toy of rich skirt-chasers like Howard Hughes and Bob Hope (she blackmailed the married Hope), and moonlighting as the playmate of B-list sexaholics like Steve Cochrane and John Ireland, she landed in a love/hate triangle with the past-his-prime actor Franchot Tone and the washed-up B-list actor Tom Neal. This led to an incident in which Tone and Neal came to blows over Payton at two in the morning, with Neal beating Tone so badly he put him in a coma. This effectively ended the Hollywood careers of both Neal and Payton, though it did not end the lurid love triangle. Payton married Tone (who was a forgiving sort, apparently) but she kept up her affair with Neal. Tone and Payton divorced in a matter of months and the ugly details of Payton's sex life hit the tabloids. A failed suicide attempt seemed to presage more darkness to come.

It was this Barbara Payton who went to England to make a little boxing and infidelity flick called *The Flannigan Boy* (its underwhelming original English title). The film stars handsome young Tony Wright as an aspiring boxer named Johnny Flannigan who gets involved with a gregarious boxing promoter named Giuseppe Vecchi (Frederick Valk) and his sexy, much younger wife played by Payton.

As with much of the Hammer/Lippert output, *Bad Blonde* is a well made variation on the film noir. Director Reginald Le Borg has an instinctive feel for the material, and his film is sexy, well paced, and exciting. The murder of Giuseppe, alone aboard a little fishing raft in the middle of the lake, is about as well done as these things get. The secret weapon of the film is the gifted cinematographer Walter J. Harvey, the man responsible for giving much of Hammer Noir its dark hue. As he did in films like *Stolen Face* and *Blackout*, Harvey gives *Bad Blonde* a gorgeous pallet of rich blacks and shimmering whites. The look of the film is at once English-countryside- pretty and deeply noir.

The main reason to see *Bad Blonde*, however, remains the bad blonde at its center. Her youthful sheen is already gone and her face is starting to look puffy and wan, yet she is still effective, a perfect match for the role of a gold-digger on her way to the gallows. After this she would close out her career with a handful of forgettable films and then descend into a sad final spiral. After 1955's *Murder Is My Beat* she couldn't get another acting gig, no matter how low rent. Before long, she was turning tricks for five dollars down on the Sunset Strip. Sexual abuse and an addiction to heroin and alcohol decimated her body, and she was found passed out behind a dumpster in the parking lot of an A&P in 1967. A few weeks later, she was dead of liver failure. She was only 39. *Bad Blonde* is an artifact of her life at the point where everything had gone wrong. Perhaps because of this, her desperation feels authentic. Never a great actor, she doesn't really seem to be acting here. She just seems like Barbara Payton.

In one respect, Payton finally lucked out. In 2007, John O'Dowd wrote a haunting biography of the actor, *Kiss Tomorrow Goodbye*. While the book is brutally honest about a life that was often lived unwisely, it manages to avoid any cheap sensationalism. Instead, it is a love letter full of pain and beauty, much like the woman herself.

III. Fallen Angel: Linda Darnell

Being beautiful was Linda Darnell's curse. She was an emotionally intuitive actor, but almost from the beginning of her career, she was typecast because of her looks. Add in alcohol problems and a series of tortured relationships, and you have the recipe for a full-tilt Hollywood tragedy.

She was born Monette Eloyse Darnell in Dallas, Texas on October 16th, 1923 to a postal clerk named Calvin Darnell and his wife Pearl. Hailing from rural Tennessee, the fiercely ambitious Pearl had sought unsuccessfully to become an actor, only to end up as a domestic servant saddled with five children. Determined that one of her children would succeed where she had failed, she focused all her energies on her beautiful second daughter. For all intents and purposes, Monette was groomed from youth to be a star. She was enrolled in music, dance, drama, and elocution lessons while still a child, and her mother entered her into an unending series of beauty and talent contests.

She started making appearances in movies in 1939 when she was still just fifteen years old (though by this time the studio, 20th Century Fox, had changed her name to Linda and tacked on two years to her official age). Already fully possessed and startlingly beautiful, she almost immediately became a star. She made four films cast opposite swarthy Tyrone Power and specialized in fresh-faced brides and ingénues.

Then in 1943 her surprise marriage to veteran cameraman Pev Marley (who was twice her age) threw her career into crisis. She was placed on suspension and relegated to small roles. During this period she made a brief appearance as the vision of the Virgin Mary that appears to a young girl in 1943's *The Song Of Bernadette*. In the studio system, however, actors were treated as commodities, and it didn't take very long for 20th Century Fox to decide that its voluptuous, newly married young actor would be better commoditized as a sex object. Henceforth, she would play bad girls. As Darnell's biographer Ronald L. Davis would note, "Beyond question Linda's being cast as a slut rather than a virgin made her a more interesting property both for her studio and the gossip columnists." Few women experienced the Virgin/Whore Complex in more literal terms than Linda Darnell.

In 1945 Darnell was cast in the role of a ruinously manipulative "dance hall girl" (which was 1945 for "prostitute") in John Brahm's *Hangover Square*. She first appears on stage, singing to a bunch of drunks. After she meets a composer (Laird Creger), she asks someone, "Is he important?" Told that he is indeed quite important, she proceeds to squeeze him for free songs she can put in her act. What she doesn't know is that the composer is a psychopath who murders people in moments of blackout delirium. This would not be the last time Darnell would play an ill-fated femme fatale.

That same year, she gave her best noir performance in Otto Preminger's *Fallen Angel* as Stella, the sexy waitress at a beachside greasy spoon diner. One day a smooth-talking drifter named Eric Stanton (Dana Andrews) blows in from the road. He thinks he can sweep her off her feet with some smooth talk, but there's more to Stella than meets the eye. She's been around the block. She's heard Stanton's line of bullshit before. He wants sex. She wants a future. Stanton promises her one and quickly deduces that the quickest way to buy Stella what she wants is to marry June (Alice Faye) the local church organist and steal her money.

The film belongs to Darnell. It lingers on her earthy beauty, voluptuous figure, and big brown eyes. It's in love with her legs, and it gives her a lot of caustic dialog to sink her husky voice into. The audience is as taken with Stella as Stanton is. She's positioned in the film as something of a "bad girl" but in the screwy gender dynamics of the time this only means that she is sexualized. Darnell was never better—sexy and angry and ultimately very touching, more of a lost soul than a "bad girl."

In the later forties, Darnell's popularity peaked. She was excellent as a gold digger in Joseph L. Mankiewicz's *A Letter To Three Wives* (1949) and followed it up the next year with a strong performance in Mankiewicz's *No Way Out* opposite Richard Widmark and Sidney Poitier (in his film debut).

At the same time, Darnell began to struggle with her drinking. Her marriage to Pev Marley had fallen apart. Tumultuous, ill-advised affairs with domineering womanizers like Mankiewicz and Howard Hughes left her crestfallen and lonely. Bouts of deep depression followed. She was one of the world's most famous beauties, but her world had begun to shrink.

The good roles dried up fast, and by 1952 she was either headlining lifeless B-grade thrillers like *Night*

Without Sleep or providing eye candy in pictures like *Second Chance* opposite Robert Mitchum. A failed marriage followed, her drinking increased, and by the mid-fifties her big screen career was all but over.

She married for a third time to a handsome airline pilot named Merle Robertson, who took control of her career and shuttled her into nightclub work. Darnell hated the demeaning gigs, and her drinking and depression increased. After a short stint in rehab she returned home to find that Robertson had knocked up a younger woman and wanted a divorce. Broke and inconsolable, Darnell tried to kill herself.

After that low point, she slowly began to fight her way back. She cut back on her drinking and went on the road with a traveling production of the play *Janus*—which turned out to be a success. She began to repair her estranged relationship with her daughter, Lola Marley. She made a final film appearance, in the B-Western *Black Spurs*.

This brief, happy period ended on April 8th, 1965 when Darnell was caught in a fire at a friend's apartment in Chicago. After suffering burns to ninety percent of her body, she lingered for an agonizing thirty-three hours before she died on April 10th.

The misfortune of Linda Darnell seemed as determined as a Greek tragedy. Raised by a mother obsessed with turning her into a star, she was pushed into the Hollywood star machine—a factory system that used her as a commodity and then tossed her aside once her economic worth had peaked. It's a brutal story, but what remains of her is a cinematic legacy of images. To watch something like *Fallen Angel* or *A Letter To*

Three Wives is to see the mystery of Linda Darnell alive and well, as beautiful and haunting as ever.

IV. The Little Sister: Martha Vickers

If you spend enough time in the shadow gallery that is film noir certain faces start to haunt you. I'm not talking here about the icons like Mitchum or Grahame or Bennett or Andrews—their legends were set a long time ago, so we approach them with the expectation of greatness. And I'm not talking about recovered figures such as Lizabeth Scott or Ann Savage, who were forgotten in their time and then reborn as stars when noir enthusiasts discovered them and enshrined them as icons.

I'm talking about Martha Vickers. She's remembered today for two roles, one she played onscreen and one she played in life. The onscreen role was her firecracker performance as Lauren Bacall's nymphomaniac sister in *The Big Sleep*. The real life role was her stormy tenure as Mickey Rooney's third wife.

Her part in *The Big Sleep* got her noticed but didn't do much for a career that began to flounder almost immediately. She always gets noticed by audiences watching the film—she's weird and sexy at the same time, always an exciting combo—and people often ask, "Whatever became of that girl who played the sister?" The answer is: she made a few more films, did some television, married and divorced Mickey Rooney, had some children, retired from films and died young at the age of 46.

Yet, if you're a noir geek, you can't help but bump into her from time to time. She never made another film as good as *The Big Sleep*, but she pops up in supporting parts in interesting pictures like Walsh's *The Man I Love*, or Ulmer's *Ruthless*, W. Lee Wilder's *The Big Bluff* or the Paul Wendkos adaptation of David Goodis's *The Burglar*. The two constants in these films are that Vickers is always good and she is always under used.

No one quite seemed to know what to do with her. Take the 1949 noirish drama *Alimony*. Here Vickers gets a rare starring role. She plays Kitty Travers, a would be singer who gets involved with a struggling composer named Dan Barker (John Beal). He's already involved with boring nice-girl Linda (Hillary Brooke), but Kitty decides to steal him away when she suspects that he's about to strike it big with a new composition.

What ensues is pure melodramatic hokum, with lots of reversals of fortune as Dan dumps Linda, and Kitty dumps Dan, and Linda takes Dan back, and Kitty comes back for Dan, and Dan dumps Linda again before Kitty turns around and dumps him again and…

Well, you get the idea. This kind of thing can be entertaining if it's done right, but director Alfred Zeisler doesn't bring much spark to the party. On top of generally flat scenes, he's yet another director who failed to really utilize Vickers. She's well cast as a gold digging vixen, yet curiously the director does nothing to showcase her sensuality, much less her oddball appeal. Vickers doesn't even get a close up until halfway through the film, and that one seems like an afterthought.

It's really too bad. Vickers had a way of teasing a man, of toying with him in a manner that was coy and aggressive at the same time. She would lower her chin and look up with her eyes and petulantly growl her dialog as if talking were a silly waste of time. She seemed like a bad girl doing a satiric version of a nice girl.

She was sexy, yes, but the real pity of her career is that she was such a quirky actor. There was no warmth to her (I'm speaking only of her charisma as it appeared onscreen, of course), and she seemed like a self-contained unit. It's part of the reason she was so good as the psychotic little sister in *The Big Sleep*. She seemed to be off in her own little world.

Despite its flaws, something like *Alimony* manages to showcase some of this appeal. Like I said, she is well cast as Kitty. But, inexplicably, the film swerves in the last few moments and (I'll just go ahead and spoil the "surprise") she realizes how bad she's been and apologizes to everyone involved. A femme fatale who learns her lesson and decides to be a nicer person. What a bummer.

And so, the fascination of Martha Vickers has at its center an absence, a desire that can never be met—the desire for that one great role which could make her a star. Hers is a legacy of fragments, pieces of film here and there which go on teasing us with possibilities.

NOTES FROM THE GOON SQUAD
ELISHA COOK JR., NEVILLE BRAND, TED DE CORSIA

I. The Funny Little Guy: Elisha Cook Jr.

Noir's most valuable supporting player was Elisha Cook Jr. At five foot five, with bug eyes and a raspy whisper of a voice, he was dubbed "Hollywood's lightest heavy" a title bestowed on him because he shot to fame playing the diminutive goon Wilmer in John Huston's 1941 genre defining *The Maltese Falcon*. In a film full of great performances, his teary-eyed psychopath stands out without seeming to do much more than mutter threats under his breath. Although he spends the whole movie getting slapped around by Bogart, there's a slow boiling rage in those big, wet eyes.

That same year he played another psycho in another early noir, *I Wake Up Screaming*. While it's not the masterpiece that *Falcon* is, and while its noir identity is not fully formed (with goofy asides and a romance thrown in) *I Wake Up Screaming* still helped lay the ground work both visually and thematically for much of what would follow it in the forties and fifties. Cook overplays his part (at the behest of the director, once can sense), but here he is, for the second time in 1941 putting a vision of violent psychosis onscreen.

Cook had actually arrived to the noir party a year earlier with a little 63-minute Expressionistic gem called *Stranger On The Third Floor*. Cook plays a nervous little cabbie wrongfully accused of murder. His part is small but showy, and in keeping with the style of this little proto-noir, which owes much to silent German cinema, Cook doesn't just decry his persecution, he explodes all over the screen, those big eyes of his filling up like water balloons. He's not subtle, but nothing about the film is subtle. It's a highly stylized nightmare, and Cook fits right in.

As the years went on, he continued issuing fine performances in a whole slew of noirs. He's the horny little drummer who drags Ella Raines into an orgy-like jazz session in Robert Siodmak's gorgeous 1944 *Phantom Lady*. He rides shotgun with brawler Lawrence Tierney in 1945's so-so *Dillinger* and teams up with him again in the far superior 1947 *Born to Kill*. He and Tierney were real-life fishing buddies, but in their movies, Cook had a habit of getting killed.

In 1946, he had one of his best roles, opposite Bogart again, in Howard Hawk's *The Big Sleep*. Cook plays a "funny little guy" named Harry Jones. In love with a no good woman, Cook wades into an underworld of killers, an underworld from which he will not return, but he's got integrity and no small degree of guts. His big scene with tough guy Bob Steele—wherein the dead-eye killer makes him drink poison—is one of the best scenes Cook ever played.

Somehow, none of his fine work ever translated into stardom. He kept on, though, just another working stiff punching in for the night shift at the Dream Factory. He worked on no-budget pictures like Monogram's 1947 *Fall Guy* and the King Brothers' *The Gangster* the same year. He worked opposite Henry Fonda in *The Long Night*, Alan Ladd in *The Great Gatsby*, and Marilyn Monroe in *Don't Bother to Knock*. He was in the first Mike Hammer picture, 1953's *I, the Jury* and gets killed again—this time while wearing a Santa Claus suit. All part of the job.

That same year he was in the Western *Shane*, getting gunned down again (of course), this time by a ferocious Jack Palance. The picture was a blockbuster success, and Cook's scene with Palance made Palance's career. But it had no impact on Cook's career. He was still dependable ol' Elisha Cook. So what if he got blown away in the biggest hit of the year? He'd been blown away in half the pictures he ever made. That same year he started doing television. Why not? Might as well get gunned down on the small screen, too.

Two career highlights lay in store for him, though, and both were in the genre with which he had by this time become synonymous. In 1956 he got the best part of his life in Stanley Kubrick's 1956 *The Killing*. One the great heist films, *The Killing* also features perhaps noir's most dysfunctional marriage, the unholy union between a pathetic racetrack clerk (Cook) and his wicked wife (Marie Windsor). Cook and Windsor do a duet here that is a note perfect vision of marital hell. The archetypal little man of noir, Cook at last finds a role that makes him a truly tragic figure, while

Windsor is a nightmare wife, sexy and horrible all at once. Watching these two together is the chief delight of the film. Windsor's eyes are as big as Cook's, but hers are filled with a mocking laughter. His pain and her scorn make for striking noir music.

In 1957, Cook issued another masterful performance in another terrific heist movie, the underrated *Plunder Road*. As part of a team that pulls off an ingenious train robbery, Cook is again at the heart of a film. By this time, he'd grown to middle age in film noir. Starting out, he was a weird young guy, so often cast as a psycho or a buffoon. In this film, he generates the only pathos in sight as a working stiff who's chosen the wrong profession. Watch how he keeps nervously flicking out his tongue as he rambles on about his plans for the future. Seventeen years in film noir, and this poor bastard still thought he had a future.

With the close of the classic noir cycle, the steady supply of crime flicks slowed down. Still, Cook never stopped working. Television never gave him a starring role, of course, but it supplied plenty of opportunities to do his thing. He worked on all the big shows: *Wagon Train, Rawhide, Gunsmoke, Perry Mason, The Untouchables, Peter Gunn, Bat Masterson, The Fugitive, The Man From U.N.C.L.E*, even *Star Trek* and *Batman*. And more, lots more. By the end of his life most people probably knew him best for his recurring role as Ice-Pick Hofstetler on *Magnum PI*.

Not much has ever been known about Cook. Born in San Francisco in 1903 to a vaudevillian father and actor mother, he made his stage debut at thirteen and was making movies before he turned thirty. Despite being widely respected in the industry, he lived a reclusive life, preferring to stay up in the mountains and fish between movie roles. After a failed first marriage to actor Mary Lou Dunckley, he married Peggy McKenna in 1943 and stayed married to her the rest of his life. They had no children. He died in a nursing home in Big Pine, California, in 1995. If the world didn't regard his passing as the loss of a giant of cinema, it's a shame. He made every movie a little better. And he made great movies even greater.

II. King Thug: Neville Brand

Neville Brand was the king of the thugs. Pure and simple. Big and beefy, built like a garbage truck, squinty-eyed and greasy-faced—he was a thing of pure pulp beauty. Almost always playing the henchman, he's the ugly hulk of muscle standing behind the main villain, waiting impatiently to be told that he can finally break your kneecaps.

The man himself was, of course, more complicated than his onscreen persona. Born in Iowa in 1920, Brand was raised in Illinois, the eldest of seven children. After graduating high school, he enrolled in the Illinois National Guard and worked a series of odd jobs (shoe salesman, soda jerk) before he was inducted into the Army at the outbreak of World War II. During the war, he served as a platoon sergeant and amassed a distinguished military service record that surpassed that of any other film star before or since (with the exception of Audie Murphy, who became a film star *because* he was WWII's most decorated soldier).

Among other honors, Brand earned a Purple Heart, the Good Conduct Medal, the American Defense Service Ribbon, an Overseas Service Bar, a Service Stripe, and the Combat Infantryman's Badge. (Later, when he became a film star, the Hollywood hacks would promote his service record—claiming falsely that he was the fourth most decorated American infantryman in the war—but Brand himself was always sheepish to talk about his wartime exploits and resented the way they were embellished.) He war time service ended when he was wounded and nearly killed in battle. "I knew I was dying," he later recalled. "It was a lovely feeling, like being half-loaded." Honorably discharged, he came home and studied acting with the help of the GI Bill.

His entry into movies seemed a harbinger of ass-kickings to come, as an uncredited heavy in the 1949 narcotics thriller *Port of New York*. He followed that with "The Man With Nothing To Lose," an episode of the anthology series *The Bigelow Theater*, about an escaped convict who breaks into the home of an elderly couple.

His big break came in 1950 in the classic noir *D.O.A* starring Edmond O'Brien as Frank Bigelow, a man who discovers he's been poisoned and has only a few hours to track down his killer. The exact *who* and *why* of the murder aren't really the point of a movie like this because a murder plot is just a puzzle, and *D.O.A* isn't really a puzzle. As directed by former cinematographer Rudolph Mate` and written by the longtime screenwriting duo of Russell Rouse and

Clarence Greene, *D.O.A* is more like a sprint through the dark environs of film noir.

While Luther Adler is silk-smooth as the gangster at the center of the mystery, it's Brand as Adler's psycho henchman Chester, who steals the whole damn show. Brand has only a few scenes, but his orgasmic *You-don't-like-it-in-the-belly-do-you-Bigelow* sniveling upped the ante on the way heavies would be played in the 1950s. Chester isn't just mean, he's a full-on nutcase who gets a psychosexual jolt from shooting people in the gut.

That same year you could find Brand playing an peculiar role in Preminger's *Where the Sidewalk Ends*. He's a thug/masseuse for a gangster played by Gary Merrill. He roughs up guys and then rubs down the boss. It's an odd job, but who better than Brand to do it?

1952 found him in one of the all time great hoodlum line-ups. *Kansas City Confidential* is a cornucopia of head-thumpings curiosity of director Phil Karlson. John Payne stars as an ex-con trying to clear his name of involvement with a daring armored car robbery. He has to punch his way through a heap of bad guys that includes Brand, Jack Elam, Lee Van Cleef, and Preston Foster. The three man duke-out in a hotel room between Payne, Van Cleef, and Brand is one of the best scenes of its kind in a film noir.

While Brand continued to notch up roles in noirs like *Kiss Tomorrow Goodbye*, *The Mob*, and *The Turning Point*, he also branched out into Westerns and war films (including Billy Wilder's classic *Stalag 17*). In 1954 he got a rare starring role as the leader of a prison uprising in Don Siegel's *Riot in Cell Block 11*. Looking beefy even by his own impressively beefy standards, Brand turns in a solid performance as Dunn, the mastermind of a large scale riot. Although Dunn has staged the riot as a way to draw media attention to the plight of the inmates, the film doesn't seem particularly interested in representing that plight. Brand works hard, but his character is underwritten. It's difficult to find the center of Dunn. Is his revolt really a public relations ploy? Does he really trust the system to keep its word to him?

The missed opportunity of *Riot in Cell Block 11* may help explain why Brand, although one of the great supporting players in noir, never really broke out of the thug tier the way someone like Richard Widmark did. Much like Elisha Cook Jr., Brand was destined to occupy the edges of the frame, stealing scenes, making things more interesting, but never really seizing the spotlight.

As the classic noir era wound down at the end of the fifties (including henchmen roles in good late era films like *Cry Terror!*), Brand moved on to the greener pastures of the Western, where he basically took his knuckle-dragging thug act into the old West. He banked an impressive run of lowlifes and sweaty scumbags (including an entertaining part in the underrated Anthony Mann flick *The Tin Star*, opposite Henry Fonda).

Once the sixties hit, Brand found himself working primarily in television. He played Al Capone on *The Untouchables* and did a guest spot on *The Virginian* playing a wisecracking Texas Ranger Reese Bennett, a role so popular it got spun-off into the series *Laredo*. Sadly, Brand's on and off set drinking caused production problems and Brand left the show early.

His drinking seemed to stabilize a bit after that, and Brand kept on working in television and film. His last film, just a few years before his death in 1992, was a cheapie horror flick called *Evils of the Night* (1985). Brand played...a psychotic henchmen.

The key to his greatness is that he was, in fact, a serious actor. "I don't go in thinking [my character is] a villain," Brand told the writer William R. Horner. "Nobody thinks he's a villain. Even a killer condones what he's done. So I just create this human being under the circumstances that are given...Everybody just condones his own actions."

III. A Real Smart Fella: Ted de Corsia

Let us establish here and now the Ted de Corsia Rule: Any movie with Ted de Corsia is worth watching. That's not to say that Ted can redeem a complete stinker but *he'll* always be worth the price of admission. You can stick that in the bank and start drawing interest on it. Ted's a sure bet.

In classic noir, he was one of the great thugs, a man who seemed to have been born with a sneer on his lips and a head full of pomade. In film after film, he's the world's biggest sleaze, grifting his way through life, hatching schemes, ogling dames, slapping around a bunch of suckers and chumps. He makes being an asshole look like the meaning of life.

When he made his film debut in Orson Welles's *The Lady From Shanghai*, he already seemed like a fully formed screen presence. Born Edward Gildea de Corsia in Brooklyn in 1905, he showed an early affinity and aptitude for accents. Starting in radio in the 1930s, de Corsia basically did it all—from newsreels like the *March Of Time* (where he did the voice of President Herbert Hoover, Huey Long, and Benito Mussolini among other notable figures) to mystery and adventure programs like *The Shadow*. He stayed a dependable radio workhorse throughout the forties before heading to Hollywood to work for Welles.

Although he had played all kinds of roles on the radio and on stage in New York, the movie camera knew a villain when it saw one and de Corsia quickly became a popular tough guy in crime films. For the next three decades, he did a little bit of everything—like any great character actor—with his baseline being the squinty-eyed bad guy. In between film and television roles, he continued to work in radio (on shows like *Night Beat*, *The Lone Ranger*, and *CBS Radio Workshop*) and raised two daughters. He died of natural causes at the age of 69 in Encino.

With charisma to burn, he invigorated every film he was ever in, but it should also be noted that he was a real professional and a dedicated craftsman. It's not for nothing that he worked with Orson Welles, Jules Dassin, Allan Dwan, and Stanley Kubrick—just to name a few of the top tier directors who regarded de Corsia as a sure bet. He sold every line with a sneer and a twinkle. I wish this guy was in every movie ever made. Every time he walks on screen, I smile.

He made six essential noirs. In *The Lady From Shanghai* (1947), he's a sleazeball named Broome. He shows up in the film with his hair slicked back and his top lip stuck to his teeth. He winds up gut-shot. This is the film debut that launched a thousand sneers and a thousand fatal stomach wounds. Jules Dassin's great docu-noir *The Naked City* (1948) features his turn as a remorseless killer named Garzah in what might be his keystone performance. The film was shot on the teeming streets of New York (it is a masterpiece of cinematography and an essential film for lovers of Manhattan), and De Corsia is as much an artifact of 1948 NYC as the Brooklyn Bridge. In *The Enforcer* (1951) Humphrey Bogart plays a DA trying to crack a murder-for-hire ring. De Corsia plays a slimy killer-turned-prosecution-witness named Joseph Rico. An underrated film in many ways, this is a nice showcase for the way de Corsia embedded a trembling coward inside the protective shell of all his tough guys. *Crime Wave* (1954) is Andre De Toth's noir masterpiece. It features de Corsia as a small time gang leader named Doc Penny who's trying to outrun an obsessed cop played by Sterling Hayden. Even in a movie packed full of great character actors (Timothy Carey, Charles Bronson, Jay Novello), de Corsia's menace shines hard and bright. In *Slightly Scarlet* (1956), playing the oily rival to crime boss John Payne, de Corsia teams up with Arlene Dahl as the psychotic little sister of Payne's girlfriend. Watching de Corsia and Dahl claw each other is like watching monsters mate. *The Killing* (1956) features another all-star cast of misfits. Sterling Hayden assembles a gang to pull off a heist a race track. Pivotal to his plan is a desperate cop played by de Corsia. Watching de Corsia play scenes with fellow noir stalwarts like Elisha Cook Jr. is as fun as noir gets.

THE NOTHING MAN

STERLING HAYDEN

There were many great leading men in the heyday of classic film noir and each one seemed to carve out a little piece of the kingdom for himself. Robert Mitchum was the King of the Suckers, ultra laidback and super smooth but always and forever a chump for the ladies. Robert Ryan was the ultimate Man on the Edge, the embodiment of unchecked fury. John Payne was The Ass-Kicker, a one man demolition crew.

And then you have Sterling Hayden. In some ways he might be the hardest to pin down. What makes Hayden fascinating is that, as an actor, he really only makes sense within the context of film noir. He made many different kinds of films, but noir is his métier. His voice, a kind of rapid-fire bellow, is made for the clipped dialog of a suspicious cop or a surly thug. His shopworn good looks and imposing physical presence make him a natural to play men stalking darkened city streets at three in the morning. What he lacks in nuance, he makes up for in essence. In crime films, he's as natural as cheap carpet and cigarette smoke. No, he couldn't act, he could only *be*. And that *being* was the key to why he was a great actor. Among noir heroes, he may well be the most intrinsically existential.

The man himself was always hard to pin down as well. Born Sterling Relyea in Montclair, New Jersey, he lost his father at an early age and took his stepfather's last name in his youth. About the same time he changed his name, he met the love of his life: the sea. He ran away to a life on boats, spending seven years working his way up to becoming and serving as a ship's captain. During WWII he served in Yugoslavia and, almost by accident, found himself in the movie business. Paramount promoted him as "The Most Beautiful Man In Movies" and as a bronzed and muscular young man with a shock of blond hair, he was indeed quite the male specimen. But Hayden loathed the movie business. After a life on the sea, squinting into the sun and living by honest toil, he hated standing around a movie set, striking poses and repeating canned dialog.

Matters became worse when the House on Un-American Activities Committee came to town. Hayden had always leaned hard to the left—having been impressed with the Tito partisans he served with in Yugoslavia he became, for a time, a Communist—and when the witchhunters cornered him, he turned rat and named names. The incident was the low point of his life. "It's the only thing in my life," he said later, "that I'm genuinely ashamed of. It still haunts me. Because I was a rat. I was weak. I have no excuse."

Haunted by what he had done and the friends he'd betrayed, fed up with the subpar movies he was making (cast in westerns, he "couldn't ride worth a goddamn" and was "the slowest draw west of the Rhine"), flat broke and waging a custody battle with his ex-wife, Hayden escaped into the arms of his first love. In defiance of a court order, he loaded up his four children on a schooner called *Wanderer* and set sail for the South Seas.

This period of his life was covered in his autobiography *Wanderer*, which might well be the best memoir ever written by a Hollywood actor. Steeped in the literature of Conrad and London, Marx and Whitman, Hayden set out to write a real book, not a trashy showbiz tell-all. He succeeded impressively at articulating the restless spirit that defined him:

Voyaging belongs to seamen, and to the wanderers of the world who cannot, or will not, fit in. If you are contemplating a voyage and you have the means, abandon the venture until your fortunes change… [W]e fling our lives beneath the wheels of routine—and before we know it our lives are gone. What does a man need, really need? A few pounds of food each day, heat and shelter, six feet to lie down in—and some form of working activity that will yield a sense of accomplishment. That's all, in the material sense, and we know it. But we are brainwashed by our economic system until we end up in a tomb beneath a pyramid of time payments, mortgages, preposterous gadgetry, playthings that divert our attention for the sheer idiocy of the charade. The years thunder by, the dreams of youth grow dim where they lie caked in dust on the shelves of patience. Before we know it, the tomb is sealed. Where, then, lies the answer? In choice. Which shall it be: bankruptcy of purse or bankruptcy of life?

Hayden was a character, no doubt. His work is a testament to a fascinating man and an indispensable artist. Consider the importance of this three key noirs. *The Asphalt Jungle* (1950), directed by John Huston, is the heist movie by which all others are judged, with Hayden leading a pitch perfect supporting cast featuring the likes of Sam Jaffe, Marc Lawrence, and Jean Hagen. Oh, and Marilyn Monroe in her first big role. *Crime Wave* (1954), directed by Andre De Toth, puts Hayden on the other side of the badge. Here he plays a relentless cop tracking three murderous punks. He thinks they're in cahoots with an ex-con played by Gene Nelson. Nelson is an innocent man just trying to go straight, but hard-driving Hayden believes "once a crook, always a crook." Gorgeous cinematography by Bert Glennon, and Hayden's freight train performance make this a classic. Two years later in *The Killing* (1956), Stanley Kubrick cast Hayden as the mastermind of racetrack heist. He plans everything perfectly, but in true noir fashion it all goes to hell. The impeccable supporting cast includes Marie Windsor and Elisha Cook Jr. as perhaps the most dysfunctional married couple in all of noir. Based on the book by Lionel White, with a script by Jim Thompson (who got stiffed on his writing credit by Kubrick), the film builds on *The Asphalt Jungle* and ups it in existential fury. While Hayden made other noirs that ranged from the quite good (*Naked Alibi*) to the quite bad (*Suddenly*), these three key films are really all the legacy he needs. If there is a film noir icon who deserves to get more credit, it's this guy.

THE ALTARS OF FORGOTTEN WOMEN

One of the ironies of film noir is that many of its lasting icons were never stars in their lifetime. While some big names like Barbara Stanwyck and Ava Gardner were noir regulars, more than any other genre, stardom in noir is retroactive. Someone like Ann Savage, for instance, had only the most fleeting taste of low-tier movie fame in her youth before Hollywood showed her the door. Yet, Savage was one the lucky people who lived to see her fame catch up to her. A cheap little sixty-seven minute crime picture called *Detour*—a picture Savage appears in for all of thirty minutes—somehow endured and prospered over the years. Savage was in her sixties and working as a secretary when she discovered that because of her fiery performance in *Detour* she was at the center of a cult.

Savage's following is just one sect of a larger cult of forgotten women. Savage was not alone in finding herself as an object of worship. Within this convocation there are many different factions, factions with passionately devoted followers. Actors like Audrey Totter, Marie

Windsor, Evelyn Keyes, and Janis Carter all have legions of admirers. None of them were really stars in their day, but their movies have had a life all their own. Long after their careers fizzled out, sometimes after their own deaths, some actors finally became stars. And that just about defines the word *bittersweet*.

Of course, major movie stars like Audrey Hepburn and Judy Garland experience a whole other level of life after death fame, and a select few even seem to reach beyond mere stardom and become a part of the larger shared consciousness of society. You could argue, at this point in Western culture, that Marilyn Monroe is nearly as iconic as the Virgin Mary.

Film noir fame, on the other hand, is born out of B-movie obscurity. Lizabeth Scott will never be as famous as Marilyn Monroe, but she is the ruler of her own dark little corner of Dreamtown because she is the woman who most deserves the title of Queen of Noir. She starred in more film noirs than nearly anyone else, and she was unique in that her filmography consists mostly of noirs. She played the entire range of characters available to women in the genre, from doe-eyed innocents (*The Strange Love of Martha Ivers, The Company She Keeps*) to world-weary lounge singers (*Dark City, I Walk Alone*) to cold-blooded femme fatales (*Stolen Face*). She starred in one of the genre's real lowlights, the misogynistic *Dead Reckoning*. She starred in what maybe the campiest noir ever made, the hilarious *Desert Fury*. And, most importantly, she starred in two of the finest noirs we have, Andre De Toth's 1948 *Pitfall* and Byron Haskin's 1949 *Too Late For Tears*.

To understand the appeal of Liz Scott, one only need look at those last two films. In the first, she plays a woman named Mona Stevens who falls into an affair with a married man played by Dick Powell. Their affair is discovered by a psychotic private detective (played by Raymond Burr) who is obsessed with Mona and proceeds to make life hell for everyone involved. The cast here is superb, and at the center, in a performance of great sympathy, is Queen Liz. She makes Mona a sexy woman (which must have been fairly easy since Scott herself was gorgeous, blonde, and had a voice that was equal parts cigarettes and silk), but she also makes Mona a sad woman. Loneliness is the undercurrent of Scott's voice, the thing that pulls you further down into her trap. Even when she's happy, you can tell that Scott is afraid of the worst. In *Pitfall*, she pretty much gets the worst at the hands of thoughtless men.

In *Too Late For Tears*, she gets her revenge. As housewife turned criminal Jane Palmer, Scott creates a portrait of coolheaded evil. Jane and her husband Alan (Arthur Kennedy) are driving home one night when someone tosses a briefcase full of money into their car. Is the money a payment for a ransom? Perhaps a blackmail payoff? Alan doesn't care, he just wants to turn the money over to the cops. His wife, alas, disagrees. She's willing to do anything to keep the cash, even after slimy crook Dan Duryea shows up looking for it and slaps her around.

These guys are toast. Neither the crook nor the husband have any idea who they're dealing with. With her performance, Scott makes a pretty good grab for the most evil femme fatale on record, yet she also makes Jane Palmer curiously relatable. Like any great femme fatale, she has her reasons. Again, there's that sadness, that aching, unfulfilled need at the center of Lizabeth Scott that comes through in her performance. Jane Palmer is evil, yes, but she's also smart, dogged, and utterly human.

It is, after all, humanity that is the great appeal of the forgotten women of film noir, our sense that we're seeing a human being alive onscreen. Movies of the forties and fifties were made to be dreamlike, and all these years later they still seem like dreams. The dreams hook us; the humanity makes us obsessives, worshipers at the altar. *Who was this woman?* we ask. Not just Queen Liz, but so many others. We watch them laugh and cry and scheme and die and then we watch them do it all over again. It doesn't take much to hook us.

Take Joan Dixon. In 1951 she starred in an underrated B-film called *Roadblock* alongside Charles McGraw. She plays Diane, a sexy conwoman who marries a straight-laced insurance investigator name Joe Peters, a marriage that will have disastrous results. I've always been hypnotized by Joan Dixon in this movie. It's not just that she's beautiful, it's that she projects that essential combination of intoxicating sexual allure and an untouchable, unknowable center. Is Diane bad? It's tough to say. With her sleepy eyes and pouty lips, Dixon might be criticized for giving a performance that's too laid back, but I would argue that very ambiguity is her greatest attribute. She doesn't set out to ruin Joe Peters, but once she meets him, he's a goner. It's an interesting take on the femme fatale. Many femmes are man-ating monsters. Diane is different. She's a catalyst who opens up all the insecurity and greed buried beneath honest Joe Peters' upright façade. It takes quite a gal to destroy Charles McGraw. Joan Dixon does it without really trying.

One thing's for sure: she never had much of a career in Hollywood. She started out at RKO under contract to Howard Hughes (which was not somewhere a fresh-faced twenty-year old from Norfolk, Virginia wanted to find herself). Hughes promised to build her career, but he was too busy running RKO into the ground. Dixon spent most of her time in low budget westerns and ended her acting career in the late fifties doing bit parts on television. By then, she'd become a lounge singer and was mostly notable in the newspapers for a string of quick marriages and messy divorces. She died in Los Angles in 1992.

She was no one's idea of the queen of anything, yet she lives on in this little-seen jewel. Her fame hasn't happened yet, unlike Ann Savage or Lizabeth Scott. Even in the insular world of film noir, Joan Dixon isn't an icon—yet. I have faith, however, that her cult is coming. If there's one thing that you can learn from the history of noir, it's that there's always time.

ACKNOWLEDGEMENTS

This book collects my writing from venues such as *Noir City, Los Angles Review of Books, Criminal Element, Mulholland Books, Bright Lights Film Journal,* and NoirCon, the bi-annual conference for noir enthusiasts held in Philadelphia. As such, I owe huge thank yous to all the editors, writers, artists, and organizers involved in these endeavors.

I owe particular thanks to Eddie Muller, Don Malcolm, Michael Kronenberg and everyone at *Noir City.* And I need to thank, extra-in-particular, Eric Beetner, who first said, "Hey, you want to write something for us?"

Thank you so much to Clare Toohey at *Criminal Element.*

Many thanks to Miriam Parker at *Mulholland Books.*

Thanks to Lisa Levy at *Los Angles Review of Books.*

Thank you to Lou Boxer and Cullen Gallagher at NoirCon.

Thanks to Gary Morris at *Bright Lights Film Journal.*

And, of course, thanks to J. David Osborne, the mastermind of Broken River Books, who asked me if I wanted to do a book on film noir.

Lastly, the most thanks go to Heather Brown, movie lover, who, when I began to explain (perhaps not for the first time) just who Dan Duryea was, said, "I know who Dan Duryea is. I can't live with you and not know who Dan Duryea is."

ABOUT THE AUTHOR

Jake Hinkson is the author of several books—including the novels *Hell On Church Street* and *The Big Ugly*, the novellas *The Posthumous Man* and *Saint Homicide*, and the short story collection *The Deepening Shade*. He has written essays and reviews for *The Los Angeles Review Of Books, Mental Floss, Mystery Scene, Criminal Element, Tor.com* and *Noir City*. Born in Arkansas and raised in the Ozarks, he currently lives in Chicago. His books *Hell On Church Street* and *The Posthumous Man* have been translated into French by èditions Gallmeister. For more visit JakeHinkson.com and TheNightEditor.blogspot.com